MONEY, GOLD, AND HISTORY

For more information about the author, Lewis E. Lehrman,

or the work of The Lehrman Institute,

please visit **www.LehrmanInstitute.org.**

To keep abreast of the latest on *The True Gold Standard:*

A Monetary Reform Plan without Official Reserve Currencies,

please visit **www.TheGoldStandardNow.org** where additional

information, breaking news, history, and research on monetary

policy, economics, and the gold standard may be found.

MONEY, GOLD, AND HISTORY

Lewis E. Lehrman

ISBN-10: 0-9840178-3-6
ISBN-13: 978-0-9840178-3-6

Published by The Lehrman Institute
www.LehrmanInstitute.org

Printed in the United States

First Edition

In honor of:

> Paul Fabra

In memory of:

> John P. Britton (1938-2010)
>
> Barton M. Biggs (1932-2012)
>
> Jacques Rueff (1896-1978)

Article I, Section 8.

The Congress shall have Power... To coin Money, regulate the Value thereof, and of foreign Coin, and fix the Standard of Weights and Measures.

Article I, Section 10.

No State shall emit Bills of Credit; make any Thing but gold and silver Coin a Tender in Payment of Debts...or grant any Title of Nobility.

– United States Constitution

PREFACE AND DEDICATION

Paul Fabra was born in Paris in 1927. I first met him, I believe, in 1972 in Paris at the home of Professor Jacques Rueff, 51 rue de Varenne. He was then the world famous senior financial writer for France's most prestigious newspaper, *Le Monde*. He remains one of the most distinguished financial commentators of France. During the past forty years, he and I forged an irreplaceable personal friendship. His intellectual influence on my writing endures. I dedicate this book to him, because without him, modest as this book is, it would be the lesser.

Paul Fabra is a philosopher-economist, a distinguished author, a peerless journalist, supremely well educated, a linguist, a man of the world.

Above all, Paul Fabra is a devoted husband and father, a patient teacher, a gentleman, and a gentle man – I cherish him and our priceless friendship.

Lewis E. Lehrman
Paris, December 15, 2012

TABLE OF CONTENTS

Table of Contents

N.B. These essays, almost forty years of published material, often analyze similar subjects at different periods. Inevitably, there is repetition which I hope the reader will indulge.

Lewis E. Lehrman
December 15, 2012

SELECTIVE CHRONOLOGY

1944	Bretton Woods Agreement
1944	Dollar becomes the world reserve currency after World War II
1948	Thomas B. McCabe becomes chairman of the Federal Reserve
1951	William McChesney Martin, Jr. becomes chairman of the Federal Reserve
1959	Europe reestablishes currency convertibility on current account
1960	Dollar crises begin and recur
1970	Arthur F. Burns becomes chairman of the Federal Reserve
1971	President Nixon closes the gold window
1973	Floating-pegged exchange rates based on the world dollar standard followed by the Great Inflation
1974	Repeal of prohibition of private ownership of gold coins, bars, and certificates
1979	Paul A. Volcker becomes chairman of the Federal Reserve
1981-1982	U.S. Gold Commission meets amidst highest interest rates in American history. Restoration of dollar convertibility to gold debated – rejected
1987	Alan Greenspan becomes chairman of the Federal Reserve
2006	Ben S. Bernanke becomes chairman of the Federal Reserve
2007-2009	Great Recession
2008-2012	Era of quantitative easing (or money printing)

Fiat Money Periods in the United States
(inconvertible paper money)
Revolutionary War (1776-1792)

War of 1812 (1812-1817)

Civil War and Reconstruction (1862-1879)

1971 to the present

Gold/Silver Standard Periods in the United States
1792-1812

1817-1834

1834-1861

1879-1971

"The dollar, and other key currencies, must be defined in law as a weight unit of gold – at a statutory convertibility rate which insures that nominal wage rates do not fall."

INTRODUCTION

The problems which affect the American economy are not new. Sadly, they are far too familiar and very predictable. Almost four decades ago, during America's worst economic period since the Great Depression, this is what I wrote in the first edition of the book, *Money and the Coming World Order* (1976):

> Today, national economic policy making is largely concerned with the problems of unemployment and inflation. More precisely, it is their simultaneous combination in nearly all Western economies which preoccupies policy makers. As these problems grow worse, the stakes rise higher. We know that either severe unemployment or sustained inflation, let alone both together, can be expected to have the most serious consequences for liberal democracy.
>
> During the post-war era, some had imagined the issue of widespread unemployment resolved by Lord Keynes who, forty years ago in the midst of a world depression, prescribed activist fiscal and monetary policies: "It may be possible," he wrote in *The General Theory*, "by a right analysis of the problem [of unemployment], to cure the disease whilst preserving the efficiency of freedom."[1] Surely, it is a proper and compassionate national goal to try to eliminate large-scale unemployment if it develops during the declining phase of the business cycle. But whether ever active monetary and fiscal full-employment policies, during *all* phases of the business cycle, are compatible with a reasonable degree of economic stability, let alone efficiency and freedom, has become a major question of our times. In fact, recurring interventionist government economic policies, in themselves, appear to be unmistakable causes of the intensifying

disorders which increasingly characterize the age.

Until recently, at least, the principal ailment of post-war Western economies has not been unemployment, but inflation. Indeed, if the post-war era in the liberal democracies can be accurately described as the age of Keynes, it is also the age of inflation. Inflation plagues all Western economies, even now [1973-1975] in the midst of recession and unemployment. Everywhere the value of money deteriorates. The burden of debt, public and private, mounts ever higher. Money, it seems, serves less well as a reliable store of value and the means of payment. In a worldwide exchange economy, money no longer impartially mediates between limited resources and rising expectations. Instead, political power, either of governments or of private corporations and trade unions, more and more shapes and supplants the market economy. Some Western nations thus move closer to civil war.

On a larger scale, the interdependent world economic system grows steadily more precarious. The disorders of the global economy, and in particular the disequilibrium of its monetary system, are inextricably tied up with this problem of inflation. Internationally as well as nationally, power replaces the market. The unrestrained use of political power, in pursuit of particular national economic interests, exemplifies an increasing tendency both to circumvent market disciplines, and to brush aside temporarily inconvenient systems of international rules. Nowhere, of course, has this tendency toward accentuated nationalism been more obvious than in the growing disorder of the international monetary system.

Today, in 2012, one is tempted to quote the inimitable Yogi Berra: "this is déjà vu all over again."

Three questions now arise: Will the perennial global monetary crisis and the century-old age of inflation still be underway forty years from now? Will the global economy have succumbed to national rivalries, mercantilism, financial disorder, and entropy? Or, will monetary order have been restored by the leading nations of the world – in their own self-interest? *The passage of almost forty years has not changed my mind; there is a necessary and sufficient solution to the problem of financial disorder.* My conviction has only grown deeper that American and world prosperity depend on monetary reform, Federal Reserve reform, and restoration of international monetary order based on stable exchange rates. American public and private finances have been sustained during the past generation by running down the immense capital laid up for us by centuries of frugal, enterprising forbearers – and by running up our debt. This liquidation of national capital for current, unrestrained, consumption may have a long, but finite life. The endgame must be financial reform or national bankruptcy. National bankruptcy (or its equivalent – systemic currency depreciation) is not inevitable. Monetary reform and budgetary equilibrium, led by America, is still plausible, especially because monetary reform has again become an international political issue.

But the nature of future monetary reform must be singular in design. Only the restoration of the gold standard, a dollar convertible to gold, can establish the stable framework for sustained global economic growth and balanced budgets. Only a stable dollar, defined by law as a weight unit of gold, can displace the speculative, paper-currency casino with incentives to save and invest in real production facilities and jobs. I have spelled out such a detailed plan for *an American restoration*, based on dollar convertibility to gold – in *The True Gold Standard: A Monetary Reform Plan without Official Reserve Currencies* (2012).

The authentic and effective American solution is neither esoteric nor complicated. It is simple and straightforward. The solution is authorized by the United States Constitution – in Article I, Sections 8 and 10 whereby the control of the supply of dollars is entrusted to the hands of the people because the definition of the dollar was entrusted to Congress. There it remained for most of American history, especially from 1792 to 1914 when the dollar was precisely defined by congressional statute as a weight unit of gold or silver. This gold standard economic era was America's longest period of rapid, non-inflationary, economic growth – almost four percent annually – with the budget under control, except during major wars.

Congress need only mobilize its unique, constitutional power under Article I "to coin money and regulate the value thereof." From 1792 to 1971, U.S. law defined the gold value of American currency such that paper dollars and bank demand deposits were convertible to their gold equivalent – by the people (1792-1914) and/or by governments (1933-1971). The last vestige of convertibility was terminated by President Richard Nixon's Executive Order of August 15, 1971.

Congress should exercise its constitutional power to restore dollar-gold convertibility, especially because of the proven, budgetary, and economic growth benefits of a dollar as good as gold.

What are the benefits?

First, the discipline of convertibility would automatically set an institutional limit on Treasury access to its limitless Federal Reserve credit card. If the Federal Reserve created more money than participants in the market wanted to hold, people would get rid of the inflationary excess by promptly exchanging paper and credit money for the gold equivalent. Moreover, under the true gold standard, the Fed and the commercial banks would be required by law to maintain dollar-gold convertibility at the statutory gold-dollar parity – or suffer insolvency. In order to maintain dollar convertibility to gold, if the people were redeeming excess currency for gold, the Fed and the commercial banks must then reduce the growth of money and credit, including credit to the Treasury – thereby also compelling government spending limitations.

Second, the empirical evidence of American economic history shows that convertibility to gold stabilizes the value of the dollar. The same evidence shows that, in a free market, a dollar convertible to gold stabilizes the general price level over the long run. For example, under the gold standard, the price level in 1914 was at almost the exact same level as it was in 1879 and 1834. That is, there was no long-term inflation, even over an 80-year period! But from 1971 – the year of Nixon's termination of dollar-gold convertibility – until 2012, the purchasing power of the dollar (adjusted by the CPI) fell 85 percent – during a short 40-year period. Every American born after 1950, who saved money in the bank, for example in 1970 and 1971, has lost 85 percent of the 1970-1971 purchasing power of those saved dollars. The depreciation of the dollar by the authorities (this is, inflation) is the cause.

Third, gold convertibility of the dollar will lead to a vast outpouring of worldwide savings from inflation hedges such as commodities, farmland, art, antiques – almost everything perceived to be a better store of value than depreciating paper currencies. Convertibility triggers the global release of speculative trillions hoarded in these unproductive inflation hedges. Stable money also creates incentives to save from income. Combined with a new level of savings from income, hoarded funds would pour into real productive facilities. The new investment would give rise to a general economic expansion – through new business, new products, new plant and equipment, creating thereby new demands for labor to work the expanding economy.

The restoration of a dollar worth its weight in gold provides not only a missing and necessary brake on government spending, but a stable dollar also supplies the missing steering wheel by which to guide efficiently the immense, new savings into long-term productive investment.

Dollar convertibility to gold is the simple, institutional financial reform which terminates the fear of rapid inflation – thus transforming unproductive store-of-value hedges into real investment capital with which to inaugurate a new American era of rapid economic and employment growth.

The true gold standard – that is a dollar convertible by statute to a specific weight of gold, combined with the windup of the official reserve currency role of the dollar – would engender a vast increase of true savings from current income made available for long-term productive investment. Confidence in a stable long-term price level would cause vast, speculative sums of worldwide savings to abandon unproductive inflation hedges. This dishoarding would yield immense, liquid savings looking for productive investment in real goods and services. Equity and true capital investment would gradually displace debt and leverage. Under conditions of stable money and stable exchange rates, savings would be redeployed by entrepreneurs and investors in new and innovative plants, products, technology, and equipment – minimizing unemployment as skilled and unskilled workers were hired to work the new facilities. The production machine of the United States would be reoriented – by a currency convertible to gold, and by the end of the reserve currency role of the dollar – to produce for the world market. Producing for the world market would engage all the positive and equitable effects of economies of scale and free trade.

It is, I believe, incontestable that all the celebrated monetary gods of the 20th century have failed. Originating in the conceits of 20th century academics, bankers, economists, and politicians, these monetary gods have sowed chaos. Now we reap the financial whirlwind.

In my book, *The True Gold Standard: A Monetary Reform Plan without Official Reserve Currencies* (2012), I charted a road to get from *here* – a world of financial disorder, to *there* – the remobilization of the gold standard. But I do emphasize that if the United States takes the lead to re-establish dollar convertibility to gold, the project should become a cooperative effort of the major powers.

To accomplish such a reform, *first* the United States announces future convertibility of the U.S. dollar – the dollar itself to be defined in statute, on a date certain, as a weight unit of gold. *Second*, a major international conference must be convened to establish mutual gold convertibility of the currencies of the major powers, the United States if necessary, proceeding to convertibility unilaterally. *Third*, the curse of official reserve currencies born of the 1922 Genoa and 1944 Bretton Woods agreements must be ruled out – gold alone designated to settle residual balance-of-payments deficits. At the same time a consolidation of official dollar reserves must be organized into long-term debt – to be funded in the very way the Founders funded the volatile national and state debts at the birth of the American republic.

It is a great lesson of American history that the classical or the true gold standard – a dollar defined as a weight unit of precious metal – is in fact the constitutional American monetary standard (see Article I, Sections 8 and 10). Let us uphold the Constitution and thereby inaugurate a new industrial revolution, rebuild America's self-respect, and with our constitutional monetary standard, restore American leadership in the global economy.

****

This book includes many, but not all, of the essays and articles on monetary policy that I have written during the last four decades. One of my first extended essays appears in *Money and the Coming World Order* (1976, 2012). There is an historical progression to the articles in this book, but each may be read in isolation. It should be remembered that each article was composed in a specific historical context. The individual articles do stand by themselves. Inevitably there is some repetition. The **Summary** at the beginning of this book is taken from testimony before the U.S. House Subcommittee on Domestic Monetary Policy and Technology, March 2011. **Part I** presents a brief history of money and the monetary traumas of the last century. **Part II** analyzes some of the problems caused by defective monetary policies of the 1980s and 1990s. **Part III** deals with more recent financial and economic traumas of the last decade in the run-up to the financial crisis and Great Recession of 2007-2009 – and its aftermath. I have not included in this book the more technical essays, some of which I wrote for Morgan Stanley during the 1980s and 1990s, although they spelled out the intellectual framework for what is presented here. Those Morgan Stanley papers and other additional articles may be found at *www.thegoldstandardnow.org*. My detailed proposals for the restoration and transition to an enduring gold standard are set forth in detail in the revised edition of my book, *The True Gold Standard: A Monetary Reform Plan without Official Reserve Currencies* (2012).

My basic argument has not changed in the five decades I have been studying and writing on monetary policy.

The true gold standard is the just, lasting, and least imperfect monetary system by which to integrate a growing U.S. and worldwide economy.

Note

[1] J. M. Keynes, *The General Theory*, Royal Economic Society edition (1973), p. 381.

SUMMARY

Testimony Prepared for U.S. House Subcommittee
on Domestic Monetary Policy and Technology,
March 17, 2011

Monetary policy, the Federal Reserve, the Budget Deficit, and Inflation

Since the expansive Federal Reserve program of quantitative easing began in late 2008, oil prices have almost tripled, gasoline prices have almost doubled. Basic world food prices, such as sugar, corn, soybean, and wheat, have almost doubled. Commodity and equity inflation, financed in part by the Fed's flood of excess dollars going abroad, has profound effects on the emerging markets. But in many emerging countries, food and fuel make up 25-50 percent of disposable income. Families in these countries can go from subsistence to starvation during such a Fed-fueled commodity boom.

The Fed credit expansion, from late 2008 through March 2011 – creating almost two trillion new dollars on the Fed balance sheet -- triggered the commodity and stock boom, because the new credit could not at first be fully absorbed by the U.S. economy in recession. Indeed, Chairman Ben Bernanke recently wrote that quantitative easing aimed to inflate U.S. equities and bonds directly, thus commodities indirectly. But some of the excess dollars sought foreign markets, causing a fall in the dollar on foreign exchanges. With quantitative easing, the Fed seems to aim at depreciating the dollar. In foreign countries, such as China, financial authorities frantically purchase the depreciating dollars, adding to their official reserves, issuing in exchange their undervalued currencies. The new money is promptly put to work creating speculative bull markets and booming economies.

The emerging market equity and economic boom of 2009 and 2010 was the counterpart of sluggish growth in the U.S. economy during the same period. The Consumer Price Index (CPI) will be suppressed because unemployment keeps wage rates from rising rapidly; the underutilization of industrial capacity keeps finished prices from rising rapidly. Inflation has shown up first in commodity and stock rises.

For Congress the irony could be that euphoria – always caused by renewed, gradual inflation – may set in once again, disarming potential budget and monetary reforms.

But commodity and stock inflation inevitably engenders social effects, not only financial effects. Inflationary monetary and fiscal policies have been a primary cause of the increasing inequality of wealth in American society. Bankers and speculators have been, and still are, the first in line, along with the Treasury, to get the zero interest credit of the Fed. They were also the first to get bailed out. Then, with new money, the banks financed stocks, bonds, and commodities, anticipating, as in the past, a Fed-created boom. The near-zero interest rates of the Fed continue to subsidize the large banks and their speculator clients. A nimble financial class in possession of cheap credit is able, at the same time, to enrich themselves, and to protect their wealth against inflation.

But middle-income professionals and workers, on salaries and wages, and those on fixed income and pensions, are impoverished by the very same inflation that subsidizes speculators and bankers. Those on fixed incomes earn little, or negative returns, on their savings. Thus, they save less. New investment then depends increasingly on bank debt, leverage, and speculation. Unequal access to Fed credit was everywhere apparent during the government bailout of favored brokers and bankers in 2008 and 2009, while millions of not so nimble citizens were forced to the wall, and then into bankruptcy. This ugly chapter is only the most recent chapter in the book of sixty years of financial disorder.

Inequality of wealth and privilege in American society is intensified by the Fed-induced inflationary process. The subsidized banking and financial community, combined with an overvalued dollar – underwritten by China – have also submerged the manufacturing sector, dependent as it is on goods traded in a competitive world market. In a word, the government deficit and the Federal Reserve work hand in hand, perhaps unintentionally, to undermine the essential equity and comity necessary in a constitutional republic. Equal opportunity and the harmony of the American community cannot survive perennial inflation.

If the defect is inflation and an unstable dollar, what is the remedy?

A dollar convertible to gold would provide the necessary Federal Reserve discipline to secure the long-term value of middle-income savings, to backstop the drive for a balanced budget. The gold standard would terminate the world dollar standard – by prohibiting official dollar reserves, and the special access of the government and the financial class to limitless cheap Fed and foreign credit.

The world trading community would benefit from such a common currency – a non-national, neutral, monetary standard – that cannot be manipulated and created at will by the government of any one country. Thus, dollar convertibility to gold must be restored. But dollar convertibility to gold must also become a cooperative project of the major powers. Gold, the historic common currency of civilization, was during the Industrial Revolution and until recent times, the indispensable guarantor of stable purchasing power – necessary for both long-term savings and long-term investment, not to mention its utility for preserving the long-term purchasing power of working people and pensioners. The gold standard puts control of the supply of money into the hands of the American people, as it should in a constitutional republic. Because excess creation of credit and paper money can be redeemed by the people for gold at the fixed statutory price, the monetary authorities are thus required to limit the creation of new credit in order to preserve the legally guaranteed value of the currency. As President Reagan said: "Trust the people."

To accomplish this monetary reform, the United States can lead, *first*, by announcing future convertibility, on a date certain, of the U.S. dollar, the dollar itself to be defined in statute as a weight unit of gold, as the Constitution suggests; *second*, by convening a new Bretton Woods conference to establish mutual gold convertibility of the currencies of the major powers – at a level which would not pressure nominal wages; *third* to prohibit by treaty the use of any currency but gold as official reserves.

A dollar as good as gold is the way out. It is the way to restore American savings and competitiveness. It is the way to restore economic growth and full employment without inflation. Gold convertibility is the way to restore America's financial self-respect, and to regain its needful role as the equitable leader of the world.

A Century of Decline in the Dollar's Value

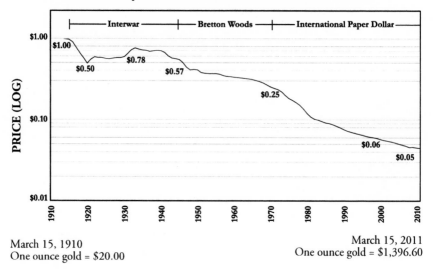

| Interwar | Bretton Woods | International Paper Dollar |

March 15, 1910
One ounce gold = $20.00

March 15, 2011
One ounce gold = $1,396.60

The Monetary Problem of the 20th Century; and its
Solution in Historical Perspective: Professor Jacques Rueff
and the dollar problem

As a soldier of France, no one knew better than Professor Jacques Rueff, the famous French central banker and economist, that World War I had brought to an end the preeminence of the classical European states system; that it had decimated the flower of European youth; that it had destroyed the European continent's industrial primacy. No less ominously, on the eve of the Great War, the gold standard – the gyroscope of the Industrial Revolution, the proven guarantor of one hundred years of price stability, the common currency of the world trading system – the monetary standard of commercial civilization – was suspended by the belligerents.

The Age of Inflation was upon us.

The overthrow of the historic gold standard, led, during the next decade, to the great inflations in France, Germany, and Russia. The ensuing inflationary convulsions of the social order, the rise of the speculator class, the obliteration of the savings of the laboring and middle classes led

4

directly to the rise of Bolshevism, Fascism, and Nazism – linked, as they were, to floating European currencies, perennial budgetary and balance-of-payments deficits, central bank money printing, currency wars and the neo-mercantilism they engendered.

Today, one observes – at home and abroad – the fluctuations of the floating dollar, the unpredictable effects of its variations, the new mercantilism it has engendered, and the abject failure to rehabilitate the dollar's declining reputation. Strange it is that an unhinged token, the paper dollar, is now the monetary standard of the most scientifically advanced global economy the world has ever known.

The insidious destruction of the historic gold dollar – born with the American republic – got underway gradually, in the 1920s, during the inter-war experiment with the gold-exchange standard and the dollar's new official reserve currency role. It must be remembered that World War I had caused the price level almost to double. But after the war, Britain and America tried to maintain the pre-war dollar-gold, sterling-gold parities. Designed at the Genoa Convention of 1922, the official reserve currency roles of the convertible pound and dollar collapsed after 1929 in the Great Depression – a collapse which helped to cause and to intensify the worldwide deflation and depression. Then, Franklin Roosevelt in 1934 reduced the value of the dollar by raising the price of gold from $20 to $35 per ounce.

But it must be emphasized that it was in 1922, at the little known but pivotal Monetary Conference of Genoa, that the unstable, gold-exchange standard had been officially embraced by the academic and political elites of Europe. It was here that the dollar and the pound were confirmed as official reserve currencies to supplement what was said to be a scarcity of gold. But there was no true scarcity, only overvalued currencies after World War I. Professor Rueff warned in the 1920s of the dangers of this flawed gold-exchange system designed "to economize gold." He predicted again in 1960-1961 that the Bretton Woods system, a post-World War II gold-exchange standard, flawed as it was by the same official reserve currency contagion of the 1920s, would soon groan under the flood weight of excess American dollars going abroad. Rueff in the 1950s and 1960s forecast permanent U.S. balance-of-payments deficits and the tendency to constant budget deficits, and ultimately the suspension of dollar convertibility to gold. His prescience was borne out by the facts.

After World War II, Professor Rueff saw that because the United States was the undisputed hegemonic military and economic power of the free world, foreign governments and central banks, in exchange for these military services and other subsidies rendered, would for a while continue to purchase (sometimes to protect their export industries) excess dollars on the foreign exchanges against the creation of their own monies. But these foreign official dollars, originating in the U.S. balance-of-payments and budget deficits, were then redeposited by foreign governments in the New York dollar market which led to inflation and excess consumption in the United States. This same process engendered inflation in its European and Asian protectorates which purchased excess dollars against the issuance of their own currencies. In a word, official reserve currencies jam the indispensable, international settlements and adjustment mechanism. Moreover, these purchases of dollars by foreign central banks have the simultaneous effect of creating inflation in these foreign countries and undervaluing their currencies relative to the dollar. Incipient mercantilism was only one pernicious result of the dollar's overvalued, official reserve currency status. The decline of the great U.S. manufacturing center was another.

Incredibly, during this same period of the 1960s, the International Monetary Fund authorities had the audacity to advocate the creation of Special Drawing Rights (SDRs), so-called "paper gold," invented, as International Monetary Fund officials said, to avoid a "potential liquidity shortage." At that very moment, the world was awash in dollars, in the midst of perennial dollar and exchange rate crises. Professor Rueff remarked that the fabrication of these SDRs by the International Monetary Fund would be "irrigation plans implemented during the flood."

The post-World War II gold-exchange standard (Bretton Woods) came to an end on the Ides of March, in 1968, when President Lyndon B. Johnson suspended the London Gold Pool. After a few more crippled years, Bretton Woods expired on August 15, 1971. The truth is that monetarists and Keynesians sought not to reform Bretton Woods, as the true gold standard reform of Jacques Rueff intended, but rather to demolish it. The true gold standard had become passé among the intellectual, economic, and political elites because of their confusion over the difference between the gold standard and the gold-exchange standard – the collapse of the latter, not the former, having intensified the Depression. I shall give you just one example of the obtuseness of the political class of the 1960s and 1970s, which happened at the height of one major dollar crisis. A friend of Professor Rueff, the American policy intellectual Henry Reuss, chairman of the Banking and Currency Committee of the U.S. House of Representatives, went so far as to predict, with great confidence and even greater fanfare, that when gold was demonetized, it would fall from $35 to $6 per ounce. (I am not sure whether Congressman Reuss ever covered his short at $800 per ounce in 1980.)

President Richard Nixon, a self-described conservative, succeeded President Johnson and was gradually converted to Keynesian economics by so-called conservative academic advisers, led by Professor Herbert Stein. Mr. Nixon had also absorbed some of the teachings of the monetarist school from his friend Milton Friedman – who embraced the expediency of floating-exchange rates and central bank manipulation and the targeting of the money stock to create a stable inflation rate. Thus, it was no accident that the exchange rate crises continued because the underlying cause, inflation, continued. On August 15, 1971, after one more violent dollar crisis, Nixon defaulted at the gold window of the western world, declaring that "we are all Keynesians now." In 1972, Nixon, a Republican, a so-called free market President, imposed the first peacetime wage and price controls in American history – encouraged by some of the famous "conservative" advisers of the era.

In President Nixon's decision of August 1971, the last vestige of dollar convertibility to gold, the final trace of an international common currency, binding together the civilized trading nations of the West, had been unilaterally abrogated by the military leader of the free world.

Ten years later at the peak of a double-digit inflation crisis, the gold price touched $850. At the time, Paul Volcker, Chairman of the Federal Reserve, declared that the gold market was going its own way and had little to do with the Fed's monetary policies. Volcker then engineered a draconian credit contraction leading to near 11 percent unemployment and a decline in inflation. At that time, Professor Henry Wallich declared that the gold market is but "a side show." Secretary of the Treasury William Miller, and a short-lived Fed Chairman, who had been selling U.S. gold at about $200 in 1978, announced solemnly that the Treasury would now no longer sell American gold. Presumably Secretary Miller, an aerospace executive, meant that whereas more than one-half the vast American gold stock had been a clever sale, liquidated at prices ranging between $35 and $250 per ounce – now, in the manner of the trend follower, Secretary of the Treasury Miller earnestly suggested that gold was a "strong hold" at $800 per ounce.

On January 18, 1980, Fed Governor Wallich, a former Yale Economics professor, explained Federal Reserve monetarist policies in an article appearing in the *Journal of Commerce*. "The core of Federal Reserve... measures," basing "control upon the supply of bank reserves," he said, "gives the Federal Reserve a firmer grip on the growth of monetary aggregates."

As subsequent events showed, the Federal Reserve promptly lost control of the monetary aggregates. The bank prime rate rose to 21 percent, inflation to double digits.

Professor Rueff's experience as a central banker had taught him from hard experience what his five volumes of monetary theory and econometrics demonstrated. That is, no central bank, not even the mighty Federal Reserve, can determine the quantity of bank reserves or the quantity of money in circulation – all conceits to the contrary notwithstanding. The central bank may influence indirectly the money stock; but the central bank cannot determine its amount. In a free society, only the money users – consumers and producers in the market – will determine the money they desire to hold. In a reasonably free society, it is consumers and producers in the market who desire and decide to hold cash balances, and also to change the currency and bank deposits they wish to keep; it is central banks and commercial banks which can supply them.

During the past forty years, the important links between central bank policies, the rate of inflation, and the variations in the money stock have caused much debate among the experts. It is still generally thought by neo-Keynesian, and some monetarist economists and central bankers, that the quantity of money in circulation, and economic growth, and the rate of inflation can be directly coordinated by central bank credit policy. May I now firmly say that, to the best of my knowledge, no one who believes this hypothesis, and, as an investor, has systemically acted on it in the market, is any longer solvent. But I do confess that the neo-Keynesian and monetarist quantity theories of money still hang on – even if their practitioners in the market cannot. In the end neo-Keynesian and monetarist economists at the Federal Reserve were ultimately required to accommodate to a reality in which, for example during 1978, the quantity of money in Switzerland grew approximately 30 percent while the price level rose only 1 percent. The quantity of money, M-1, grew in 1979 about 5 percent in the United States while the inflation rate rose 13 percent. The Fed learned that the CPI inflation rate cannot be precisely associated with the quantity of money in circulation.

If then, a central bank cannot determine the quantity of money in circulation, what, in Rueffian monetary policy, can a central bank realistically do? To conduct operations of the central bank, there must be a target. If the target is both price stability and the quantity of money in circulation, one must know, among other things, not only the magnitude of the desired supply of money, but also the precise volume of the future demand for money in the market – such that the twain shall meet. It is true that commercial banks supply cash balances, but individuals and businesses – the users of money – generate the decisions to hold and spend these cash balances. Thus, the Federal Reserve must have providential omniscience to calculate correctly, on a daily or weekly basis, the total demand for money – assuming the Fed could gather totally reliable statistical information – which it cannot; and even if the Fed's definitions of the monetary aggregates were constant – which they are not.

Jacques Rueff, himself the deputy governor of the Bank of France, clarified this fundamental problem in the form of an axiom: Because the money stock cannot be determined by the Federal Reserve Bank, nor can it determine a constant rate of inflation, the monetary policy of the central bank must not be to target the money supply or the rate of inflation. The Federal Reserve Bank simply cannot determine accurately the manifold decisions of the public to hold money, for individual and corporate purposes, in order to make necessary payments and to carry precautionary balances. Therefore, the leaders of the European Central Bank and the Federal Reserve System, indeed all central banks, cannot and should not try to determine the quantity of money in circulation.

But, if the true goal of the central bank were long-run stability of the general price level, the operating target of monetary policy at the central bank must be simply to influence the supply of cash balances in the market, such that they tend to equal the level of desired cash balances in the market. To attain this goal, the central bank must abandon open-market operations and simply hold the discount rate, or the rediscount rate, above the market rate – when, for example, the price level is rising – providing money and credit only at an interest rate which is not an incentive to create new credit and money. Indeed, if the target of monetary policy is long-run price stability, the central bank must supply bank reserves and currency only in the amount which is approximately equal to the desire to hold them in the market. For if the supply of cash balances is approximately equal to the desire to hold them, the price level must tend toward stability. If there are no excess cash balances, there can be no excess demand, and, thus, there can be no sustained inflation. There also can be no sustained deflation, caused by scarcity of cash balances, because the target of monetary policy is a stable price level and, in these circumstances, the central bank supplies the desired cash balances.

An effective central bank policy, therefore, must reject open-market operations. Professor Rueff shows further that, in order to rule out inflation, and unlimited government spending, the government treasury must be required by law to finance its cash needs in the market for savings, away from the banks. That is, a government treasury, in deficit, must be denied the privilege of access to new money and credit at the central bank and commercial banks, in order also to deny the government the pernicious privilege of making a demand in the market without making a supply – the ultimate cause of inflation. That is, since the Federal Reserve creates new money and credit to finance the Treasury deficit, but the Treasury creates no new goods and services, total money demand will exceed supply at prevailing prices. Prices must rise. At first, commodity and equity prices advance. Then the general price level rises gradually. This exorbitant U.S. government financing privilege, a function of total Fed discretion and of the dollar's reserve currency status, is a necessary cause of the balance-of-payments deficit and persistent inflation. It is also a fundamental cause of unlimited budget deficits and bloated big government. So long as new bank credit is available to the government, so long will the budget deficit persist and grow.

One can see that the monetary theory and policy of Jacques Rueff finally does come to grips with, indeed it modifies, the famous Law of Markets of Jean Baptiste Say, building of course on Say's insights, but perfecting the flawed Quantity Theory of Money. Jacques Rueff reformulated the quantity theory of money, definitively, in the following proposition: aggregate demand is equal to the value of aggregate supply, augmented (+/-) by the difference between the variations, during the same market period, in the quantity of money in circulation and the aggregate cash balances desired. This is a central theorem of Rueffian monetary economics. Rueff demonstrated that Say's Law does work, namely, that supply tends to equal demand, provided, however, that the market for cash balances must tend toward equilibrium. Any monetary system, any central bank, which does not reinforce this tendency toward equilibrium in the market for cash balances destroys the first law of stable markets, namely, overall balance between supply and demand – a necessary condition for limiting inflation and deflation.

It is conventional wisdom that Milton Friedman and the monetarists try to regulate the growth of the total quantity of money and inflation through a so-called money stock rule designed to constrain the central bank monopoly over the currency issue. In practice, the Federal Reserve has failed, and will fail, to succeed with such a flawed, academic, and impractical rule. Professor Friedman himself humbly admitted failure in a remarkable 2003 interview. The much simpler, more reliable, market-biased technique – proven in the laboratory of history as Professor Rueff demonstrated – would be to make the value of a unit of money equal to a weight unit of gold, in order to regulate, according to market rules, the same central bank monopoly. But academics have argued for a century that a monetary "regulator," such as gold money, absorbs too much real resources – by virtue of the process of gold production – and is therefore, in economic terms, too costly.

Whatever the minor incremental mining cost of a gold-convertible currency, it is a superior currency stabilizer, as history shows. The empirical data also demonstrate that it is a more efficient regulator of price stability in the long run. The gold standard was no mere symbol. It was an elegantly designed monetary mechanism – carefully orchestrated over centuries by wise men of great purpose – who developed convertibility into a supple and subtle set of integrated financial and credit institutions organized to facilitate rapid growth, quality job creation, a stable price level, above all, social stability amidst free economic institutions. Thus did the free price mechanism and the international gold standard become the balance wheel of rapid economic growth during the long-lasting Industrial Revolution. Who can deny that two generations of floating-exchange rates, pegged undervalued currencies like the Chinese yuan, and discretionary central banking, have burdened the world with booms, panics, and busts, producing immense inflation and uncertainty costs, much greater than the comparatively modest cost of mining gold?

Therefore, in order to bring about international price stability and long-run stability in the global market for cash balances, the dollar and other key currencies must be defined in law as equal to a weight unit of gold – at a statutory convertibility rate which insures that nominal wage rates do not fall. Indeed, nothing but gold convertibility, without official reserve currencies, will yield a real fiduciary monetary standard for the integrated world economy.

At the end of the first decade of the new millennium, the world requires, a real monetary standard, a common non-national monetary standard, to deal with the monetary disorder of undervalued, pegged currencies and manipulated floating-exchange rates – the diabolical agents of an invisible, predatory mercantilism. Despite all denials, the currency depreciations of today are, without a doubt, designed to transfer unemployment to one's neighbor and, by means of an undervalued currency, to gain share of market in manufactured, labor intensive, value-added, world traded goods. If these depreciations and undervaluations are sustained, floating-exchange rates combined with the twin budget and trade deficits will, at regular intervals, blow up the world trading system. Great booms and busts, inflation and deflation, social instability must ensue.

To head off the mercantilism of present floating-exchange rates, and the consequences of exchange rate disorders caused by official dollar reserves, an international monetary conference is indispensable. The present high rates of unemployment and perverse trade effects, associated with floating-exchange rates, require an efficient and stable international monetary reform. Not least because floating-exchange rates reprice entire national production systems at unpredictable intervals. Such monetary perversity cannot be sustained. A European Monetary Union may be necessary; but it is not sufficient.

Now we see clearly, what before we saw in a glass darkly -- the dollar's official reserve-currency status still gives an exorbitant credit privilege to the United States. Professor Rueff spoke of American "deficits without tears," because the American budget deficit and balance-of-payments deficits were – they still are – almost automatically financed by the Federal Reserve and the world-dollar reserve-currency system – through the voluntary (or coerced) buildup of dollar balances in the official reserves of foreign governments. These official dollar reserves were, and still are, immediately invested by foreign authorities, directly or indirectly, in the dollar market for U.S. securities, thus giving back to the United States, at subsidized rates, the dollars previously sent abroad as a result of the persistent U.S. balance-of-payments deficit and budget deficits. This is the subtle mechanism by which excess American domestic consumption and budget deficits are financed. To describe this awesome absurdity, Professor Rueff invoked the metaphor of the king's overworked tailor, yoked permanently to fictitious credit payments by His Majesty's unrequited promissory notes. Despite his purchases, His Majesty's cash balances and euphoria kept rising, blinded as he was to his ultimate, debt-induced insolvency.

There is not sufficient time to dwell on all the intricacies of the superior efficacy of the balance-of-payments adjustment mechanism grounded in domestic and international convertibility to gold. But it can, I think, be shown that, in all cases, currency convertibility to gold, without official reserve currencies, is *the least imperfect monetary mechanism*, both in theory and in practice, by which to rule out currency wars, to maintain global trade and financial balance, a reasonably stable price level, and economic growth – while ensuring budgetary equilibrium. This proposition has been proven in the only laboratory by which to test monetary theory – namely, the general history of monetary policy under paper and metallic regimes, and, in particular, the history of the international gold standard.

Whereas, by contrast, when one country's currency – the dollar reserve currency of today – is used to settle international payments, the international settlement and adjustment mechanism is jammed – for that country – and for the world. This is no abstract notion. An example from the past: during the twelve months of 1995, one hundred billion dollars of foreign-exchange reserves were accumulated by foreign governments which were directly invested in U.S. Treasury securities held in custody at the New York Federal Reserve Bank – thus financing the more modest U.S. current account and U.S. budget deficits of the time. Between March 10, 2010 and March 9, 2011, foreign governments monetized 415 billion dollars in the form of U.S. securities held in custody at the Fed. This is only a fraction of the $3.5 trillion of official dollar reserves, held in custody at the Fed, accumulated by March, 2011, over two generations. This accumulation of foreign dollar reserves is a gigantic mortgage on America. It is the infernal mechanism by which the government budget deficit and balance-of-payments deficits are financed. Along with the Fed, foreign dollar reserves are sufficient today to finance domestic over-consumption in the United States at below market interest rates.

It is essential to understand the nature of this ongoing process of currency degradation – because the dollar's reserve currency role in financing the U.S. budget and balance-of-payments deficits certainly did not end with the breakdown of Bretton Woods in 1971. The perennial and extraordinary U.S. budget and balance-of-payments deficits still persist because there is, today, no efficient international monetary mechanism to forestall the American deficits. Indeed, Professor Rueff argued that if the official reserve role of the dollar – i.e., the world dollar standard – were abolished, and convertibility restored, the immense U.S. budget and current account deficits must end – a blessing not only for the United States, but for the whole world. This is so because the Fed and the Treasury would be bound by statute and treaty to maintain the gold convertibility of the dollar. It is true that both law and international treaty may be violated, but they do create the only barriers to the license of rogues.

The reality behind the "twin deficits" is simply this: the greater and more permanent the Federal Reserve and foreign reserve facilities for financing the U.S. budget and trade deficits, the greater will be the twin deficits and the growth of the Federal government. All congressional, administrative, and statutory attempts to end the U.S. deficits have proved futile, and will prove futile, until the crucial underlying flaw – namely the absence of an efficient international settlements and adjustment mechanism – is remedied by international monetary reform inaugurating a new international gold standard and the prohibition of official reserve currencies.

By pinning down the future price level by gold convertibility, the immediate effect of international monetary reform will be to end currency speculation in floating currencies, and terminate the immense costs of inflation hedging. Gold convertibility eliminates the very costly exchange of currencies at the profit-seeking banks. Thus, new savings will be channeled out of financial arbitrage and speculation, into long-term financial markets.

Increased long-term investment and improvements in world productivity will surely follow, as investment capital moves out of unproductive hedges and speculation – made necessary by floating-exchange rates – seeking new and productive investments, leading to more quality jobs. Naturally, the investment capital available at long-term will mushroom, inspired by restored confidence in convertibility, because the long-run stability of the price level will be pinned down by gold convertibility – as history shows to be the case in previous, well-executed monetary reforms of the past two hundred years. Along with increased capital investment will come sustained demand for unemployed labor, at quality wages, to work the new plant and equipment.

The world now awaits a far-seeing leader to carry out the international monetary reform proposed by the great monetary statesman of the 20th century, Professor Jacques Rueff.

PART I: THE HISTORY OF MONEY, DEBT, AND INFLATION

National economic policy making is largely concerned with the problems of unemployment and inflation. More precisely, it is their simultaneous combination in all Western economies which preoccupies policy makers. As these problems grow worse, the stakes rise higher. Either severe unemployment or sustained inflation, let alone both together, can be expected to have the most serious consequences for democracy. The history of money can explain how our current economic problems emerged and how they can be solved.

Throughout history, many different commodities – such as wampum, tobacco, and stones – have served as monetary standards. But each of these monetary standards quickly failed. Over centuries of evolution, gold was freely selected as the stable monetary standard that men must have for the combined purposes of exchange, rational calculation, and monetary saving in sophisticated, rapidly growing industrial economies. Merchants, consumers, traders, and producers gradually selected gold coins as the most desirable money. Over time, gold exhibited certain stable characteristics that no other medium of exchange exhibited.

As originally envisioned in the 1913 Federal Reserve Act, the credit and currency of the Federal Reserve System was to be based essentially upon the most liquid monetary assets, gold, and self-liquidating commercial bills – short-term, secured notes issued to finance goods in the process of production. In a word, the Federal Reserve Act of 1913 was designed to reinforce American participation in the international gold standard.

However, the two catastrophic world wars of the first half of the 20th century, combined with the conceits of academics and central bankers, derailed the classical gold standard and replaced it with defective gold-exchange standards – early official reserve currency systems. By the 1970s, the global monetary system, constructed in July 1944 at Bretton Woods, had fallen apart under the effects of easy money, the welfare state, the oil crisis, and wage and price controls. The end of Bretton Woods and the resulting stagflation of the 1970s had first been predicted by the great French economist, Jacques Rueff. He saw that the loose-money policies of the Federal Reserve, combined with the reserve currency role of the dollar, would create inflation and excess demand, in the United States and worldwide – especially at full employment; and that without a reform based on a true international gold standard, this excess demand, and the inflation it caused, would destroy the Bretton Woods reserve-currency system and lead to higher gold prices, rising prices in general, high unemployment, and world monetary disorder.

18

"Ancient merchants found in gold money, above all, a universally acceptable article of wealth in exchange for which they could obtain from farmers and artisans the products of painstaking labor. Working people had good reason to exchange their hard work for good money."

Chapter One
WHAT IS MONEY AND CREDIT?
ORIGINS: 700 B.C.-1700 A.D.

In the Beginning There Was Barter

Forerunners of man lived upon the planet several million years ago. But the unique, modern, social order of man – civilization – emerged only four to five thousand years ago. Historical and archaeological evidence suggests that the institution of money evolved coterminously with civilization. From the standpoint of the 100,000-year history of *Homo sapiens*, civilization and money are but young and fragile reeds. Today their very existence is threatened by financial disorder.

As even a moment's reflection suggests, modern civilization is unthinkable without money. What accounts for the appearance of money in the civilized affairs of men? In fact, what is money?

The economist defines money as a *medium of exchange*. It is the token we supply in order to effect payments for the goods we demand. Money is especially a standard like a yardstick – a unit of measure by which we value and price economic goods. Money units express prices which are the vital information necessary for efficient exchange. Money is surely a *store of value*. Many different forms of money have been selected in the market to serve the practical purposes of working people. True money is an article of wealth in which we have confidence to save part of the value of our labor for future contingencies. Indeed the money which emerges in history is no ivory tower abstraction. Until recently, it was real – a tangible article

19

of wealth. Money is a convenient, marketable substitute for the wealth we produce. It is the superior *marketability* of money over other forms of wealth which make it *generally acceptable* in exchange for other real goods and services. Thus, money is above all an agent of human trust by which we hold and exchange the cherished value of our labor and intelligence.

Money evolved through an historical process not unlike that of trial-and-error or natural selection. But money as civilization came to know it – standardized and certified coins – originated as an act of human creativity around 700 B.C. in the cradle of civilization – the Near East. Throughout history, many crude forms of money have been tried and discarded. Each form of money had to meet the test of acceptability established by working people – because it was they to whom money was supplied in return for the product of their labor. Seeking ever more marketable and efficient articles with which to transact household and business affairs, the merchants, farmers, and workers of different cultures experimented with different early currencies – cattle, iron, and in the 7th century B.C., primitive gold and silver coins. Over time, freely acceptable, widely circulated, reasonably stable forms of precious metal money did evolve. Some of these early, stable, indestructible monetary tokens, i.e., coins, survive unto this very day.

In a word, money is a commercial, political, and legal *institution* of the market with a long history. Because it is an institution based on trust, money entails moral obligation. Like the wheel, money is an *invention* of civilized man. But as some forms of the wheel have worked better than others, so is it with money. Not all forms of money are equally acceptable to free men. Nor do all wheels rotate evenly. Like a wheel without its spokes, money without real substance tends to break down. As with all breakdowns, disorder follows. The breakdown of money is associated with the depreciation of its value, or the long-term decline in its purchasing power. This social and economic disorder goes by the name of inflation. Ours is an era wherein stable monetary institutions have broken down. Historians will recall our era as the Age of Inflation – a monetary breakdown, a systemic decline in the value of money.

Inflation means the destruction, or the overturning, of an essential instrument of the market place – the political institution of stable, trustworthy, money – money which preserves purchasing power over the long term. The endurance of civilization is linked to a stable monetary standard. When the overturning of stable political institutions occurs, it is called revolution. Inflation or monetary depreciation entails a price revolution. It often precedes, indeed it may cause, a more thoroughgoing political revolution. Inflation prevails in America and the world today because of a breakdown of the institutions of trust that convertibility to gold once provided for the dollar. People no longer gladly accept and hold the dollar for long periods. They try to get rid of it for something real such as commodities, a car, real estate, equities, art, antiques, or coins – almost anything real and lasting. Producers and consumers have lost faith and trust in the dollar because the U.S. government and the Federal Reserve System have created more dollars than participants in the market desire to hold. Excess dollars have been created because the government has overproduced money and credit in order to finance its colossal deficits and also in order to manipulate the economy, prices, demand, and employment levels. As a result, the inconvertible paper dollar has ceased to be real money. Paper money is neither an article of wealth requiring labor to be produced, nor is it today linked permanently to anything of real value. The marginal cost to the Federal Reserve of adding one more paper or deposit dollar is zero.

It may be worth a moment to reflect upon this view in order to determine its merit. We know from history that civilization advanced beyond the primitive conditions of a barter economy by means of increasingly standardized commodity money. Commodity money requires human effort to be produced – copper, gold, silver. A barter economy consists in the moneyless exchange of one man's goods for the goods of another. The transition from a barter economy to a money economy was the first and most important commercial revolution. Instead of each family storing varied goods – such as wheat, wood, and venison to exchange directly for the goods of others such as cows, tools, and coal – civilized man gradually learned how to substitute an indirect, more economical means of exchange. Over a long period, working men and women invented money – simple, convenient tokens – which they labored to produce or obtain in order to exchange them for the goods they desired. To supply money for goods and goods for money, namely indirect exchange, is the hallmark of commercial civilization.

21

The long historical transition from the barter economy was marked by many different forms of indirect premonetary commerce, such as potlatching and other primitive forms of investment and risk sharing. Potlatching means to give a gift with the hope but not the certainty of a return. Potlatching is superior to barter because barter cannot always work. For example, what I produce may not be desired by the person to whom I try to barter it. Indeed such a person may supply me in exchange with a product which *I* do not desire. Thus, to potlatch, to "give" my supply of goods to others hoping that later they would reciprocate, actually advances the social order beyond inelastic direct barter. Everyone continues to produce, some more than others, without an immediately satisfying barter. Potlatching overcomes the rigidity of barter and tends to encourage indirectly the unconditional production of wealth. Production in a potlatching community goes on as if all members freely make goods for another, receiving in exchange unwritten "promissory notes", implied liabilities (or claims) of their grateful fellows to make goods for them. These implicit liabilities form the invisible currency, "the money," of a moneyless community of producers. These invisible claims of the producers are the circulating medium of potlatch. They are redeemed in the future by gifts of goods from the "debtors." Thus, the recipients of gifts make good on the essential faith and trust of the giver. The counterpart of the gift – the liability of the receiver somehow to repay the producer – is often repaid in kind and more. As George Gilder puts it, this productive circle of givers, or investors, increases the sympathy of its members for the special needs of one another. Potlatch amplifies barter, making for more efficiency and growth. Reciprocal faith is the moral currency of potlach. Barter and potlatch are way-stations of exchange on the road to civilizations characterized by a universally acceptable, real, trustworthy monetary standard.

Commercial civilization is especially a monetary economy. A monetary economy is one in which indirect exchange dominates almost all transactions. The institution of money separates into *two* transactions the primitive single act of bartering goods directly in exchange for other goods. But in the market economy, all people must first make demands with money in exchange for a supply of goods. But to obtain money, in the absence of subsidies, one must first make a supply. In a just and equitable society, the supplier, the producer, is primary. The demander is contingent because wealth is created only by the producer. Settlement in modern exchange between the supplier and the buyer takes place because the supplier of goods is willing to accept money as a substitute for goods. The supplier of goods can hold the money or he can in turn make a demand with the monetary token for goods he desires to consume, or for goods, or financial claims, which produce other goods. In this process of *indirect exchange*, a fundamental purpose and effect of money is to economize the scarce resources of the community. Money reduces the working capital otherwise invested by the producer or the consumer in a wide array of goods for which money is now an acceptable substitute. Money diminishes the storage space required for large and varied inventories held perforce by each family, enterprise, and community in a barter economy. Real money, lasting monetary tokens, also reduces the inherent risk, the contingency, and uncertainty of other forms of indirect exchange such as potlatching, which depend upon an implied currency of unrequited obligation. Such invisible claims come to be replaced by the diffusion of dependable coin, or currency convertible to real money. Standardized metallic, coined money – real money – gradually permeated the "overcapitalized," inefficient, barter economy inducing thereby a mutation in the scale and character of all ancient economic institutions of pre-commercial civilization by releasing enormous amounts of working capital to produce additional goods.

Along with the wheel, money joined parochial and tribal communities to one another, enlarging the fellowship of production by trade based on a common, metallic monetary standard. In a mere four thousand years, money transformed the closed economy of the tribe into the open and integrated economy of the whole world.

As with all human inventions, civilization increasingly improved upon its money, choosing between real money (e.g., coined precious metal), or nominal money (e.g., paper), or a combination (paper currency convertible to precious metal). Ancient and modern merchants and producers gradually embraced real money as an article of wealth, universally acceptable to all, in exchange for which they could obtain from farmers, miners, manufacturers, and artisans the products of painstaking labor. Working people had good reason to accept good money for desired goods. Often they did not want the goods produced in the neighborhood which others wished to exchange. Sometimes the producers did not know exactly when and what they wanted in exchange for their goods – after basic, life-giving needs were satisfied. At other times suppliers wished to sell the products of their labor but had no desire at all to purchase any available goods right away. They desired to defer repurchases; that is, they desired to save the product value of their effort and intelligence. By means of tested and true money, producers and merchants realized that they could exchange and save efficiently and reliably; because a real article of wealth, hard standard coin, was now available – itself the most desired, marketable, and lasting article of wealth on the market. Working people and producers understood metallic currency because, like all other goods, men had labored to discover and produce it. Coined wealth, like all produced goods, was substantially stored labor and intelligence. Such money enabled workers to wait – to defer buying – because money became a lawful, concrete token encompassing an irrevocable right to demand future goods. Money enhanced the options of all those who toiled and their families, augmenting their freedom to provide for themselves as they pleased, even to lay up efficiently a surplus for their children in the future. Real money lasted. It could be inherited and passed on. True money was universally accepted, spurious money rejected.

Money was a sacred link among people because it represented saved labor, the permanent link between work, family, past and future. It had become no less than the lifeblood of an enduring culture, the hemoglobin of commercial civilization.

The Nature of Civilized Money

In the real world of work, not every article of wealth could effectively qualify as money, the exchangeable token of stored labor. Indeed, the necessary and enduring properties of real money emerged only gradually in history. Certainly, no medicine men or academics created it according to an abstract design. In fact, enduring monetary tokens evolved gradually with the institutional advance of the social, commercial, and legal order. The first standardized and certified coins appeared in Lydia, Asia Minor, around 650 B.C. At this time the original Sumerian civilization was in its fourth millennium of development. The Lydians discovered and used a natural

mixture of gold and silver called electrum (primitive coin). In this kind of
coin, as we shall see, centuries of near eastern commercial evolution and
experimentation had bequeathed an equitable, efficient, dependable, lasting
form of money. Lydian coins exhibited specific properties, uniquely suitable
to perform the functions of money. They were small and portable. Made
of scarce precious metal commodities, they were beautiful and cherished.
Men had exerted great work effort and intelligence to produce them. These
primitive coins were very valuable to all who produced them, and others
who desired them. As a store of value, they were portable, solid, stable,
and enduring, even indestructible. As a medium of exchange, these coins
were convenient, compact, and because of their special properties ever-more
universally acceptable in ever-widening trade. Merchants and producers
knew that more of this kind of money could only be produced, over time,
by discovery and the steady application, the metering out of a certain
quantity of both capital and labor. The coins became, therefore, a useful
measuring rod by which to meter out the value; i.e., the price of the other
products of human intelligence (labor) and capital available on the market.
No one from the local "Bureau of Engraving" inaugurated such a coin from
purely abstract considerations. Nor was it foisted upon civilization. Nor
was it a government-forced currency. Instead, after centuries or millennia
of experimentation and innovation, traders and their customers came freely
to select these coins for their intrinsic monetary properties – their utility,
indestructibility, and marketability.

Merchants and artisans readily perceived that precious metal Lydian
coins could be easily handled. They were malleable, divisible, immutable,
storable, attractive, and because of their uniformity they could be easily
exchanged among merchants of many tongues in the Levant and the Near
East. The test of time had proved their lasting worth as a useful market
institution of exchange, thereby enhancing their *marketability*. Because
of the enormous labor and time invested to discover and produce these
small coins, they were prized by all and priced for the density of labor value
bestowed upon them. Each small precious metal token was one of the most
valuable articles of wealth on the market. Thus, the high value of these
coins, relative to their small size and lightweight, made them easily tradable
for large quantities of other goods. The high value-to-weight ratio also

made them an ideal means of saving the value of much of one's work and production. Enterprising producers could withdraw some of their working capital from costly warehouses and re-concentrate these ungainly hoards in secure, simple, standardized coin, expanding their options to repurchase a diversity of goods. History taught them that the value of these precious metal coins endured. In a very uncertain and risky world, merchants discovered that the purchasing power of the coins remained reasonably stable from year to year, even generation to generation. Moreover, with monetary coins, real wealth could be stored in such a little space, whereas to save other forms of real wealth required big buildings and elaborate security arrangements. But the simplest explanation for the universal acceptability of money coins by uneducated workers lies elsewhere. Plain working people could intuitively and directly compare the quantity and quality of the production value of their own labor to the value of the labor of those who had discovered, mined, and produced the lasting, real money which they desired to hold for future contingencies.

Money continued to evolve and change its form as commercial civilization gradually engirdled the earth. During the modern era, merchants and bankers learned to substitute inexpensive and easily handled fiduciary paper for coin. At first paper money consisted of bank notes or bills, convertible or exchangeable at a constant rate into a specific weight of gold and silver. The bank deposit convertible to precious metal, became even more abstract. For example, a piece of paper, certified by a bank or the government, came to substitute contractually for a certain quantity of real money – coin or bullion. By means of the lawful stamp of convertibility to gold, a near-worthless paper was suffused with a monetary life of its own. It circulated in place of coins and bullion because it was even more convenient, equally divisible, and above all secured by the substance of real money. Moreover, convertible paper and deposit currencies conserved still further the scarce mineral, labor, and capital resources previously invested in the production and circulation of precious bullion or coins. One sees in the evolution of this extraordinary commercial institution of exchange that money became a unique conservator, and the effective mechanism of growth of a civilization born of scarcity.

The Math of Modern Banking

Double-entry bookkeeping developed in 14th century Italy, whence the precise, simplified ledger and balance sheet accounting basis for the development of a "fractional" reserve banking system emerged. In such a banking system a new kind of "abstract" fiduciary money developed – subject to transfer by checks. They came to be called book entry bank deposits, bank advances, credit money, or checking accounts, sight liabilities, or demand deposits. The banks held bullion or coin reserves against this new credit money. The precious metal reserves were equal to a prudent "fraction" of the total bank note and deposit money circulation, hence the phrase "fractional reserve banking system". But, the value of the new monetary substitutes, the check and the transferable bank deposit, were upheld by convertibility to gold in the same manner as the value of paper currency or bank notes. Evolving as they did in the 17th and 18th century, bank deposits or credit money were convertible into a fixed weight unit of the original gold or silver coin, or real money, they represented. The coin and bullion were held by the banks in reserve by which to redeem fiduciary paper bank notes and deposits for real money equivalents – gold and silver.

But not all depositors wanted to redeem their deposits simultaneously. So only a fractional gold and silver reserve might be held by the banks. But a depositor could demand a warehouse receipt for his gold and silver deposits, whereupon the gold was immobilized for the depositor's account and unavailable for lending. European goldsmiths and silversmiths of the 17th century, acting as depositories, were in part the forerunners of modern commercial bankers, just as producers, merchants, shippers, and monetary depositories – at about the same time – elaborated more intricately the ancient practice of trading on credit. Commercial banking joined these two trade practices – gold and silver deposit banking and transferable credit bills of exchange – in an organic fusion which, to this very day, confuses the concepts of credit and money. By the 17th century, goldsmiths had discovered that most clients who, for a fee, deposited gold money for safekeeping, did not need their gold immediately. Though deposit receipts, or bank notes, issued for the gold could be presented on demand (hence demand deposits) to reclaim the gold, it never happened that all deposit receipts were presented for redemption simultaneously. Thus, goldsmiths (bankers) developed the practice of lending at interest a portion of the depositors money (gold and silver bullion, and coin) to others for short terms, holding only fractional reserves in order to redeem that regular fractional percentage of deposit receipts presented for redemption in coin or bullion. Over time, in a larger monetary economy, these fledgling bankers learned that only a regular percentage of depositors presented demands for redemption daily – except during periods of financial panic and war. Rules of thumb developed from this experience and bankers came to believe that a certain percentage, say 10 percent of deposits (or more), should be held on reserve to meet the depositors' demands for coin or bullion. But this rule of thumb was no more than the distillation of historic wisdom about the recurrence of demands for redemption.

Commercial Banking Traces to the Early Institutions of Credit

Trading on credit is an ancient practice, but early modern Europe had mostly developed the institutions of credit to the point we know them today. The essential instrument of commercial credit arose because the entrepreneur often did not have the cash, coin, or bullion to pay for his desired purchase of production goods. But he did have a creditworthy reputation. The goods he needed, say cloth or metals for a productive process, could be visible security for a loan. Thus the supplier of cloth would ship his goods to a textile maker, who could not pay cash, accompanied by a bill of exchange, that is a trade bill of credit. The bill of credit always accompanied the goods. Upon arrival, the textile maker received the cloth goods, verified the invoice, signed the bill of exchange, and returned the credit bill with security documents to the shipper (the cloth producer or merchant). The security documents provided that the cloth was pledged to the cloth maker until the textile maker completed the process of production (generally in 90 days), and had sold the processed goods for cash. Therewith payment was remitted to the shipper – whereupon the bill of credit was requited and cancelled. Note that the bill of exchange, a liability of the textile producer, was a form of credit in place of scarce cash (coin). It entailed a credit risk, like potlatching, but much less so, since the sale of cloth goods for the credit bill of exchange was legally secured by the goods themselves.

In a way, such an exchange of goods for credit bills, secured by the same goods, may be considered a sort of barter – the cloth (a good) in exchange for the secured bill, i.e., one thing for another. So, when the credit bill of exchange (or trade bill) had been signed by the buyer and secured, the claim itself (the bill of exchange) could then circulate as currency (means of payment) among merchants and banks until paid at maturity. Coin and bullion were thereby conserved.

As we have observed, early commercial banking in the 17th century merged the function of the goldsmith, who accepted gold and silver on deposit – issuing redeemable certificates in exchange – with the function of the merchant or producer, who extended credit through credit bills of exchange. The 17th century banker accepted not only money deposits (i.e., coin and bullion) against the issuance of certificates, notes, or deposits, but the bank accepted (purchased) credit bills of exchange from merchants and producers (who wanted money right away) in exchange for demand deposits or bank notes convertible to gold or silver. Thus suppliers were able to receive cash promptly for their sales of goods on credit by discounting their bills of exchange for money at the bank – if they did not desire to hold the credit bills of their customers until maturity. Commercial banking grew out of the desire (inspired by the profit motive) to conserve cash (gold) and by means of credit to provide financial elasticity and growth in the commercial process of exchange. That is, all producers (sellers) who desired true money (gold), instead of the short-term secured credit bills – promissory notes of their customers (the buyers) – could, through the mediation of goldsmiths-turned-bankers and bill-merchants-turned-bankers, obtain real money by discounting their bills of exchange for gold with the emerging commercial bankers of early modern Europe.

The combined institutions of stable money and secured credit enabled commercial civilization to make of the entire world the only closed economy.

"Economic exchange is uniquely a human activity."

Chapter Two

MODERN MONETARY HISTORY: 1700-1974 A.D.

By 1700, the banking system of Europe had elaborated most of the institutions of money and credit we know today. England had taken the lead. For almost 200 years, from 1717 until the onset of World War I in 1914, the British pound sterling, a weight unit of metallic money, set the example for modern monetary systems. Significantly, standard British money was called the *pound* – a standard *weight* of precious metal, originally one pound of silver – mined from the Earth's crust, then refined into coined money. The English word *money* originates in the Latin word moneta, literally meaning coin or mint. Real money is coin, that is, minted currency. On the other hand, inconvertible paper is nominal money – a monetary token without substance – generally maintained by a regime requiring taxes to be paid with inconvertible paper money. Historic standard money of the Western world, during its rise to preeminence, was coined metal, generally silver or gold.

The pound of precious metal would be "monetized" by coining standard units of *money* (coins) for circulation. Within a nation or community, the domestic issuance of such money, combined with the quantity of precious metal imported or exported, tended to equal the quantity of money desired to make payments and to hold for contingencies. But also, the value of mined, minted, and imported monetary metals in the community (i.e., money) was approximately equal to the value of all the products and services exchanged in the community. Thus, over the long run, the quantity of (coined) money in circulation was always in reasonable balance with the quantity of goods and services produced in the monetary economy plus the money held for contingencies. Under such a naturally balanced monetary system, there could be little excess coin or undesired money. Thus, there could be no great inflation. Nor could there be a "shortage" of money. All producers made a supply of goods in the market for money, the total quantity of which was determined by the amount mined or imported and then coined for those who desired to hold it instead of goods, or with it to make a purchase. Thus, there could be no great deflation caused by insufficient money because the community was free to produce or import the coin, or money, it desired to hold. In a reasonably free economy, the money prices of all goods fluctuated, but workers received money wages, or purchasing power, the real value of which tended to rise with needs and wants.

It is true that prices *gradually* rose when large, new mine discoveries amplified the quantity of monetary metal on the market. Such an example occurred during the 16th century, known to historian as "The Price Revolution." But the average annual rise in the price level during this period, contrary to conventional wisdom, was around two percent. It is also true that the price level *gradually* declined during periods of diminished rates of discovery of the monetary metals – causing real wages to rise. Such a period was the late 19th century in the United States, known to some historians as "The Great Deflation." The average annual decline in the price level during this period was one to two percent. But this fall in the price level was associated with one of America's greatest periods of economic growth – three to four percent annually. Compared to the Great Depression of 1930-1933 – caused by monopoly central banking, protectionism, trade barriers, and the official reserve currency roles of the dollar and the pound – the monetary deflation of 1870-1900 was but a gentle decline amidst a remarkable economic expansion, productivity and wage growth.

It was no accident that the effective monetary standard of the Western world was a definite *weight* of a real article of wealth. English currency had taken its name from the pound weight of precious metal, the customary unit of value at the town of Sterling in ancient Anglo-Saxon England. It is true that the metallic monetary unit in medieval Europe never contained the precise weight indicated by its name. In addition, the weight measures of money actually varied from locality to locality and were arbitraged in market places by moneychangers with accurate weights and measures. But the standard monetary unit, the measuring rod of value, was nevertheless agreed privately and publicly to be a true weight unit of bullion or coin. Intuitively, a weight unit of money enabled its users to compare the value of labor and capital and natural resources – i.e., the "weightiness" of precious metal money, to the value (or "weightiness") of other goods and services requiring labor, capital, and natural resources to be produced. Standard coined money, therefore, exhibited *real* earmarks of an acceptable, universal standard of economic value by which to gauge all *real* products and services.

Even more important was the fact that a real, *specific* weight unit of precious metal – not a nominal stamped paper note decreed by the monarch – had emerged as the standard of value in international trade. Just as political authorities cannot vary the true yardstick from its prescribed standard length of 36 inches, lest all trade-based length measurement must break down in chaos; so the community of workers and wealth producers embraced a monetary standard selected in the market, fixed by weight, in the absence of which the measurement and exchange of economic values, domestically and internationally, might become unreliable and break down through inflation, deflation, and economic contraction.

Now, the reason a unit of weight emerged as the measuring rod of economic value is transparent. Economic exchange is uniquely a human activity. Wealth consists of real articles of wealth and services offered in the market, which originate in human labor and intelligence. Wealth is created by human capital applied to natural resources, financed by capital accumulated by saved labor. Historic money of the market, i.e., metallic money, was selected because it, too, was a desired real article of wealth produced in and for the market. It was also desired for enduring beauty (ornamental savings). But standard metallic money measured the value of the amount of intelligence and effort (human capital) and financial capital (saved labor) that was required to produce a certain quantity (or weight) of metal which could be exchanged against the intelligence and work effort required to produce other real goods in the market. All goods or services require for production a certain amount of intelligence, labor, capital, and natural resources. Therefore, an intuitive proportionality – an underlying equitable relationship of value among all goods – may be measured best by a unit of measure (a monetary standard) which is common to all these goods.

After millennia of evolution, the market discovered such a unit of stable measure to be the weight unit of precious metal, gold and silver, which the empirical evidence shows, can only be produced by the application of a relatively steady amount of human intelligence, effort, and capital. The trading market discovered that a weight of gold metal exhibited the property of long-run steady value (purchasing power) and permanence (indestructibility) better than all other competing monetary standards. Thus it was that by about 1880 the value of human economic activity came to be measured worldwide by a defined weight unit of gold. Indeed, in many geographies gold prices are still the historic standard of economic measurement. The gold standard had become the golden yardstick of commercial civilization by the 19th century; and, as we shall see, acted as the gyroscope of the Industrial Revolution – the longest period of sustained and rapid economic expansion in human history – marked by rising standards of living and price level stability.

How did modern commercial communities organize money? The historic pound sterling, for example, was divisible by law and practice into weight units of gold and silver money. Paper pound notes (or bank notes) after 1717 were issued and redeemable into their equivalent weight in gold. By the late 19th century, checks drawn on the expanding demand deposits of the sterling banking system were acceptable throughout the commercial world. Acceptability of bank checks drawn on bank deposits depended on their prompt redeemability in English bank notes, themselves convertible into gold coin or bullion – a real money which under British leadership had become world money.

Gold money had proved itself in the market as the least imperfect monetary standard. But England dominated world commerce; so gold money rapidly became world currency. The integrated and expanding industrial world economy of the 19th century was based on a common, efficient currency. The network effects of a common world money proved irresistible; western capitalism comprised a family of competing nations with currencies mutually convertible to gold at a stipulated parity. The coincident occurrence of expanding trade and stable money was not accidental. Each needed the other. Throughout history, a reliable and efficient money had accompanied the development of an ordered and growing exchange economy. It was not by chance that the destruction of stable money in ancient Greece and Rome brought inflation, price and wage controls, rationing, tyranny, contraction, and decline. The monetary process of debasement, or currency depreciation, or inflation occurred over centuries, but the hindsight of the historian shows the link among a continuous depreciating money, a systemic rise in the cost-of-living, and a doomed civilization.

World War I ended the preeminence of the classical European states system and its monetary basis, the true gold standard. No less significantly, on the eve of war, the rules of the international gold standard – the proven guarantor of one hundred years of price stability – was suspended by the belligerents. From the standpoint of history, we know that total war can destroy all the institutions of civilization. Money could be no exception. No monetary standard can survive total war. In order to stem a bank run in 1914 by fear-stricken citizens on the limited gold supplies of the banking system and the central banks, the governments of Europe suspended the gold standard which for more than a century had anchored the value of bank deposits and currency in circulation. Between 1914 and 1924, expansionary central bank credit policies of war-torn European nations destroyed or depreciated many national paper currencies.

The Age of Inflation was upon us. At the time of the Paris Peace Conference of 1919 (before his later government planning phase) John Maynard Keynes argued that there was no surer means of "overturning the existing basis of society than to debauch the currency." The process of inflation, Keynes warned, "engages all the hidden forces of economic law on the side of destruction, and does it in a manner which not one man in a million is able to diagnose." Keynes was a shrewd man, and in this single phrase he depicted the satanic forces released by the destruction of the value of money. Keynes understood inflation. He knew its effects destroyed the wellsprings of the future because he had observed the catastrophic devastation firsthand after World War I. Shortly thereafter, Keynes wrote that under the conditions of inflation "a country can, without knowing it, expend in current consumption those savings which it thinks it is investing for the future....When the value of money is greatly fluctuating, the distinction between capital and income becomes confused. It is one of the evils of a depreciating currency that it enables a community to live on its capital unawares. The increasing money value of the community's capital goods obscures temporarily a diminution in the real quantity of the [capital] stock....For these profound reasons Europe is in danger of a lasting degradation of her standards, unless bold and conservative wisdom can take control."

But Keynes was more than an analyst of the defects of inflation and deflation. He knew something about its remedies, for he wrote after World War I as if for our own age: "If gold standards could be introduced throughout Europe, we all agree that this would promote, as nothing else can, the revival not only of trade and production, but of international credit and the movement of capital to where it is needed most. One of the greatest elements of uncertainty would be lifted...and one of the most subtle temptations to improvident national finance would be removed; for if a national currency had once been stabilized on gold basis, it would be harder (because so much more openly disgraceful) for a Finance Minister so to act as to destroy this gold basis."

So much for the man who (when he found it in England's interest and his own) would later expediently and contemptuously dismiss the discipline of the gold standard as "a barbarous relic." It is not by chance that the decline and fall of British capitalism (that is, the collapse of British power, as Correlli Barnett calls it) was closely associated with Britain's permanent suspension of the classical gold standard and the rise of the Bank of England's manipulated, inconvertible paper money, and the financing of the Treasury's budget deficit by the Bank of England and foreign banks.

The end of the international gold standard in 1914 led during the next decade to the great paper and credit money inflations in France (1924-1926), Germany (1920-1923), and Russia (1916-1918) – among other European countries. The ensuing convulsions of the European social order – and the virtual obliteration of the savings of its middle classes led directly to the rise of Bolshevism in Russia and Nazism in Germany. Revolution, during and following the Great War of 1914, was closely associated with the ruination of *inconvertible* European paper currencies.

Clio, the muse of history, instructs us that to desire a peaceful and prosperous world trading system is to desire the means by which to achieve it – or to court disaster. A world trading system needs leadership and a common underlying currency, independent of national currencies. To maintain a global, integrated market requires a common currency – one universally accepted and trusted after centuries of trial and error. It is an errand into the wilderness to desire an end without desiring the effective means by which to attain it. Under current circumstances, to desire peace and world economic order is to desire strong international leadership and the international gold standard.

Today, four generations after the Great War of 1914, one observes – at home and abroad – the disintegration and fluctuation of the value of all paper and credit monies. The scourge of inflation ever so gradually overtakes us. Today it is often described as "too much money chasing too few goods." In fact, inflation represents *a decline in the value and the destruction of the preeminent economic institution of civilization* – money. The astronomical rise of the price of gold – from $20 to $35 per ounce in 1934, from $35 per ounce in 1971 to $500 in March of 1981, to $1,700 in 2012 is merely the other side of the same debased coin – the decline and fall of the dollar. This corrosive process of systemic inflation got underway in 1913 with the founding of the Federal Reserve System. World War I intensified the breakdown of monetary institutions. After the international monetary conference of Genoa in 1922, and the inauguration of the official reserve currency system based on the dollar and the pound, inflation again picked up momentum in Europe. The central bank inflationary bubble of the 1920s collapsed in depression. After the early phase of the Great Depression (1929-1933) the process of worldwide inflation got underway again, which carries on to this very day – punctuated by brief periods of disinflation.

The historic signal for the great American inflation occurred in 1933-1934 when Franklin D. Roosevelt abruptly terminated the domestic gold standard (1933). He expropriated and paid $20 for all gold and gold coins owned by U.S. citizens. Then in 1934, FDR reduced the value of the monetary standard by reducing the weight of the gold dollar; or as it is said, by raising the gold price from $20 to $35 per ounce. The effect of this devaluation was, overnight, to collect for the government and spend the higher value for the gold which had rightfully belonged to the American owners of the gold who had been dispossessed by the authorities. In this way, one sees that the depreciation of the law of contract in a free society goes hand-in-hand with the depreciation of the currency.

It is important to remember that, under the classical gold standard, there is no such thing as "the dollar price for gold." This phrase improperly construes the definition of the monetary standard. The United States Constitution, in Article I, Sections 8 and 10, authorizes Congress alone to define in law the precious metal value of the American monetary standard. Under the gold standard, the dollar is defined by statute as a weight of gold. The dollar is so many fractions, or grams, or grains, of a troy ounce of gold. Confusion arises when one refers to the "price of gold" in 1932 being $20, or $35 in 1933 or 1970. (There are 480 grams of gold in a troy ounce. Therefore, if the dollar by law is 24 grams of gold; then 480 divided by 24 grams (one dollar) = 20 dollars. That is, 20 gold dollars can be coined from the weight of one troy ounce, or 480 grams of gold metal. This essential point must be kept in mind as one considers the riddle of the dollar price of gold under a future international gold standard.)

Constitutional questions arose during the 1930s over the authority of the President to violate the value of lawful contracts and debts which stipulated payments in gold dollars. The doubtful power of Congress to pass ex post facto laws prohibiting the implementation of gold clauses in already existing U.S. contracts gave rise to landmark Supreme Court Decisions. The law's validity was challenged by damaged plaintiffs but the Supreme Court upheld President Roosevelt and the legislature. Existing gold contracts were pronounced dead: they were declared by congressional resolution to be "against public policy." Otherwise free American citizens were prohibited by law from owning gold – a right only restored by statute in January 1975 after years of public debate.

It was clear that the dollar after 1934 was not "as good as gold." Americans could not exchange their paper and bank deposit money for a specified weight of gold, as they could under the classical gold standard, even though in law the dollar was still nominally defined as a certain weight of gold. Ironically, foreigners were still permitted to exchange their undesired paper dollars for American gold. The way had therefore been opened in the future for the dollar to become a fully managed currency, whose value would be substantially determined and regulated by the opinions of politicians and the Board of Governors of the Federal Reserve System.

Near the end of World War II, ten years after Roosevelt's devaluation of the dollar, and thirty years after the founding of the Federal Reserve System, the Bretton Woods Agreement of 1944 elaborated a new international Monetary System. Bretton Woods codified and institutionalized certain decisions by the monetary authorities taken at a previous world monetary conference held in Genoa during 1922.

The inauguration in 1913 of the U.S. Federal Reserve System, followed by the 1922 conference at Genoa were two events which changed the financial history of the world. In 1922, Europe was trying to recover from World War I. The general price level had doubled, and in some places much more than doubled, throughout Europe during the war-torn period of currency inconvertibility. But the statutory value of the gold currency did remain the same in America. The British government contemplated a restoration of the pre-war gold value of sterling, despite a wartime doubling of its price level. Naturally, under these conditions, a scarcity of undervalued gold developed. The monetary authorities of Europe agreed at Genoa in 1922 to three basic expedients, given the post-war undervaluation of gold: (1) to attempt to stabilize the existing general price level or the gold value of the currency – instead of devaluing the currency which would have acknowledged the great inflation of World War I; (2) to coordinate central bank credit policies in order to "manage" the value of their linked currencies more effectively; and (3) to modify the rules of the international gold standard and to institute more or less officially the "new" *gold-exchange standard* – substituting foreign exchange (dollars and sterling) to replace gold settlements. In order "to conserve," or economize, the existing supply of gold they hoped to facilitate the international movement of goods and capital without adjusting gold parities, thus ignoring the adjustment mechanism and settlements procedures of the classical gold standard, namely unrestricted currency convertibility to gold at sustainable parities.

The first point was best exemplified by Chancellor of the Exchequer Winston Churchill, who in 1925 restored the pre-war value of the pound, a policy which engendered deflation and unemployment in Britain for the remainder of the decade. The 1925 restoration of sterling convertibility at the pre-war parity overvalued the pound and overvalued the level of wages in England in international competition. Austerity, unemployment, and the destruction of much British industry were the consequences. John Maynard Keynes was inspired to write his *General Theory* (published in 1935) as an analysis and remedy for the defects of profound unemployment and stagnation of the post-war economy in England. Keynes realized that deflation and unemployment were partly caused by overvaluation in 1925 of the pound sterling at its pre-war parity, wages not adjusting to falling world prices. It is true that British prices fell; but manufacturing wages remained high because of protection, subsidies, and the dole. Thus, foreign competitors invaded English and foreign markets formerly dominated by English producers. This displacement created the havoc of unemployment in traditional British industries like coal, steel, textiles, and shipping. The General Strike of 1926 was the result.

The second Genoa policy – central bank coordination of credit policies – began the practice of substituting central bank money market manipulation for the impartial and efficient adjustment mechanism of the classical gold standard which tended to preserve among nations a true balance-of-payments equilibrium. The adjustment mechanism of global rebalancing operated through gold flows and interest rate movements, the effect of which was to balance and rebalance supply and demand in domestic and world markets. Rebalancing the global economy had been a natural outcome of international trade under the classical gold standard.

The third Genoa policy altered the method by which money was issued under the original gold standard mechanism. Under the true gold standard, a central bank creates money (its liabilities, or deposits) by purchasing gold or domestic financial claims, such as commercial loans or securities. Under the gold-exchange standard – an early form of the reserve currency system of today – a bank, or central bank, can create (issue) money (deposits, bank notes, or bank liabilities) by purchasing foreign exchange or foreign securities. Modern inconvertible money is in part made up of the liabilities or the deposits of the banking system.

But there are two sides to every balance sheet. The counterpart of money exists in the loans or securities, i.e., the bank assets against which the money (or deposit liabilities and banknotes) has been issued. Under the Genoa agreement, central banks endorsed the risky practice of issuing domestic money (deposits or currency) such as francs or marks against the purchase of foreign assets such as dollars or U.S. Treasury securities.

The problem thus created is straightforward. Under the gold-exchange standard, if the foreign currency *assets* (say dollars or pounds) held by the German central bank decline in value, or collapse, the domestic money (the *liabilities* of the bank) cannot be redeemed at par value because the assets, valued at market, are less than the value of the liabilities. The gold value of the mark must therefore be repudiated because there would be insufficient values backing the German currency. Devaluation must be the consequence. Such a process occurred in 1931 when sterling collapsed and destroyed the value of the sterling backing of foreign currencies in many other countries; and after 1971 when the dollar collapsed and caused all nations to repudiate the implied gold link of their currencies. Moreover, the reserve currency system duplicates purchasing power for the reserve currency country. America can buy abroad and again at home, because the dollars going abroad are reinvested under the reserve currency system in the United States. Systemic inflation must be the result unless the economy is underemployed.

In 1944, near the end of World War II, the Bretton Woods Agreement reestablished the dollar alone as the post-World War II official reserve currency. Sterling continued until 1975 as an unofficial reserve currency for some nations tied closely to the so-called sterling bloc. But the dollar became the "numéraire" of all world monetary values between 1944 and 1971. The values of foreign currencies were to be determined by their relationship to the dollar. In turn, the paper dollar derived value, under the agreement, by virtue of its convertibility into a fixed weight of gold – convertible for foreigners, but not for American citizens. Thus, the Bretton Woods Agreement wrote into international law the "official reserve currency status" of the dollar which, as a practical matter, had prevailed for the preceding 22 years (since Genoa in 1922).

But the story of Genoa, World War I, and Bretton Woods is incomplete without grasping the importance of the Federal Reserve System. Established in 1913, the central bank of the United States was designed for the express purpose of creating an "elastic currency" and fully integrating the U.S. financial system with the international gold standard. An elastic currency was thought to be one which could expand with the needs of trade, one which could resist the contracting forces implicit in a financial panic.

Briefly, the idea of the Federal Reserve System was born in the aftermath of the severe banking panic of 1907. A national monetary commission was appointed to study institutional remedies for the defects of the American banking system. The most profound influence on the legislative process was, of course, the bankers and legislators themselves, as well as certain luminaries like German-born Paul Warburg. Five years of study and debate gave rise to the Federal Reserve System, which was modeled to some extent on the German Reichsbank and the Bank of England. Essentially, the Federal Reserve System was created under the legal fiction of a private corporation with a statutory monopoly over the currency issue and a near monopoly regulating the banking system. Just as the Federal Communications Commission regulates the airwaves, so does the Federal Reserve regulate monetary institutions. It is not well-understood that the Federal Reserve has no constitutional status; it is a mere agency of Congress.

The power of the Federal Reserve consists not only in its regulating power, but more so in its influence over the supply of credit and money to the banking system. Under the original statute the Fed could create new credit and money primarily by purchasing gold and by advancing money or credit against secured, short-term promissory notes of merchants and producers. Under the design of the Federal Reserve Act of 1913, the government was not preferred as a client for credit at the Fed, and thus a government deficit was not primarily to be financed by the central bank, but instead in the capital markets. Additionally, the Federal Reserve System was limited by the workings of the gold standard. Since the dollar was defined in law as a fixed weight of gold, and the law required the Fed to maintain this value, the Fed could create credit, such as new deposits and Federal Reserve notes up to the limit defined by the desire to hold these cash balances. If the limit was not observed, holders at home and abroad of excess dollar deposits and currency would redeem them for gold, thus jeopardizing the legal guarantee of unrestricted convertibility of bank deposits and currency for standard money, namely gold dollars.

Oversimplified, this description characterizes the Federal Reserve System in 1913. But World War I brought major changes. First, European gold flowed to the United States as a result of panic and in order to finance war purchases. Second, the Fed extended credit, at interest rates below market, to commercial banks in order to finance the U.S. government's "Liberty Bonds" (a practice it would continue to this very day). Above all, the power to create money and expand credit, inherent in the monopoly powers of the Federal Reserve System, became evident during the course of World War I. During the recession of 1920-1921, these credit creating powers were activated through open-market operations, i.e., the technique by which the Fed issues money to purchase government and market-based securities. In buying treasury bonds, the Fed was and is able to extend massive credit to the Federal government unassociated with the production of new goods and services. Given hypothetical conditions of a permanent budget deficit and the need for government financing, all the potentialities of the Federal Reserve System as an engine of world inflation and currency depreciation were opened up. Only one check remained on this monetary engine of government deficit finance – the gold standard. In its absence, there would be no limit, no discipline, no restraint on the Fed's charter to create money and credit.

In effect, World War I was a catastrophic and suicidal act which destroyed not only the European peace and the flower of its manhood; but it also destroyed the monetary system characterizing the unprecedented prosperity of Western civilization. World War II and its aftermath were the next historical acts of the unfolding drama.

All European countries struggled with inflationary disorders during the war-torn 1940s and the reconstruction efforts during the 1950s. In the mid-1950s the world passed through what was forecast by the experts of the time as a "permanent dollar scarcity." Remember that the U.S. economy dominated the planet as no country ever had before, accounting for fifty percent of world output, and seventy-five percent of global gold reserves. During this period the gold-linked Bretton Woods dollar remained a reasonably stable epicenter around which other fluctuating currency systems orbited. But after 1958, a momentous monetary event took place. The western European governments restored the mutual convertibility of their currency systems on current account, abolished most exchange controls, and sought to establish budgetary equilibrium. Dollar primacy began to wane. From that very year, when the once prostrate nations of Europe hardened the value of their national monies, the United States began to experience a "near-permanent" overall balance-of-payments deficit. Economists and experts were confounded, as overnight the "permanent dollar scarcity" of the 1950s became "the permanent dollar glut" of the 1960s and 1970s.

Throughout the 1960s, inflation and the external deficit of the dollar, generated by expansive U.S. monetary policies, and budget deficits, led to foreign-exchange crises and ultimately to foreign-exchange controls under Kennedy and Johnson. This was the period of "the permanent balance-of-payments crises." The Bretton Woods system groaned under the flood weight of excess U.S. dollars, awash in financial markets abroad, where perforce they were accumulated in the official foreign-exchange reserves of our trading partners. This was also the period when politicians and civil servants led by academic neo-Keynesians Paul Samuelson and Walter Heller suggested that a little inflation was controllable and desirable.

Since the U.S. dollar was *the* primary reserve currency under the gold-exchange standard embodied in the Bretton Woods treaty, foreign central banks were in effect required to purchase undesired dollars held by their citizens and to hold them as official reserves against the creation of their own domestic money. It was also during this period (1967) that an international "paper" money, Special Drawing Rights (SDR), was invented by the International Monetary Fund in order, it was argued, to avoid a potential "liquidity shortage." Indeed, it was even said that the SDR, an artificially fabricated reserve asset, to be allocated among its members by the International Monetary Fund, was necessary to finance growing world trade. But as one foreign economist remarked, the creation of the SDRs, under the existing conditions of inflation and permanent U.S. deficits, amounted to irrigation plans during a worldwide flood of excess dollars.

From 1965, the Federal Reserve had been required to hold gold reserves equal to twenty-five percent of Federal Reserve notes and deposits (the monetary base) of the Federal Reserve System. Now when President Lyndon B. Johnson decided simultaneously to expand the Vietnam War and to build the Great Society welfare system – with the consent of Congress

– he moved to void the statutes of the Fed which limited, by virtue of a stipulated gold cover, the amount of currency and credit which the bank of issue, the Federal Reserve System, could create. The full inflationary potential inherent in the Federal Reserve Act of 1913 was about to be realized. The institution of financial discipline – the gold-link or legal gold cover for the currency – which had limited the creation of paper and credit dollars – was to be terminated. And predictably, with the ultimate discipline of a legally required gold cover brushed aside, budget deficits, Fed credit expansion, inflation, and the balance-of-payments crises intensified. Unimpeded by any statutory rule limiting either budget deficits or the growth of the money supply during the late 1960s, the Federal Reserve System had discretion to create, subject only to demands for gold from foreign governments, the new credit and money required by the Congress to finance President Johnson's war budgets and the welfare state.

Lyndon Johnson even put an end to the historic use of silver in the production of the subsidiary coinage of the United States. The vast silver hoard of the U.S. Treasury, part of the patrimony of every American taxpayer, was liquidated in the market at about 90 cents per ounce. Next, in March 1968, Johnson suspended the London Gold Pool as the foreigners began to cash in their excess dollars for more gold than we were willing to supply. Between November of 1967 and March of 1969, the United States lost one-fifth of its gold reserves. Beginning in 1960-1961, the Gold Pool – originated by the developed countries – had underwritten the Bretton Woods convertibility agreements. But the Gold Pool had grown increasingly shaky by excessive credit expansion in the United States and the United Kingdom. By selling gold at the stipulated dollar-gold parity of $35 per ounce in order to redeem excess dollars accumulating abroad, the Anglo-American powers had been able to finance their extravagant domestic and foreign policies. After 1968, the United States refused to supply gold for dollars to the London Gold Pool. The linchpin of Bretton Woods, the link between gold and the dollar, had been ruptured if not definitively broken.

These dramatic changes in the international monetary system were welcomed by most of the academic and policy-making communities, and the politicians. The Bretton Woods agreement was an unnecessary discipline. Gold and silver were "outdated," declared these "experts."

Professional economists – neo-Keynesians and monetarists alike – gladly dismissed the Bretton Woods fixed-exchange rate regime, a reserve currency system, as the last vestige of the pre-World War I classical gold standard. They heralded the coming of a new era of central bank "managed money" and floating-exchange rates.

From 1945 to 1965, the neo-Keynesians had ruled economic policy-making in Washington and in academic circles. Their demand management policies, especially during recessions, relied on budget deficits, financed by the creation of new credit at the central bank, the Federal Reserve System. The neo-Keynesians were indifferent to the consequences of expansive credit and monetary policy. Fiscal policy, the budget deficit, was their primary tool to manage the economy. Then came the counter-revolution of the monetarists who captured much of the field of economic policy and university departments in the late 1960s. From them one learned that money matters as much, or more, than fiscal policy. And in particular, one learned from the monetarists that governments can manage inconvertible paper currencies according to certain prescribed monetary manipulations, even by a computer as Milton Friedman suggested. Their favorite technique for controlling the money supply was so-called open-market operations, the buying and selling of government debt securities by the Federal Reserve System in order to manipulate the credit and money supply. Simply stated, monetarists promoted the idea of a gradual growth in money and credit by means of a so-called steady increase in the money supply engineered by the Fed – say, 3 percent money growth per annum. Neo-Keynesians had, of course, offered their "countercyclical" monetary management – that is, a discretionary arrangement whereby money and credit growth was geared to national demand management policies and adjusted as well to finance the budget deficits caused by their "compensatory" fiscal policies.

Both warring schools of thought criticized the faltering Bretton Woods reserve currency system based on the dollar, itself a form of the ill-fated official gold-exchange standard originating at Genoa in 1922. Ironically, the monetarists and neo-Keynesians did agree on one major issue – but not upon the reform of Bretton Woods. Instead they advocated its demolition. In its place, monetarists and neo-Keynesians alike endorsed central bank managed currencies; floating-exchange rates ("clean" for some, "dirty" for others); and the demonetization of gold. Simply put, they wanted an end to any international exchange rate regime, any limitation on the discretion of central bankers to manage domestic economies. The historic institution of the real monetary standard, a defined yardstick of value, had been destroyed. These monetary doctrines soon became the fashionable credo propagated by the Fed, academic economists, and policy makers everywhere.

President Nixon followed Johnson and under the influence of his "conservative" advisors gradually went through his own conversion to Keynesian economics. But Nixon also absorbed some of the teachings of the monetarist school under the influence of Milton Friedman – in particular, the importance of a so-called independent monetary policy and the desirability of replacing the Bretton Woods fixed-rate system with floating-exchange rates. On August 15, 1971, Nixon acted. European governments had become increasingly impatient to exchange their excess dollars for gold. Nixon responded by defaulting at the gold window: he refused to redeem the excess dollars for gold, as the British government a few days earlier had demanded under the terms of the Bretton Woods treaty. In one of those curious historical ironies, it was the anti-New Deal Nixon who affirmed in 1971 the final demonetization of gold, begun at home by the liberal FDR in 1933-1934. On August 15, Nixon abolished by executive order the last vestige of dollar convertibility to gold. Nixon followed up, outdoing FDR by imposing the first comprehensive peacetime wage and price controls in American history. The remnant of an official domestic and international gold standard had been abrogated by the undisputed leader of the free world.

The dollar had ceased to be *real* money, linked directly to an article of wealth such as gold. It would henceforth be a *nominal* paper money, a monetary token empty of substance, linked to nothing but the judgment of its regulators at the Federal Reserve System.

"Since...the stable expectations of our citizens stem largely from the stability of their political institutions, we now can understand why they must be so concerned with the stability of the key financial institution of their political economy, the monetary unit."

Chapter Three

INFLATION AND CIVILIZATION: MAN'S FATE AND HIS MONEY

We identify civilization by its etymology – from the Latin "civis", or "civitas", meaning citizen or city. That is to say, civilization is characterized by the economy of city life. By this definition, hunting and gathering cultures are, in the literal sense of the word, not civilized. Indeed, the emergence of early urban cultures occurred, over five thousand years ago, coterminously with the intensification of agricultural and commercial exchange in the village markets of the Near and Middle East. In a word, the city and commerce are one.

From the standpoint of economic development, a study of history confirms that the money exchange economy, a widespread division of labor, and large-scale accumulation of productive capital were economic phenomena coextensive with the origin of the early city-states. Of the many civilized institutions which originated over four millennia ago (in the urban cultures of the "Tigris and Euphrates," the Nile Delta, and the Indus Valley), the economic institution of money was a social and political innovation as significant as the development of the city itself. A unique medium of exchange, the institution of money, was a social invention which provided the economic means by which sophisticated commercial communities could minimize, once and for all, their capital investments in the mere process of voluntary exchange itself. As I shall try to explain, these complex economic activities and widespread commercial exchanges are, if one reflects for a moment, unimaginable without money. It is no exaggeration to say that the struggle for civilization was inseparable from the origin of its monetary institutions.

We know now that the universal success of the monetary token represented a far-reaching mutation in the economic affairs of men. Its general acceptance freed man from the insularity and inefficiency of barter, releasing a veritable flood of human resources, the rising tide of which led inexorably to man's dominion over nature and all her creatures. Man's dominion is part of what we mean by the idea of civilization. Viewed in the austere light of history, moreover, the culture and stability of the cities seems to be inextricably bound up with the utility, or, more quaintly, with the soundness of its monetary institutions. Let your imagination and your understanding be persuaded as we wander through the past.

Consider, for a moment that *Pithecanthropus erectus* emerged from the dark rain forests, savannahs, the primeval ooze over a million years ago. Then, his proud heirs, *Homo sapiens*, ushered in the urban era, beginning with the blazing glory of the golden city of Ur in Sumer, a mere two thousand years before the advent of the Christian era. In your mind's eye, imagine the volatile nomadic hunting and gathering cultures which had preceded the coming of the Sumerian towns and their markets. Contemplate the improbable contingency of this urban social order which, from the standpoint of eternity, appeared almost overnight on the banks of the Tigris and Euphrates rivers. Reflect moreover on the unceasing march of its commercial civilization as urban culture spread its tenuous dominion over life and nature. The history of the city is so brief, its life so fragile a reed, that it is fair indeed to ignore its improbable origin, unless we can ascertain the ineluctable cause of the city's development and permanence. That cause, the evidence suggests, was nothing other than the systematic accumulation of productive capital in the market through the agonizing labor and savings of men. When the tribe ceased to consume all the products of its capital, even the capital itself, when our tribal forbears determined to defer present consumption – that is, to save and to invest, in order to produce for the future – a new society, civilization was born.

The city then is quite literally the creature of saving and capital. Only its peace and order, free from the violence of hunting and gathering, could have inspired stable expectations among men and women, especially as their civilized efforts increasingly bore fruit in freedom from want and pervasive violence. Just as urbanity was the social condition which gave rise to exponential growth in the power of *Homo sapiens*, so the characteristic financial institution of the city's political economy, the monetary unit, became the means of diffusion and expansion by which the currency of commercial civilization encircled the globe in a mere 4,000 years.

Money is then a necessary, if insufficient, condition of urban civilization. Specialization and exchange, even in the most primitive commercial society, is unthinkable in the absence of money. Consider, for a moment, an ancient village and its commercial life carried on in the farmers' markets on the streets and in the dwellings of its merchants. Imagine the innumerable economic exchanges among men in the absence of money: The farmer, burdened by his undesired surplus grain production, must find just that merchant or housewife who reluctantly might barter for only some of the grain. But the very same merchant or housewife who, at that moment, actually desired cloth, must now, having reluctantly accepted the farmer's grain, find an unlikely seamstress who might be prepared to take his undesired grain inventory in payment for her cloth. Conceive therefore the required and bewildering diversity in the "portfolio" of assets (that is to say, the varied inventory) of every farmer, merchant, seamstress, laborer, and housewife), were our primitive city bereft of the institution of money. Is it reasonable to believe that every enterprising citizen, every merchant, every housewife, albeit in a most prosperous market place, could create the necessary, vast storage for deteriorating wheat, cloth, vegetables and firewood in order to be in a position, every day, to supply the desired products to whomever would provide them the basic desired products of life?

The very description of such a marketplace evokes the absurdity of such a capital-intensive exchange process. Our historic village would have been the most overcapitalized, uneconomical village in the world. A community without money, we now see very clearly, must overinvest too large a part of its savings and scarce resources in the very process of exchange itself. The real economic result of a moneyless economy is to impoverish a community which might otherwise have used the real capital resources required by barter (i.e., excessive personal inventories) to produce new goods and services, thereby adding to the general economic welfare. For the purpose of economic exchange, the monetary unit is an efficient substitute for the varied and burdensome inventories required of both producers and consumers in a barter economy. But inventory is working capital. Money conserves this scarce capital. So the monetary unit is, among many other things, the paramount conservator of capital in a civilized community. Every producer and all consumers, by reason of the universality of the monetary unit's acceptance, reduce the capital they might otherwise have invested in a diverse stock of goods which, in our imaginary city of barter, they were required to hold in order by indirect exchange to supply what was demanded for day-to-day necessities. If the historical origin of the city coincided with the sustained accumulation of productive capital, then the monetary unit may be seen as the preliminary condition of the city's very existence. The monetary token is not only the means of exchange, nor is it simply an article of wealth, a mere good available in the market. It is above all the hemoglobin which actuates the lifeblood of commercial civilization.

Even an aesthete might reasonably conclude, after having contemplated all this, that money, no less than art, is the hallmark of civilization. But the statesman must perceive that the monetary unit is so central an institution of society that its political uses are surely as important as its economic functions. It should be no strange thing to us, therefore, that from time immemorial, the power to mint the coin of the realm has been, but for rare episodes, a sovereign prerogative. Nor is it an accident to discover that the Congress of the United States, in Article I, Sections 8 and 10, should have reserved to itself the same dominion, over issuing, and "regulating," the coin of the realm. If, as it is often said, war is too important a matter to be left to the generals, then the same statesman might have said, with equal effect, that money is too important a political institution to be left to the economists.

The monetary unit, we observe upon reflection, is much more than the adolescent totem of a capitalist society's greed from which, according to some Marxists, post-industrial society will liberate itself upon maturity. We now recognize money as the means by which society conserves its scarce resources and removes from each citizen the intolerable economic burden of over-capitalizing and over-diversifying his personal assets. In a world of scarce resources, money liberates man from poverty, from the uneconomical yoke of barter, enabling him to make an efficient demand (with a simple monetary token) for what he needs from the supply of goods offered by his neighbors. Money is a foundation stone in the political framework of a civilized community, the stable structure of which is the necessary condition for the development of extensive, even global voluntary exchange.

But stable community requires a stable currency. It follows that if the value of money is unpredictable, then its utility will be impeached, and a just civilization itself, given its monetary origins, will be impeached. Let me develop this argument further. If money is the universal standard, the medium of exchange, by which we measure economic value, we intuitively presume it to be what it must be, namely, a reasonably stable unit of account. Cash money is not unlike a yardstick (invariably 36 inches!), similar to other universal standards of weights and measures upon which the inhabitants of our ordered city may fairly well rely. Stable expectations, in general and in particular, about the future value of cash balances form the bases of trusted, enduring money in a civilized community, just as stable expectations about the absence of violence in society undergird a lasting legal order. For we recall that money is a political institution; and if the police and the courts are the regulators of an enduring legal order, we should not be surprised to discover that dependable money is the constabulary of a stable economic order. It is a silent monarch.

We agree then that the monetary standard, or money, is the most efficient voluntary and universal means by which, with cash, we can make an immediate demand. If we assume that the actual cash balances of the members of society are equal to their desired cash balances, we know then that one must first offer a supply to the market in order to get incremental cash to make a demand. That is, if we will not give up any cash in order to make our economic demands, then we have no alternative but to produce (supply) something new for the market in order to consume. And in civilized communities we must always accept money in exchange for what we produce anew. This unconditional style of exchange mobilizes the force of law in the obligatory phrase on every currency note: "This note is legal tender for all debts, public and private," the coercion mitigating pure voluntary exchange. Now, in a well-ordered and equitable society, the incapacity to make a specific demand on society, without first supplying it with something of equal value, completely alters human behavior. As one is required to accept cash money, legal tender, for production and labor of a stipulated value, we naturally expect the money we receive to retain a stable value in the future. This is what economists mean when they say of money that it is a store of value: The cash balances we save are the means by which we conserve the value of our labor which we choose not to expend on current consumption, perhaps to consume in the distant future. Money, therefore, if it is to be anything, must be at least an efficient instrument by which plain people accumulate savings for future consumption.

Since, in our peaceful and ordered country, the stable expectations of our citizens stem largely from the stability of their political institutions, we now can understand why they must be so concerned with the stability of the key financial institution of their political economy, the monetary unit. Men and women carefully save cash balances from the proceeds of their honest labor. Surely they will insist that the future value of their money, itself one necessary condition of their original decision to save, must be directly proportional to the present value of their labor. This relationship must be so, our citizens intuitively sense, because the value of most products, offered in a free and open market, is in the long run proportional to the quantity and quality of labor bestowed upon them before they are offered in the market.

Now, if the factors of production are mobile and the price mechanism is flexible, then the value of a product, or service, must be proportional over the long run to its real costs of production. And these costs, (along with the anticipation of a modest profit which induced our citizen's effort in the first place) constitutes an objective basis for determining the specific value of money wages. We will not save and labor for money wages – we can almost hear the citizenry murmuring – if the real value (the purchasing power) of our money savings will not endure. And therein lies the hard-and-fast connection, the implied convertibility if you will, between a unit of real money, on the one hand, and an article of wealth produced by labor for the market, on the other. In order to assure the retention of the monetary standard's value, irrespective of the power of enemies and tyrants, the monetary unit must itself be convertible into a unit of a lasting article of wealth, itself requiring labor to be produced.

Why is that, you say? If in the long run the objective economic value of a product is regulated by its proportionality to its real costs of production (primarily labor), then the value of inconvertible paper money will have no regulator – because the marginal cost of production of one more flimsy piece of paper approximates zero! But if the monetary unit must be an unvarying standard, like the yardstick, and it is set equal to a specified weight unit of a scarce and fungible real commodity which men labor to produce, then there will be an enduring relationship, a proportionality, between the value of labor and savings, and the objective value of the monetary unit.

In the end, the fundamental relationship, the moral covenant between the worker, and the value of the product of his labor and his savings (in a civilized community) must be joined by a real money whose value endures. From time immemorial, civilized men have chosen to set the monetary unit equal to a specified weight unit of, among other real articles of wealth, gold. By establishing a real money, men rule out its arbitrary debasement toward worthlessness. By choosing a monetary institution worthy of the moral covenant between working men and women and their beneficiaries, civilized men chose to rule out inflation. In the long run, the value of an ounce of gold is proportional to the immense quantity of labor and capital invested to mine and to fabricate it, in order to supply it to those who, since the dawn of civilization, have desired it. It is real, scarce, storable, measurable, immutable, transportable, malleable, and fungible. But above all these things, the value of a monetary standard, defined by a weight unit of gold reinforces a fair and efficient regulator of its value in a civilized community, namely, its real costs of production. If it requires 50 man-hours to produce one ton of coal, and 100 man-hours to produce one ounce of gold, then approximately two tons of coal will be exchanged for monetary units sufficient to buy one ounce of gold. If in the market this relationship were to change substantially, say men could for a time exchange one ton of coal (50 hours of labor) for the money to buy one ounce of gold (100 hours of labor) – men would gradually cease to labor to mine gold and they would come to labor enthusiastically to mine coal. They would produce coal for money and purchase the gold they desired – until the increased supply of coal and the increased monetary demand for gold once more reestablished an equilibrium ratio in the underlying value of the two commodities, a ratio proportional, but not equal, to the quantity of labor required to produce them.

You see, the real costs of production (primarily labor) are the underlying regulator of the value of a convertible monetary unit – just as these real costs will be the objective regulator of the value of all other articles of wealth produced for the market. Contrast this to the value of an inconvertible paper currency produced at will, under monopoly conditions, by a sovereign government. Such a currency can have no objective and reliable regulator, since the quantity and value of inconvertible paper money largely depends upon the subjective whims of the government monopoly which produces it. Human nature and history suggest that government money monopolies will in the long run overproduce such paper money until its value approximates its marginal cost of production, that is to say, zero. And indeed, it is just such a fall in the purchasing power of inconvertible paper money which characterizes the age of inflation through which we are living. Today, the world is inundated by inconvertible currencies and it should be no surprise to us that we are being carried away by a global inflation.

We know now that the social invention of a stable monetary unit was a midwife of our ordered and urban civilization, itself no more than an improbable contingency in this vast and expanding universe. So also must we know that the contemporary instability of the monetary unit, inflation and depreciation will give rise to the disintegration of the precious social order we call Civilization. History suggests to us that the sustained fall in the purchasing power of an inconvertible paper money, toward its zero marginal cost of production, generates first social distemper (revolutionary France), then decline (England), and finally entropy (Ancient Rome). There is no inevitability to this devastating inflationary and currency depreciating process. But only a bold act of political courage will arrest its frightening momentum. What must Americans do?

To assure the future of a free and ordered global economy we must restore to the world a real money. To restore the spirit of free men and women, willing to labor and to save in money wages, we must restore their belief in the enduring and objective, even the moral, relationship between the value of their labor and the objective value of the monetary standard. If we would inspire once again – in all the heirs of civilization – the incentive to work and to save, that is, the desire to create capital, and therefore to provide for the future of our children and of our children's children, then we must provide for them a monetary standard with enduring purchasing power. If the third century of our great nation is to be what it might be – truly a beneficent American century – we must restore the hallmark of its birthplace, the monetary gyroscope of its leadership, a sound and stable currency. Indeed, to raise up America as it falls, to elevate her people to a just preeminence once again, confident in an honest and enduring reward for work and saving, to set all her people free from the satanic scourge of inflation, we will have to restore to America a real money, that is to say, a dollar defined in law as a weight unit of gold.

"The fundamental problem of Federal Reserve monetary policy is that the amount of money in circulation cannot reliably be determined by the Federal Reserve Board of Governors. Therefore, the Fed should stop trying to do so. The Fed simply cannot either accurately know the demand for money in the market or fix precisely its supply."

Chapter Four

AN EXCERPT FROM "REAL MONEY"

Harper's Magazine, August 1980

...When President Nixon demonetized gold in 1971, Henry Reuss, chairman of the House Banking and Currency Committee, predicted that the price of gold would fall to $6 per ounce. It is true that gold remained below $40 until 1972. But by January of 1980, the price of gold was soaring above $800. Recently it has fluctuated between $500 and $600. What caused the exponential rise, fluctuations, and fall of the gold price? The cause of the violent rise was the same as the cause of other commodity price rises. Indeed, the same cause was behind the balance-of-payments deficits of the 1960s and the inflation of the 1970s: quite simply, the expansion of money and credit in excess of real economic growth, engineered by the Federal Reserve System, in order to finance the Treasury deficit and fine-tune the economy.

The credit policy of the Fed can be observed in the following numbers.

TOTAL FRB CREDIT EXPANSION
(Average annual compound rates)

1960-1965	8.6 percent
1965-1970	8.8 percent
1970-1975	8.4 percent
1975-1979	8.7 percent

As the table shows, the expansion of central-bank credit has for two decades been almost three times the rate of economic growth. Some of the excess credit created by the Fed went abroad in the 1960s when it was known as a balance-of-payments deficit. The same excess credit also caused domestic prices to rise in the late 1960s. During the 1970s, the excess money created by the Fed caused inflation at home and the decline of the dollar abroad.

Thus, there is irony in the comments of the monetary authorities who declaim that gold is too volatile to stabilize the monetary system once again. On the contrary, it is not the gold price that is unstable. From 1540 to 1976, the purchasing power of gold has remained constant, demonstrated empirically by the distinguished monetary historian and statistician, Professor Roy Jastram, in his book *The Golden Constant*. In fact, it is the value of the managed-paper dollar that is unstable, an instability caused by the Fed's unpredictable and expansionary monetary policies.

The truth is that the Federal Reserve managers are honest and well-intentioned. But they believe they can achieve a goal that is not within their power to achieve, namely, to manage the currency. Moreover, they believe they can fine-tune the world's most complex economy by changes in credit policy. The Fed's ever-changing open-market interventions to this end have only created uncertainty and disorder in the financial markets.

The fundamental problem of Federal Reserve monetary policy is that the amount of money in circulation cannot reliably be determined by the Federal Reserve Board of Governors. Therefore, the Fed should stop trying to do so. The Fed simply cannot either accurately know the demand for money in the market or fix precisely its supply. Nor does the Fed possess the information, the operating techniques, or the provision to bring about a certain rate of growth of money supply and credit. Nor could this growth of supply be consistent with the precise demand for money in the market. Moreover, as history shows, no stipulated level of money supply during a specific market period is necessarily correlated either with a specified rate of inflation or deflation or with price stability.

Previous experience also gives one little confidence in the limitless discretion of the Federal Reserve governors, or any central bank, under the present system of floating-exchange rates. Consider what the Federal

Reserve is: First and foremost, it is a bank. More precisely, it is the "bank of issue." It has a balance sheet and it has an income statement. As a banking institution it can perform no magic with money. The Fed buys assets with the resources provided by the liabilities it takes on. But it is important to recognize that, within limits, the central bank can also vary the quantity and composition of Federal Reserve credit, its assets. Federal Reserve credit is a precise magnitude that tends to regulate the rise and fall of credit and money supplied by the Fed to the banking system. If the credit or money supplied is actually desired in the market, the price level will tend to be stable. If some of the new credit created by the Fed is undesired, it will quickly be lent or spent at home and abroad, the price level will tend to rise, and the value of the dollar at home and abroad will tend to fall; that is, the price level will tend to rise.

This problem of equalizing the supply of credit and the demand for it in the market illustrates the problem of monetary policy and central banking. To conduct the operations of the central bank, there must be a goal. If the goal is the level of employment, price stability, nominal GDP, or a specific amount of money in circulation, the Fed must know precisely, among other things, not only the amount of money in circulation but also the volume of money and credit actually desired in the market – and the tools to attain these goals. For only when the supply of money equals the amount desired in the market will there be no inflation or deflation. If by open-market operations the Fed unwittingly creates excess money in the market, prices will rise, as the excess money is rapidly used for purchases.

But if instead, the goal of the central bank were primarily price stability, the Fed would promptly reduce the amount of credit it made available to the commercial banks when excess credit was causing inflation. As Fed credit growth contracted, so would the money stock. As a result, excess money would be reabsorbed until the level of actual cash balances in the market was equal to the amount of cash balances desired in the market for economic growth. During such a market interval, inflation – or excess demand – would dissipate and prices would gradually stabilize.[1]

If the goal of the central bank during a period of inflation is to restore reasonable price stability, then the central bank should reduce the quantity of money in circulation such that money once again is about equal to desired cash balances in the market. Under such a monetary policy the banking system must tend to avoid making new bank loans. This is a monetary policy that will work, because the supply of money and credit will, as a result, tend to decline and to equal the desired amount. If cash balances in the market are equal to the level of desired cash balances, the general price level will be stable. If there is no excess money in the market, there can be no inflation.

The consequences of such a monetary policy will make themselves felt throughout the economy. Since the supply of money will tend to equal the level of money desired by participants in the market and enterprises, consumers as a whole will not wish to make purchases with their existing cash balances until they first produce something new. In a word, consumers will not make demands in the market without first offering supplies. Under these conditions the price level must be stable. Total demand will equal the supply level. The level will vary moderately around unity, and there will be no inflation arising from excess cash balances created by the central banking system.[2]

History and economic analysis show that the policy best suited to reinforce price-level stability is to make the value of paper and bank money equal to a defined weight of gold. Thus the volume of currency would be linked to a real commodity, gold, the supply of which grew during the past century at about two percent a year, roughly proportionate to the rate of GDP per capita over long periods.

A currency convertible at a fixed price into gold is the long-run stabilizer of the money supply, while central banking discretionary instruments are useful only for providing elasticity to credit and currency supplies in the short and intermediate term.

Although one wants to give the managers of our central bank a certain degree of discretion in order to supply money desired in the market, one doesn't want to give them so much discretion that in the short run, for political reasons, they might abandon the goal of reasonable price stability – a goal that only the convertible currency will ensure.[3] Indeed, a convertible currency constrains all central banking techniques. For if undesired money is pumped into the convertible currency system, there will appear on the market a surfeit of cash balances. Those receiving money in excess of desired levels would then appear at the bank or the central bank with a demand for currency redemption in gold. Such evidence of excess money offered for redemption in gold will signal unequivocally to the monetary authorities that there are indeed excess cash balances in the market. The true signal of excess money on hand can be given only by people and firms, concretely expressed by those who would desire to convert such excess funds for gold. Such money would clearly be unwanted or else it would not be brought in for redemption at the bank. On this signal the Fed or the banks would gradually reduce credit to reabsorb these excess cash balances. The inflationary episode would be cut short because of the requirement to sustain the fixed convertibility ratio between bank reserves and the undesired currency in circulation.

Some would argue that a gold-backed currency is costly, in social and economic terms, compared with a pure paper currency. But whatever the minor resource cost of a currency convertible at a fixed parity into gold, it is a superior monetary stabilizer and a more efficient price regulator. As Professor Roy Jastram shows in *The Golden Constant*, the history of the gold standard provides evidence of reasonable, long-term price stability. If the goal of the United States is an end to inflation and reasonable price stability, it is a modest cost to allocate a minor share of our resources to the all-important regulating mechanism of the money supply. Nothing else but real money, a currency defined as a weight unit of gold, will assure the indispensable virtue of trust in the monetary standard. Without real money, saving evaporates, investment languishes, and the future is impoverished.

Consider also that Americans are required by law to accept paper and credit dollars in exchange for production and labor of a stipulated value. Money, therefore, if it is to be anything, must be at least an efficient and trustworthy instrument by which working people are paid and accumulate savings. Men and women carefully save cash balances from the proceeds of their labor. Surely they intend that the future purchasing value of their money closely approximates the objective present value of their labor. The convertibility between a unit of real money, such as gold, produced by labor, and every article of wealth created by human labor for the market is the essential equation of economic justice. Therefore, the value of the monetary unit should have a real objective regulator. But the value of money has an objective regulator only when it is linked to a real commodity, like gold, itself requiring the cost of human labor to be produced. By comparison, the value of inconvertible paper money has no objective regulator, its marginal cost of production being nearly zero.

The covenant between any worker and society must be underwritten by something more lasting than a nominal paper currency or mere monetary tokens. In exchange for work, there must be the payment of real money, the value of which endures, lest the worth ethic erode. Over thousands of years, a gold-related currency has performed this function for civilized men. By establishing real money, men rule out its debasement. In the long run, the value of an ounce of gold is proportional to an objective quantity, namely the amount of labor invested to mine and to fabricate it. Moreover, a gold currency exhibits the properties that make real money the trustworthy foundation of an exchange economy. It is scarce, storable, measurable, divisible, immutable, transportable, malleable, and fungible.

Therefore, in order to end inflation permanently and to bring about stability and trust in the U.S. currency, the dollar must be defined in law as equal to a weight unit of gold, at a statutory convertibility rate that ensures that average wages do not fall. Nothing less will yield an enduring currency and a stable social order. Currency convertibility into gold at a fixed-rate is virtually a constitutional guarantee of the purchasing power of money and, therefore, of the future value of savings. The legal framework of a convertible currency makes of money a constitutional institution.

As a result of a true international gold standard, no central bank, not even the Federal Reserve System, could expand credit beyond the desired level in the market. This self-denying ordinance is the principal foundation of financial order. The ordinance must work, because to create an excess supply of money and credit in the market would cause the price level to rise and the exchange rate to fall – while the gold convertibility price of the currency would remain the same. Therefore, the stable gold price would be falling relative to the rising price level. The demand for the relatively cheap gold would create an increasing cash demand for the gold reserves of the banking system. This unique signal of excess cash balances now offered for redemption into gold at the bank would alert the banking system to the danger of inflation.

An Excerpt from "Real Money"

It is clear that a true gold standard will assure that the supply of money will tend to equal the quantity of money desired for steady economic growth. To sustain this condition, the amount of cash balances and the level of interest rates must be determined in the open market, not in the Open Market Committee of the Federal Reserve System. There is no need in a free market order, based on the classical gold standard, for monetarist and Keynesian fine-tuning of the money stock through continuous open-market operations. Indeed, the effects of fiscal fine-tuning and money-stock fine-tuning are the same: they create chronic instability of the price level and, in this expansionist era, inflation.

Notes

[1] Cash balances, metallic or credit-based, are the ready means of payment we hold in our pockets or at the bank. So is money. Money is often used by people to mean wealth. But money is not the same thing as wealth. Modern money consists of currency and checkbook deposits. Money is, therefore, that balance of our wealth that we choose not to hold in the form of financial assets, goods, and services. This money balance is cash. Money, strictly defined, is a synonym for cash balance.

[2] This concrete monetary policy finally comes to grips with the quantity theory of money and Jean Baptiste Say's Law of Markets, famous classical issues of economics that preoccupied Lord Keynes in *The General Theory*. Say's Law holds that the value of total supply always equals total demand. Keynes disagreed, and he was right. If Say's Law were correct, there could never be an imbalance between supply and demand; therefore, no inflation or deflation could occur. But they do occur.

The monetary policy to be derived from a modified Say's Law is clear: minimize the difference between actual and desired cash balances, and supply through the regulating mechanism of private banks or the central bank only the amount of money actually desired in the market.

[3] A favorite gambit of Presidents seeking reelection is to throw monetary sheets to the wind and expand the money supply, thus inducing a false sense of prosperity among the electorate.

PART II: MONETARY DISORDERS AFTER THE NIXON SHOCK

Since 1932, the U.S. Comptroller of Currency has issued new Federal Reserve Notes to the regional reserve banks at their request, provided that the Federal Reserve board guarantees that an equivalent amount of collateral has been posted with the Federal Reserve agent – i.e., segregated from the general portfolio of the regional reserve bank. (The Monetary Control Act of 1980 removed the collateral requirement for notes not yet in circulation.) Such collateral was almost exclusively U.S. government debt securities until 2007. Through Federal Reserve open-market operations, a portion of new issues of Federal debt securities are monetized as backing for newly issued currency. Excess demand for Treasury bills – as backing for Federal Reserve Notes and U.S. banking system reserves, as well as official monetary reserves in foreign central banks – weakens or ends disciplines that curtail budget and trade deficits.

The close of the gold window in 1971, the end of all institutional restraint on the discretion of the Federal Reserve, triggered a period of growing inflation and speculation. Both neo-Keynesians and monetarists agreed: (1) on the superiority of a central-bank-managed currency (a quantity rule, variable or fixed) over a currency with a fixed real value (a price rule); (2) on the superiority of a floating exchange rate system over a fixed rate system and (3) that in an era of modernity, the irrelevance of gold to contemporary monetary theory and policy.

Regrettably, government officials chose to muddle along with policies that postponed rather than prevented disaster. In the 1970s, inflation exploded and "stagflation" ensued. In the 1980s, the economy grew, but the twin deficits – that is the budget deficit and the current account of the balance-of-payments – expanded.

*"We must remember that the Federal Reserve is
above all a bank, though a bank with the monopoly powers
to issue legal tender currency and to regulate the banking
system. It is not a magical government agency, nor should
it be confused with the Yale Economics Department or a
classroom at the University of Chicago."*

Chapter Five

GOLD IS NOT A "SIDE SHOW"

The Wall Street Journal, February 20, 1980

Lenin once observed that gold should adorn the floors of latrines. Keynes labeled it a "barbarous relic," and Milton Friedman has recently been saying that for a monetary standard you may as well use pork bellies.

President Jimmy Carter inaugurated his administration in 1977 with the rhetoric of austerity – pledging, among other things, to balance the federal budget. The price of gold promptly rose over $150. Mr. Carter replaced Arthur Burns with William Miller as chairman of the Federal Reserve Board. By the autumn of 1978 the dollar was collapsing and gold was approaching $250. Then, on November 1, 1978, new policies to control the money supply and defend the dollar were announced by Chairman Miller. Gold fell to $200 within 30 days. But by the middle of 1979, gold was once again rapidly rising to $300.

In July 1979, amid much fanfare, Paul Volcker was summoned to replace Mr. Miller. Gold vaulted to $450 in September. In a crisis atmosphere, Mr. Volcker returned from the International Monetary Fund meeting at Belgrade to announce his new monetary guidelines on October 6, 1979. They stressed "a new method" – targeting bank reserves – focused on the goals of a stable dollar, a slower rate of money and credit growth and an end to excessive commodity speculation in general and gold speculation in particular. Over the next few weeks, the gold price fell to $372.

Going Its Own Way

Three months later, as the gold price soared over $800, Mr. Volcker observed that gold was going its own way and that its movements had little to do with the success of failure of his October 6 monetary policies. Treasury Secretary Miller allowed that the Treasury would sell no more gold during these "uncertain and uncharacteristic times," evidently meaning that for him gold was a good sale at prices ranging from $40 to $200 but now a strong hold at $800. Fed Governor Henry Wallich said the gold markets were no more than "a side show."

Yet on February 5, 1980, commodity future prices, following the earlier gold lead, closed at a record high, up 26 percent from a year earlier on the Commodity Research Bureau futures index. The market for U.S. government securities had suffered a devastating collapse. Gold closed around $665 on February 15, more than 20 percent below the early January peak but 83 percent above its bottom of October 1979. It has risen back above $700.

What caused the exponential rise and violent fluctuations of the gold price? The surging gold price, commodity prices, and interest rates suggest that the so-called anti-inflationary money policy proclaimed by Paul Volcker on October 6 had intensified rather than quelled speculation. The contradiction between Mr. Volcker's goals and the results achieved requires explanation.

An explanation for the Volcker contradiction – and for that matter the earlier monetary problems of Arthur Burns in 1972-1974 and the failure of William Miller in 1978 and 1979 – must ascertain what policy the Fed has actually pursued, as opposed to its announced goals. The economists have focused our attention on monetary aggregates such as M-1. Laying aside the problem of how to define these numbers – the Fed switched definitions only last week – the fact remains that the Fed does not actually control M-1, however it is measured. The money stock depends partly on Fed policy and partly on events elsewhere in the economy. Consumers and producers in the market largely determine the demand for money, while the Fed does influence its supply. That is, market participants alone determine the level of cash balances they will hold.

For any real understanding, we must remember that the Federal Reserve is above all a bank, though a bank with the monopoly powers to issue legal tender currency and to regulate the banking system. It is not a magical government agency, nor should it be confused with the Yale Economics Department or a classroom at the University of Chicago. To study the policies of a bank, you study its balance sheet, to see what its officers are actually doing. The only elements its managers control, within limits, are the volume and composition of the assets of the balance sheet. Line items will show the amount of credit the Fed is extending to the commercial banking system.

The Fed's credit operations are revealed in the balance sheet item called Total Federal Reserve Bank Credit. FRB credit is the Fed's financial assets – the amount of government securities, acceptances, advances, float and so on. Changes in FRB credit reflect the net operations of the Fed's open-market desk, foreign-exchange desk and discount window – the various ways the Fed influences the expansion and contraction of credit in the economy.

To achieve its announced October 6 goal of restraining the growth of credit, the Fed would have to restrain the growth of FRB credit.

Let us go back to 1977 and look at recent history. Both FRB credit and the gold price were relatively calm in 1977, but in the second half of 1977 FRB credit rose toward $120 billion and gold toward $175. As expected, FRB credit peaked seasonally at year-end; the gold price topped out two months later. By October of 1978, FRB credit had expanded above $130 billion, while the gold price rushed to $250.

FRB credit peaked again after the Miller monetary changes of November 1, 1978, and so did the price of gold. FRB credit declined and stabilized through the winter of 1978-1979, and so did the price of gold, which remained below $250 through the winter. Beginning in April of 1979, total FRB credit advanced rapidly from $125 billion reaching $143.5 billion during the week ending January 2, 1980. During this period FRB credit did stabilize for six weeks starting with the week of October 3, reflecting the Volcker October 6 moves. But it started to rise again by November 14 about the time of the Iranian deposit freeze. From November 14 to January 2, total FRB credit startled most Fed watchers by rising from $135 billion to nearly $144 billion.

In parallel, the gold price took off from $250 in the spring of 1979, and topped out at $450 with the October 6 Volcker moves. Promptly the gold price declined to under $450 and steadied along with FRB credit, which remained steady in October and early November. Gold then vaulted to $850 on January 15, peaking just weeks after FRB credit. FRB credit declined from its high of $142.5 billion on Jan. 2 to $134.5 billion during the week ending February 6. By February 15, the gold price fell to $665.

The lagged correlation between the rise and fall of FRB credit and the rise and fall of gold is not perfect, but there is a compelling association between the two. Indeed, even taking into account seasonality, almost every reacceleration of FRB credit between January 1977 and January 1980 tends to be accompanied, after a varying but short lag, with an acceleration in the price of gold.

This relationship reflects the impact of expectations, well known to classical economists. Market participants in a fully employed economy are increasingly sensitive to information that suggests the Fed is expanding credit rather than, as the Fed chairman says, contracting or stabilizing credit. In response to each new injection of Fed credit, individuals and businesses move ever more decisively to protect themselves against inflation.

It is essential to point out that the price of gold seems to respond directly to the monetary policies *actually pursued* at the Federal Reserve open-market desk. But the gold market often ignores what the Chairman says. In a word, the rise of the price of gold is just one more reflection of excessive credit growth, as shown by the Fed's own balance sheet. If war-scares, oil-price hikes and Iranian asset freezes did not exist, but the same expansionary credit policies prevailed, Fed apologists would find other plausible political events with which to rationalize the advance in the price of gold.

The Fed managers do not deceive us intentionally. Instead they deceive themselves. They believe they can achieve what is not within their power and tools to achieve – namely, a certain quantity of money consistent with a certain level of employment and consistent with a stable price level or inflation rate.

The Fundamental Problem

The fundamental problem of Federal Reserve monetary policy can be stated quite simply. Because the quantity of money cannot be controlled effectively by the Fed, the goal of the Fed's monetary policy must not be to control it. The Fed simply cannot determine *precisely* either the demand for money in the market or its supply. Nor does the Fed possess neither the information, the operating techniques, nor the perfect foresight to bring about a certain rate of economic growth and money and credit, especially through its chosen technique, open-market operations. As history shows, open-market operations succeed only in destabilizing interest rates and the money markets, creating bubbles and financial panics.

Ultimately, achieving the goal of price stability will require comprehensive reform of the monetary system. But for now, in their efforts to sustain a managed currency, Fed policymakers often misunderstand market data and the effects of their own hyper-interventionist open-market operations. They even have difficulty insuring that announced policies of the Fed governors are actually implemented by the staff at the open-market desk. Still, in the absence of comprehensive reform, it would help if the men at the Fed and Treasury stopped belittling the importance of the gold price. Their policies since October 6 would have been better if they had recognized that it is no "side show," but a highly sensitive scoreboard for the main event.

"...the elementary cause of America's decline abroad is defective national leadership at home. The problem lies not so much with our people but with our elites who, during the past decade, have suffered a failure of nerve. The consequences of our moral collapse have been catastrophic."

Chapter Six

STOP THE BATTLE FOR REAGAN'S SOUL

The Wall Street Journal, June 16, 1980

There is intellectual combat going on in Governor Reagan's camp. Some call it a struggle for Reagan's soul. The subtle arguments of the opposing sides make a battleground of many editorial pages, for it is clear that Governor Reagan may be our next President. But the primary goals of his national policy, and the means to achieve them, are not yet crystal clear. The disputes arise over both national security and economic policy.

The fundamental issue seems to be whether the greater threat to our country comes from abroad or from within. There are essentially two points of view. Both agree that we must restore America's position as a preeminent world power, but they disagree on the source of the primary threat. One group asserts that the most fundamental threat to America today is the decline of the economy and rising unemployment at home. The deterioration of American productivity, the enervation of American enterprise, the disincentives of our tax system, the inordinacy of the federal budget and the depreciation of the dollar preoccupy these advisers. In their view, renewed vitality of American capitalism is a precondition for restoring the security of the nation.

The other group argues that threats from the Soviet Union and other foreign enemies constitute the fundamental challenge. In this view, the elementary cause of America's decline abroad is defective national leadership at home. The problem lies not so much with our people but with our elites who, during the past decade, have suffered a failure of nerve. The consequences of our moral collapse have been catastrophic.

We now risk Finlandization of Europe, loss of our economic oil lifeline in the Persian Gulf, and demoralization of our allies in the Middle East, Egypt, and Israel. And because of our inferior military position and weak leaders, every vital American interest is threatened by the intimidating policies of an aggressive Soviet imperialism. From this standpoint, it is necessary to change leaders, chase the fallen elites from power, steel our national nerve, rebuild our fighting forces and assert America's interests abroad. Such a forward foreign policy itself would do much to protect American values at home while upholding and extending Western civilization abroad.

Terms of the Struggle

In economic policy, it appears that the struggle for Reagan's soul consists, in part, of a fight between two groups over tax policy. On the one hand, many well-known economists believe that the path to economic stability is lined with signposts leading directly to reduced government spending and a gradually balanced budget. To reduce the rate of growth of government spending, they plausibly argue, is an indispensable condition of tax rate reduction. Republican leadership, it is argued, must re-establish discipline in America and, in particular, fiscal discipline in the spending habits of Congress.

On the other hand, there is a group of Republican advisers who argue that substantial reduction of personal income-tax rates is of paramount importance. They believe in increasing after-tax rewards for work – thus leaving the sweat on a worker's brow rather than draining it into the government trough in Washington. They support the Kemp-Roth Bill, a 30 percent reduction in tax rates over a period of three years. Only thereby, argue these advisers, can we create the incentives to work, to save and to invest, and thereby restore the necessary conditions for economic growth and full employment

Another dispute is over how to stop the depreciation of the dollar at home and abroad. In a word, how do we end inflation? This is the issue of monetary policy. One group of advisers argues: Let the Federal Reserve System regulate the quantity of bank reserves and the money stock so as to provide a steady rate of increase in their supply. By establishing a steady, long-run relationship between commercial bank reserves and the supply of money, the rate of inflation may be brought down. These experts say, moreover, that the discretionary authority to manipulate bank reserves through buying and selling government securities, so as to provide a certain quantity of money, should belong to government officials at the Federal Reserve System.

On the other hand, there is another group which argues that the monetary problems of the last 50 years – deflation in the 1930s and inflation in the 1970s – have been caused by the fact that the discretionary management of the money supply has been in the hands of politicians and civil servants (the Federal Reserve Governors). Often they try to achieve conflicting economic and political goals rather than reasonable stability of the price level. These advisers argue that the key to restoring the stability of the dollar is to make the value of the currency subject to the rule of law rather than to the rule of men. To do this, they reason, it is necessary to limit the power of the Federal Reserve governors, politicians, and bureaucrats who make monetary policy.

They assert that the only effective instrumentality for achieving a stable price level over the long run is to make the value of a paper dollar equal by law to the value of a unit of a real commodity. The dollar would be made convertible into a weight of gold, as it was for most of the 200 years of U.S. history. Gold, unlike paper currencies has preserved its purchasing power for hundreds of years. As a result, the value of the dollar and the variations in its supply would be stabilized, because the quantity of dollars would be linked by law to the historically stable, century-long growth in the supply of gold (about 2 percent per year), proportional that is to the growth of output. Thus would inflation come to an end.

Each of these views is put forth by their advocates as the vital issue. The tax cutters say theirs is the real economic issue; the currency stabilizers say theirs is the fundamental issue; the budget balancers say theirs is the popular and crucial issue. And the national security strategists say making America number one abroad again is the enduring issue. All of them struggle for Governor Reagan's soul.

End Inflation Now

But in reality, all four of these views are of a piece. Alone, each is unavailing. If in order to restore incentive we reduce the tax rates on the American people, what do we really achieve if the dollar depreciates and inflation continues? For inflation merely transports all working people into higher and higher progressive tax brackets, even though we may delude ourselves by reducing the tax rates on rising nominal incomes. Therefore, in order to give lasting incentive effects to reduced tax rates, we must end inflation now by limiting permanently the Fed's excessive expansion of money and credit.

If we reduce the tax rates and also end inflation, the incentives to work and save may be restored; but if we do not gradually balance the budget, the federal government may still enter into the market and preempt all the new savings for its deficit spending programs – the very capital which we need to develop new energy sources, create new jobs, and rebuild our nation's beleaguered economy.

If we achieve only one or two of the following – (1) a stable currency and an end to inflation; (2) lower tax rates on work, savings, investment and, therefore, increasing employment opportunities; and (3) a gradually balanced budget thereby releasing capital from the public to the private sector for new job creation – we shall not create all the necessary conditions for stable, long-run economic growth. But only substantial, economic growth and full employment will provide the required resources with which (4) to rebuild our national defense in order to secure our vital interests. In the absence of economic growth, we cannot finance a forward foreign policy worthy of the name. And without a national defense capability second to none, we cannot insure our economic interests and opportunities at home and abroad. In truth, national security and economic growth are indissolubly joined.

In the interest of our country's future, this struggle for Governor Reagan's soul must cease. Instead, the task before us must be the development of a coherent and comprehensive economic and national security policy, linked together by mutually compatible goals and sustained by the will to achieve them. For in our economic policy at home and in our relations abroad, we must try to achieve all four necessary goals together or we shall not achieve them at all.

*"The budget should be balanced, the Treasury should
be refilled, public debt should be reduced, the arrogance
of officialdom should be tempered and controlled .... "*
– Marcus Tullius Cicero: 106 B.C.

Chapter Seven
HOW TO END INFLATION

Washington Post, January 18, 1981

Inflation is the transcendent issue of our times. Inflation is to our generation what depression was to our parents and grandparents. Inflation, if not stopped, will revolutionize our nation and its social institutions.

There are at least two separate schools of thought about how to end inflation:

First, there are professional policy analysts who believe that overdemanding working people create inflation by spending too much money. President-elect Reagan captured the perversity of this elitist view when he asked why it is inflationary when working people spend money – but not inflationary when the government spends it. In the past, these same analysts have recommended austerity as a remedy for inflation: simply reducing the number of working people (i.e., recession and unemployment) in order to reduce or "fine-tune" private demands for goods and services.

A true understanding of inflation begins with a second and entirely different view of its causes and origins.

In this view, the correct one, the government causes inflation. Not the oil sheiks, not the oil companies, not greedy labor or avaricious big business. Inflation is a *monetary* and a *financial* disorder, engendered by the federal government. This interpretation explains why working people voted on November 4, 1980 to reduce the size of government, *not* to restrict further the world of work and enterprise.

In this view of inflation, the remedies logically follow from the analysis of the defects. The remedies constitute a coherent economic policy:

1) Reduce as rapidly and humanely as possible the federal budget deficit, especially on current account. Reorganize the government capital account, including federal credit programs, such that government demand for credit is substantially less than the volume of total savings available in the market.

2) Reform the tax structure and restore work incentives in order to encourage the production of new goods, which will help to balance supply and demand conditions and thereby to mitigate inflation. The tax legislation must reduce marginal income tax rates and capital gains rates. Tax reform must abolish the inane distinction between taxes on savings and taxes on wages (so-called "unearned" and earned income). Savings are, in part, stored wages and must be taxed the same way, or savings will evaporate.

3) Renovate the regulatory policy. Decontrol of energy prices would be the symbol of serious intent to sweep away excessive impediments to commerce and economic growth.

4) Encourage the Federal Reserve System to moderate creation of money and credit, such that the supply of new credit is strictly consistent with the demand for credit by producers who need it to create new goods and services during the same market period.

5) Commit, publicly and unequivocally, to a free and open world trading order under American leadership. The indispensable conditions for achieving such an open world order are twofold. At the earliest possible moment, perhaps January 1982, the President should announce his intention to restore a stable dollar to the world by creating a gold-based currency. Second, the President should call for an international monetary conference, to be held in January 1983, to reform the world monetary system, to uphold an open trading system, to contain the rising tide of protectionism.

Each of these five policies is, by itself, necessary. But alone, each will be unavailing. Therefore, all should be done together, for only together will the new economic policy be sufficient.

The new financial policy to end inflation would rely on the creation of real economic growth and *more jobs* – not on unemployment and reduced demand in order to produce *more* goods, not less.

President-elect Reagan...must move soon and with profound understanding and conviction about the course to be followed.

There are six months in which to decide and to act. There is a way out of the maze of inflation. But in this particular crisis, the economic stabilization plan must not be characterized, as in past emergencies, by price and wage controls. On the contrary, the new program for economic renewal will deal with the crisis by *a systematic reformation of economic institutions.* Economic recovery must rely upon a reawakened nation, market institutions, free prices, mobile factors of production and stable currency.

It is true that, in the absence of sound policy, we shall survive this crisis too. It is the lot of businessmen and working people to accommodate and to survive. But to what end? Eight percent unemployment? Twenty percent interest rates permanently? Ten percent inflation rates? Bankruptcy? Wage and price controls?

It cannot be that these are the results we desire. Our goal is an end to inflation. President Reagan was elected to do it and now he must.

"Instead of fixing a specific quantity of money, the goal of the central bank should be reasonable price stability, or even better, a stable value for the dollar. The means by which to achieve this goal is a remobilized discount rate joined to a true international gold standard."

Chapter Eight

THE MEANS TO ESTABLISHING FINANCIAL ORDER

The Wall Street Journal, February 18, 1981

Recently on this page Milton Friedman wrote: "Despite vigorous efforts by the Fed to implement the [October 6, 1979 Volcker] policy, monetary growth has varied over a wider range since October 6, 1979, than in any period of comparable length for at least the last two decades. That fact is recognized by the Fed itself, by its defenders and by its critics." Professor Friedman's remarks go to the heart of the problem of the Federal Reserve System.

The Fed's governors honestly believe they can attain a goal that is not within their reach – namely, to fix the quantity of money in circulation. They also believe they can fine-tune the world's most complex economy by changes in credit policy and monetary base manipulation. Monetary base manipulation leads to the Fed's daily interventions in the open market for government securities, creating uncertainty and disorder in the credit markets. In recent years, Fed open-market operations have led to the systematic expansion of its portfolio of government securities. Not only has this process indirectly financed the government deficits; but, along with reduced reserve requirements, open-market operations have been the primary source of the perennial 8-9 percent increase in total adjusted Federal Reserve Bank credit – about three to four times the average growth of output. Through this mechanism of open-market operations, the Fed has become the engine of world inflation.

It is important to understand that in a free market order neither the amount of money in circulation, nor its growth rate, can be determined by the central bank. For, quite simply, the Fed does not possess all the necessary market information, the proven operating techniques or the foresight to bring about a predictable rate of growth of money now or in the future. It is true that the Fed does influence conditions governing the supply of money; but it is the users of money in the market who alone determine their demand for it.

An Elusive Abstraction

Indeed, the money supply cannot be precisely defined or measured. How can the Fed control such an elusive abstraction? Moreover, no money-supply growth rate during a specific market period is necessarily correlated with a specified rate of inflation, deflation or with price stability. For example, during part of 1978 the quantity of money in Switzerland grew approximately 30 percent, while the price level rose about 1 percent. Conversely, in the United States in 1979, the money supply grew about 5 percent while the consumer price index rose 13 percent. In 1980, MIA grew at 5 percent; MIB grew 7.3 percent, while the CPI rose 13 percent. It is clear that the Fed cannot precisely control the relationship between the rate of growth of the money supply and the rate of inflation.

This should come as no surprise. Consider the institutional constraints on the Federal Reserve System. First and foremost, it is a bank. More precisely, it is a monopoly – the "bank of issue." The Fed has a monopoly over the issue of paper currency; that is, Federal Reserve notes. But it also has a balance sheet, which limits even the actions of a government monopoly. The Fed buys assets (Fed credit) with the resources created by its liabilities (largely the monetary base). Total Federal Reserve credit is a precise magnitude which regulates the rise and fall of credit supplied by the Fed to the rest of the banking system. If the new credit supply is actually desired in the market, the price level will tend to be stable. If the new credit created by the Fed is *forced* on market participants, it will quickly be spent by them at home and abroad, thus tending to cause inflation and a depreciating dollar.

Therefore, in the future, the Fed should allocate credit by mobilizing the superior technique linked to the *price mechanism* – not the mechanism of open-market operations, a blunt and unwieldy quantity technique. If we must have the central bank, then remobilize the discount rate, which is the price of credit for loans from the Fed to the commercial banks. Recently the amount of this type of Fed credit has ranged from $1 billion to $3 billion – 5-10 percent of bank reserves held at the Fed. The present discount rate constitutes a subsidy rate to substantial commercial bank credit expansion – because it is below market rates. During periods of inflation, the discount rate should be above market rates – for example the rates on Treasury bills or Fed funds. Thus the subsidy would be eliminated. The discount rate, as a market-related technique of central banking, was repudiated long ago by the money-supply fine-tuners; and not coincidentally, so was a stable value for the dollar.

The problem of equalizing the supply and demand for credit by means of the discount rate illustrates the fundamental issue of monetary policy and central banking. *Instead of fixing a specific quantity of money, the goal of the central bank should be reasonable price stability, or even better, a stable value for the dollar. The means by which to achieve this goal is a remobilized discount rate joined to a true international gold standard.*

When excess credit causes inflation, the Fed, by raising the discount rate (of the Fed funds rate) above market rates, should promptly eliminate the subsidy to bank credit expansion, thus removing the stimulus to inflation. As a result, excess money and credit will be reabsorbed in order to hit the correct target: *the volume of money in circulation should always be equal to the amount of money actually desired in the market.* Inflation is caused by excess money. If there is no excess money, there can be no inflation. Such a monetary target can be hit so long as the government does not finance its inflationary deficit spending by continually demanding new money at the Fed and at the banks. That is why a balanced budget is crucial. It keeps the government from demanding new money at the Fed and the commercial banks.

To establish financial order, a sound Fed credit policy is a necessary condition; but it is not sufficient. History and classical economic analysis show that the policy best suited to ensure stable money over the long run is to define the dollar as a weight of gold. But a domestic gold standard is not enough, because our national economy is fully integrated with the free world economy. It follows that only a world monetary system can provide an impartial, common currency, not subject to sovereign political manipulation. Such a world monetary system is the international gold standard. *This is the classical monetary policy.*

As a monetary standard, the value of gold compared to other goods in the world economy is determined by its relative costs of production, while the costs of production of one more unit of a paper currency is almost zero. Zero production costs explain why most government currency monopolies have overproduced paper money and thereby destroyed its value. On the other hand, gold is an ideal monetary standard because its real costs of production cause it to have a relatively inelastic supply curve. It cannot be overproduced. Its rate of growth of production over a century has been about 1.5 to 2 percent – proportional, that is, to the rate of long-term economic growth and population growth in the industrial world. It is this unique and stable long-run relationship between the rates of increase of the supply of gold and of economic growth which, among other reasons, makes gold the optimum monetary standard.

Gold Is Least Imperfect

Unlike paper and credit money, the supply conditions of gold cannot be fundamentally and swiftly altered by politicians. Supply conditions for gold depend upon the real-world economics of gold production, which are, in general, not susceptible to scale-techniques of mining. When scale techniques of production are applied to other, more easily mass-produced commodity money standards, oversupply results and the monetary standard depreciates. In an imperfect world, the gold standard is, therefore, the least imperfect of the monetary standards. That is why over the centuries a gold currency was *freely* selected as money by the market.

Under conditions of modern central banking, a disciplined discount policy at the Fed is only useful for providing elasticity to the supply of credit in the short and intermediate term. But a gold currency is an independent long-run stabilizer of the supply of money and credit in the world economy

– the stable price level gyroscope, if you will, of a free world-market-order. The true gold standard rules out excessive manipulation of money by politicians and bureaucrats. Therefore, in order to end inflation and to restore trust in the U.S. currency, the dollar must be defined in law as a weight unit of gold. A modernized gold standard would be a guarantee of the purchasing power of money and, therefore, of the future value of money savings. And we know that in the absence of increased savings there can be no long-term economic growth.

Thus, given President Reagan's unequivocal commitment to stable money and a policy of economic growth, it is time for the United States to offer the free world a real money, and to call for monetary reform based on the international gold standard.

"Paper money has been the handmaiden of war, protectionism and big government. But the gold standard was the symbol of peace, free trade and limited government."

Chapter Nine

THE CASE FOR THE GOLD STANDARD

The Wall Street Journal, July 30, 1981

The U.S. dollar today is an inconvertible paper currency. But this is nothing new. In 1690, the Massachusetts Bay Colony promised a limited issue of 7,000 pounds in paper notes. But by 1714, the colony had issued 194,000 pounds worth, and the value of the paper pound had fallen 70 percent. Naturally, the politicians blamed the currency depreciation on the people, they being "so sottish as to deny credit to the government."

During the Revolution, the Continental Congress financed the war with paper money. "Do you think, gentlemen, that I will consent to load my constituents with taxes," said one member of Congress, "when we can send to our printers, and get a wagonload of money, one quire (25 sheets) of which will pay for the whole?"

Congress issued $2 million worth of continental currency in early 1775. At first, the law required two congressmen to sign and number each note – a sunlight procedure that much appeals to me. But that implicit restraint limited the number of paper notes, and the issuing technique was soon changed. By 1779 Congress had issued $200 million in continental currency and its purchasing power had fallen to $1/1000^{th}$ of gold.

American patriots suffered most of the depreciation, wrote William Gouge, President Andrew Jackson's financial adviser, since they accepted and held the paper money. "The Tories...made it a rule to part with it as soon as possible." More than two centuries later, we still hear the phrase "not worth a continental."

Paper Money

During the Civil War, both North and South printed paper money. The Union issued $450 million worth, and the price level more than doubled. Every American knows what happened to Confederate paper money – total worthlessness.

In our own time, President Nixon officially uncoupled the last link between the dollar and gold. The U.S. currency became once again an irredeemable paper money issued at will by the government. Since that act in 1971, the money supply has more than doubled, and so have prices.

Irredeemable paper money has almost always been accompanied by unbalanced budgets, high inflation and high interest rates – except during financial collapse and depression. But the true gold standard has been associated with balanced budgets, reasonable price stability and low interest rates amidst economic growth. Paper money has been the handmaiden of war, protectionism and big government. But the gold standard was the symbol of peace, free trade and limited government.

At one time, American companies could sell 100-year bonds. Because of the gold standard, Americans saved and lent their savings for generations to growing corporations. People saved because the gold dollar's purchasing power did not decline. The price level was no higher in the 1930s, when we left the domestic gold standard, than it had been under President Washington.

Today, we must decide whether to have a nominal dollar – mere paper – or a real dollar, defined by its weight in gold; whether to have a budget balanced at current tax receipts, or continued deficits.

The road to the balanced budget is paved with the gold standard.

To choose the gold standard and the balanced budget is to choose stable prices, low interest rates and economic growth. To some, that choice seems too simple – a prime reason many economists, politicians, and intellectuals reject the gold standard. Even a balanced budget is too straightforward for them. They want more complex institutions and problems to manipulate on behalf of special interests.

But a gold-based currency is the only money worthy of a free people. Most Americans cannot afford sophisticated financial and tax advisers, nor an economist to figure out the Fed's actions. Gold money, on the other hand, can be easily understood by everybody, and working people can control the quantity of convertible dollars they desire. People, free to choose, decide for gold, because it is democratic money.

Gold is also the best coordinator of a world market order. For centuries gold has been a common international currency. A gold dollar would benefit all nations because there is only one economy, the global economy. Through the mechanism of arbitrage, the prices in all national economies are linked. This is, of course, a good thing. It leads not only to the maximum amount of individual liberty, but also to the maximum production of goods and services, to the special benefit of the poor. To choose the gold standard is to choose openness over isolation.

Inflation is profoundly imperfect and immoral. The gold standard, being a human institution, is imperfect. But it is the least imperfect of all monetary institutions. Paper currencies and unbalanced budgets are dishonest and disorderly. The depreciation of the dollar deranges the movement of relative prices and interest rates around the world, and it causes unemployment through misdirected investments and uncertainty.

Above all, inflation fraudulently transfers hundreds of billions of dollars from the weak and honorable to the slick and well-placed financial class. This wealth transfer – from the thrifty to the speculator, from the small businessman to the giant government contractor, from the saver to the spender from the aged and poor to the rich and powerful – violates our religious ethical and constitutional heritage, makes a mockery of honest work, and erodes our faith in constitutional government.

Today, interest rates are at the highest levels in American history: higher than during the Civil War, when the very life of the nation was in question. The real value, the purchasing power, of the average worker's paycheck is 14 percent less than 10 years ago adjusted by the CPI. Small business access to credit is being crushed by government bond sales, the result of federal deficits. At present interest rates, Americans can no longer afford to borrow money for a car or a house. They are not consoled by government officials who preach sacrifice for working people while spending more on the public sector.

Almost impossible

The Dow Jones Average is 52 percent lower, in real terms, than in 1971. The bond market is 61 percent lower, and most companies find it almost impossible to raise long-term capital.

As a remedy we are offered austerity and monetarism. But these well-meaning policies will not work here. Compassionate and enterprising Americans reject such an outcome here.

What America needs is a policy of financial order, the Reagan tax program and economic growth. That is why the establishment of the U.S. Gold Commission by Congress was so timely. The commission will consider, in the words of the Helms-Paul Amendment, what role gold should play "in the domestic and international monetary systems."

The National Monetary Commission of 1908 led to the creation of the Federal Reserve System in 1913. The Gold Commission could be as significant, inspiring a national debate about the choice between inconvertible paper money and the gold standard. There is nothing like the free market and stable money to determine the real value of a product or idea.

As in the marketplace of ideas, so in the world of money: every American must discover what is false, and what is true.

*"My argument has always been that the gold standard
is an imperfect institution. All institutions are imperfect.
But it's the least imperfect institution that's been tested in a
laboratory of history to yield reasonable price stability
and to provide for a stable dollar."*

Chapter Ten

SHOULD WE (AND COULD WE) RETURN
TO THE GOLD STANDARD?

The New York Times, September 6, 1981

Keynes called it the "barbarous relic." Lenin said it was fit only to adorn
the latrines of the world. Ten years ago President Nixon, in effect, tore the
world's currencies loose from it by pulling the dollar away from a gold peg.
Still, gold has lost neither its romantic allure nor its practical attraction.

President Reagan recently appointed a commission of 17 experts, mostly
government officials, to review the issue again. Its specific task is to
determine whether the metal should once more play a dominant role in the
domestic and international monetary system. The Week in Review asked
two members of that commission, Henry C. Wallich and Lewis E. Lehrman
to talk about the gold standard. Mr. Wallich, a former economic professor
at Yale, has been a governor of the Federal Reserve Board since March
1974. Mr. Lehrman, chairman of the executive committee of the Rite Aid
Corporation, a discount drug chain, was one of the inner core of supply-
siders in the Reagan transition team. Excerpts of their separate interviews
with Clyde H. Farnsworth, a reporter in *The New York Times*'s Washington
bureau, follow.

Question. Is the gold standard, as some advocates argue, a cure-all or is it a patent medicine?

Answer. My argument has always been that the gold standard is an imperfect institution. All institutions are imperfect. But it's the least imperfect institution that's been tested in a laboratory of history to yield reasonable price stability and to provide for a stable dollar.

The dollar would have a permanent fixed value. Think of it the following way. The dollar is the monetary standard, and the monetary standard is defined permanently as a weight unit of gold.

Q. But there can be gold strikes, or shortages.

A. Well, with respect, the truth about the production of gold is very different from some of the mythology. The rate of gain in gold output has averaged around 2 percent, since the industrial revolution.

Q. The severe shortages and booms of the late 19th century had great economic consequences.

A. The consequences were all very beneficial. [Real economic growth averaged almost 4 percent.] From 1875 until about 1912, the average rate of variation of the price level never exceeded 2 percent. Compare that to the last 10 years of the manipulated paper currency system, where the price level has varied as much as 13 percent above the previous year several times.

Q. How would going on a gold standard affect wage increases locked into contracts?

A. We all want to see the rate of gain in wages be approximately equal to the rate of gain in productivity. The gold standard gives people today confidence in the future purchasing power of the dollar. As a result, working men believing in an honest dollar begin to ask for reasonable wage increases, proportional, that is, to the gain in the productivity in their own labor.

It's almost as if the gold standard were an insurance policy, an actual reminder to all who participate in the market that the dollar in 10 years instead of being 50 percent of what it is worth today would be approximately equal in purchasing power as it is today.

Q. If you're going to establish a gold standard, you have to set a price. What happens if the price is too high? All the gold would come to the United States. If it's too low, the United States would lose gold, or go into some kind of economic contraction.

A. Under the gold standard there is no price for gold. The dollar is the monetary standard, set by law equal to a weight of gold. The price of gold does not exist. As a matter of fact, you may even look at the gold standard as the end to the speculation in gold in terms of paper dollars.

Q. But in the real world, you would be using paper dollars and you could turn them in to the Treasury for so much gold. So the gold does have a dollar value.

A. And I live in the real world. I'm a businessman and I'm very concerned about just the character of our monetary standard. Under the gold standard, the paper dollar is a promissory note. It is a claim to a real article of wealth defined by law as the standard.

Let us say, for example, that in January 1982, we would announce that two years hence the monetary standard of the United States would be established as a dollar equal to a weight of gold. About 90 days before the period in which the price, as you call it, would be fixed, the gold markets would be tending to stabilize because they would know that the President and the Congress, under statute, would be about to fix (the dollar) equal to a weight of gold.

Q. In other words, that's the market price and that would be the fair price for gold.

A. The market price would be the lead indicator. On the other hand, other indicators are important – the assignment of the experts assembled around the President in writing a statute. There's no substitute for judgment.

Q. Wouldn't we be mortgaging our future by founding our whole monetary system on the amount of gold coming out of, say, South Africa?

A. Generally that criticism is made by people who have never bothered to study the statistics of gold production. South Africa and the Soviet Union first of all would act in their own self interest because in order to obtain foreign exchange to buy Western technology and Western grain they would want to sell the gold in an orderly manner. On the other hand, if they chose not to sell their gold for foreign exchange they do not produce enough to disrupt the total gold market, of which they are less than one percent.

Q. But why should we guarantee the price of the chief source of foreign exchange for them?

A. We are not guaranteeing a price for them. We are establishing a monetary standard for us.

We've all learned that we don't cut off our nose to spoil our face. If something is good for the United States, namely a monetary standard, a gold dollar and a price level that's stable, we don't worry too much about other countries who may get a minor benefit. Indeed, I would argue that South Africa and the Soviet Union have a stake in inflation, because they get a high price for gold when the United States inflates.

Q. Why is dependence on 'the barbarous relic' better than the rational creation of reserves by rational men?

A. Your phrase – quote, the rational creation of reserves, unquote – is precisely the technique that the Federal Reserve and central banks all over the world during the last 10 years have been using. Not only have they succeeded in destroying almost all currencies; they have succeeded in disrupting the trade patterns based upon a stable exchange rate.

Q. So you don't trust the Fed or the politicians?

A. Well, not that. I do trust them. I do not believe they have the proven techniques to rationally provide for reserves by manipulating the money supply.

In the abstract, especially in the classrooms of Yale where I went to school, it was always easy for professors to draw on a blackboard equations which showed why bank reserves could be provided rationally to the market. As a businessman I have learned that under the gold standard these reserves were provided much more rationally by virtue of the operations of free markets.

"Confidence in the fixed value of the monetary standard, the measuring rod of economic value, is similar to our enduring trust in the fixed value for the principal measure of length, the yardstick – always 36 inches. Who would arbitrarily depreciate the value of the yardstick to 30 inches tomorrow or gradually augment its value to 40 inches one year from now?"

Chapter Eleven

GOLDEN ANTIDOTE TO HIGH INTEREST

The Wall Street Journal, June 29, 1984

The threat of inflation and punitive interest rates is the transcendent economic issue of our times. Financial disorder is to our generation what depression and unemployment were to our parents and grandparents. Searching the 200-year history of the Industrial Revolution to find *a full decade* of average interest rates as high as those during the period of 1974 to 1984, it is necessary to go back to the French Revolution and the total financial collapse of France in the years 1789 to 1799. The modern history of interest rates shows that in periods such as ours there has been only one way to return to relatively low, long-term interest rates and rapid economic growth; and that is by a monetary order based on a gold-backed currency. The alternative is low interest rates and slow growth.

For example, the period of the American Revolution was a time of paper-money hyperinflation, immense budget deficits and high interest rates (for example, 26-40 percent on long-term government bonds in 1787). As a result of this experience, the founders in 1789 established the new constitutional republic upon the bedrock of a convertible currency and government credit reform – largely the initiative of Secretary of the Treasury, Alexander Hamilton. Along with the Coinage Act of 1792 Hamilton refinanced the public debt and established a dollar based on a gold-and-silver standard. As a result, Federal government interest rates fell to 6.5-7.5 percent for long-term government bonds. After the monetary reform, between 1792 and 1801, budget deficits were actually exceeded by budget surpluses. A decade of economic boom without inflation followed domestic monetary reform.

Restoration of Gold Franc

By means of a very similar monetary reform – restoration of the gold franc – Napoleon ended the French revolutionary period of inflation, floating-exchange rates and high interest rates (average yields of 34 percent in 1799 on government bonds). These high interest rates, like our own, had been brought about by government-manipulated "assignats," the inconvertible paper-money issues of the French revolutionary government. The return to gold convertibility brought down interest rates to 6 percent (or lower) on government bonds from 1806 – with a few years' exceptions – until World War 1.

As recently as 1959, after two decades of a depreciating franc and comparatively high interest rates, French President Charles de Gaulle and Professor Jacques Rueff reformed the domestic monetary system and launched the Fifth Republic on a decade of economic growth, exceeding even Germany's growth. The Rueff reforms restored a franc convertible to gold, ended France's inflation, lowered interest rates, led to a balanced budget and linked the gold franc to the Bretton Woods system of fixed-exchange rates.

A century and a half earlier in Britain, the 1819-1821 restoration of the gold standard had ended an era of comparatively high interest rates, floating-exchange rates and parliamentary paper-money experiments. These experiments also had begun during the Anglo-Napoleonic wars – a 24-year financial nightmare (1795-1819) of alternating wartime inflation and peacetime austerity and deflation. For example, British long-term government bonds yielded 3 to 4.5 percent from 1735 to 1785. From 1795, when pound convertibility was suspended, yields almost doubled, peaking at nearly 7 percent in 1798. But in expectation of the return to gold convertibility of the paper pound in 1819, yields declined almost 50 percent, and continued to decline thereafter. The capital markets of London revived, undergirded by sterling convertibility to gold, officially ratified in 1822, and offered interest rates of 2 to 4 percent for British government bonds for almost a century.

In 1879, the United States officially ended a 17-year epoch of inconvertibility of the dollar to gold, and the financial disorder it engendered. The Civil War and Reconstruction period, with its paper money ("greenbacks") and floating-exchange rates, was also marked by comparatively high interest rates. For example, the average yield on long-term government bonds during the 1850s was 4.33 percent. In the first year after the suspension of dollar convertibility in 1861-1862, yields ran about 50 percent higher, to average about 6.5 percent. Peak rates also occurred in 1861-1862 – 6.75 percent as measured in greenback yields, higher if measured in gold prices.

During Reconstruction, in expectation of the return of gold convertibility in 1879, market yields on long-term government bonds declined to 3.75 percent, a 40 percent decline from the peak in 1861-1862. During the decade after dollar convertibility was restored (1879-1889), average yields declined radically to 2.13 percent in 1889, averaging 2.71 percent for the entire decade. The U.S. monetary reform of 1879 had reestablished a necessary condition of low interest rates – the gold dollar – and linked it to the international monetary order of the day, a general system of multi-national currency convertibility to gold and free trade, upheld at the center by the convertible, gold-backed British pound.

Why do freely convertible currencies and an international monetary order based on the gold standard produce such positive financial effects? Because only a fixed value for any unit of measurement can bestow reliability and trust on the chosen standard. Faith in a just and lasting value for an objective standard of economic measurement and exchange, namely money, is crucial for commerce. Confidence in the fixed value of the monetary standard, the measuring rod of economic value, is similar to our enduring trust in the fixed value for the principal measure of length, the yardstick – always 36 inches. Who would arbitrarily depreciate the value of the yardstick to 30 inches tomorrow or gradually augment its value to 40 inches one year from now? Such manipulation would cause the collapse, for instance, of the textile industry – any industry based on constant, reliable standards of measure.

That is precisely the arbitrary power we give today to the Federal Reserve – to depreciate and appreciate – to manipulate – the value of the monetary yardstick, the dollar. That is because there is no longer any legal requirement to maintain the value of the monetary standard. And because of universal floating-exchange rates, the Fed is in fact free, through open-market operations, to increase or decrease the supply of credit and money without limit. The financial markets are fully aware of this fact, reminded as they are by the open-market operations of the New York Fed at 11:45 a.m. almost every day. Indeed, total Federal Reserve financial-market purchases and sales of government securities have reached $52 trillion in a single year. Imagine the destabilizing effect of $2 trillion of government purchases and sales in the market for any other product.

By means of open-market operations, the Fed creates and destroys bank money without creating or removing new goods and services during the same market period. Thus, on the one hand, too expansive open-market purchases of government securities by the Fed cause demand to exceed supply at prevailing prices, inflation, and dollar depreciation gets under way, as happened between 1971 and 1980. Or, on the other hand, open-market sales of government securities by the Fed often reduce credit too abruptly and cause demand to fall short of supply, and a drift toward deflation gets under way. This happened in the fourth quarter of 1981 and more recently in the third week of May 1984 when, just after the collapse of Continental Illinois, the Fed sold $4 billion of government securities adding to the largest ever weekly drop in Federal Reserve credit. Uncertainty about such Fed operations has raised the risk premium in interest rates.

Only a stable monetary standard can abolish this risk premium in long-term interest rates and renew faith in the fixed value of all future money payments on borrowings (mortgages, and other long-term financial contracts). Confidence in the stable future purchasing power of a convertible dollar leads directly to a boom in the supply of savings offered for long periods at fixed, low rates. This new supply of savings will tend to lower the price of credit, i.e., interest rates. Only a real currency, legally convertible to gold at a fixed rate, can bring about these effects in the capital markets. That is why the Constitution of our country – originating as it did in 1789 after a catastrophic inflation of the previous currency of the Continental Congress ("not worth a Continental") – upholds a gold- or silver-backed currency.

With this general understanding, a comprehensive economic reform, containing the solutions to the related problems of inflation, the budget deficit, high interest rates and the hidden threat of deflation follows directly from the analysis:

1) Reduce as rapidly and humanely as possible the federal budget deficit. But the President cannot currently control the deficit without using an indiscriminate, broad-brush veto of multibillion-dollar appropriations bills. The President needs the line-item veto he has requested and the legal forces of a constitutional amendment in order to require Congress to balance the budget annually in the future.

2) The economic-reform program also should include a renovation of the federal tax structure – a low, simple, fair flat tax. This would create compelling incentives for more work, saving, investment, new jobs and the production of new goods, and therefore tend to balance supply and demand conditions in the market through economic growth, without creating disincentives by raising tax rates. In truth, an authentic demand for a balanced budget and low interest rates can only mean a demand for raising tax revenues through rapid economic growth without inflation.

New Monetary Philosophy Needed

3) At the same time, the Fed must abandon its failed quantitative monetary targeting. A new Federal Reserve monetary philosophy must be adopted – one that will supply, at market rates, the new money and credit currently needed by small enterprises, farms and entrepreneurs for the profitable production of new goods and services. So long as new money is borrowed at market rates to create new goods and services, there can be no inflation. If the ratio of new goods to new credit stays approximately in balance over the long term, it does not matter how much new credit and money is created.

4) This new Fed target should be part of a domestic and international monetary reform designed to restore a gold-backed dollar.

We know that sustained economic growth and full employment require a long-term investment boom and the rebuilding of a competitive American economy. And that a long-term investment boom requires the means to finance it. To restore ample, long-term bond markets at low, fixed interest rates, we must ensure the value of all future money payments to those willing to lend their savings for the long term. This means, by every careful study of history, a true and reliable monetary standard, and only a gold or silver-backed currency has been proven such a money standard throughout history.

*"The First Amendment wisely prohibits government
censorship (that is, the devaluation) of speech; the
gold standard prohibits government devaluation (censorship)
of money – the currency of honest labor."*

Chapter Twelve
TO MOVE FORWARD, GO BACK TO GOLD

The New York Times, February 9, 1986

The damage inflicted on our workers and industries by the overvalued
dollar has demonstrated that free trade without stable exchange rates is
a fantasy. The trade crisis caused by overvaluation has also given us a
clear choice: Either we continue to live with floating-exchange rates, in
which case we will face bitter trade wars and the gyrations of inflation and
deflation, or we can choose a stable currency based on the gold standard.
The argument for gold has rarely been stronger than it is today.

During 1985, almost 200,000 blue collar jobs, mostly in manufacturing,
and an equal number of farms disappeared from the economic landscape.
Our budget deficit rose above $200 billion. Our trade deficit with Japan
climbed to almost $50 billion up from $1.7 billion in 1974. The trade
deficit was the result of an overvalued dollar (and the reserve currency role
of the dollar) that made foreign imports cheaper and our own exports more
expensive – and left our industries gasping for relief.

President Reagan's effort to persuade the Group of Five industrial nations
– the other members are West Germany, Britain, France and Japan – to
restore balance among the leading currencies has managed to deflect same
protectionist sentiment in Congress. But this is only the first step toward
thorough, equitable monetary reform.

To achieve such reform, and thereby stabilize exchange rates, we must
re-examine the post-war Bretton Woods system, which lasted from 1944
to 1973, as well as the system of floating currencies begun in 1973. The
common flaw in both dollar-based systems is the official reserve currency

status of the dollar, a role that jams the market adjustment mechanisms needed to regulate currencies and [rebalance world] trade. Both a burden and a privilege, the world dollar standard creates an extra demand for the dollar to supply the reserves of foreign central banks, which tends to keep the real value of the dollar higher than it would otherwise be. Gradually, overvaluation has reduced the competitiveness of American industries, helping to increase our trade deficit from small figures in the late 1960s to a staggering $148 billion in 1985.

A lasting and just solution to the dilemma of the world paper dollar standard would require the leading nations to share a common monetary standard, a reserve currency independent of any national currency and not controlled by any self-interested sovereign government. The solution to the trade problems caused by unhinged currencies requires key currencies to be directly convertible into an impartial monetary standard. Indeed, a common monetary standard underlying the different convertible currencies is precisely the international adjustment mechanism needed to coordinate and discipline the global balance-of-payments and bring about the convergence of national fiscal and monetary policies.

The only secure approach would be a system of fixed exchange rates based on the convertibility of key currencies into gold, a neutral and independent monetary reserve. No other commodity will do: Governments have accumulated a billion ounces of gold, not pork bellies or bricks.

Conceivably, we could instead create a World Central Bank, whose independent credit would serve as neutral reserves for all national central banks – a system proposed by John Maynard Keynes in 1944 at Bretton Woods. But such a bank could not be expected to exercise impartial discipline on the international monetary system any more than its counterpart, the United Nations, acts impartially on the world political scene. Therefore, we must consider the gold standard, which has been tested by the commercial experience of advanced civilizations for 3,000 years.

If we also ask that the world monetary system be neither inflationary, nor deflationary over the long run, history shows there is no practical alternative to the convertibility of key currencies at fixed rates into a common monetary standard, defined by law as a weight unit of gold. Each disruption of convertibility, such as the currency float of the 1930s, led to financial turbulence similar to our volatile inflationary and deflationary experience since 1971. Today, some commentators sincerely but mistakenly associate the gold standard with the causes of the Great Depression. This notion is false. Among others, the economist Milton Friedman has shown that government mismanagement and the Federal Reserve System caused both the Depression and the destruction of the gold standard.

A comprehensive plan for monetary reform based on an international gold standard could be established during the remainder of President Reagan's second term.

First, he should arrange for the Treasury and Federal Reserve to cooperate with the Group of Five to stabilize the value of key currencies – which essentially means agreeing upon the relative purchasing powers of these currencies on world markets. Indexes of currency purchasing powers can be agreed upon at the forthcoming economic summit meeting in Tokyo in May.

Second, the President should send legislation to Congress establishing a gold dollar as this country's constitutional monetary standard. Limited convertibility would take effect in May 1987, one year from the Tokyo meeting.

The price of gold must be set at a level that will cover the cost of producing the gold that constitutes the monetary standard. Otherwise there is no incentive to produce that gold. Under current market conditions, and given a Federal Reserve policy consistent with stable economic growth, I estimate that the gold price should be approximately $400 to $500 per ounce – the marginal cost of production of gold in the United States. Such a price prevents a decline in nominal wages.

Third, the President should convene an international monetary conference to agree upon the reciprocal value of all major currencies and to refund official reserve currencies. The conference agenda should then move to the question of dismantling protectionism.

One must emphasize that the new international monetary system could accommodate generous social policies in every country. But social policy would be based on the essential justice of a constitutional order, not on the present tendency among governments to finance social policy by inflationary means.

Moreover, currency convertibility alone could end the varying dollar premiums now awarded Soviet and South African gold through speculation on future inflation. Far from helping the South Africans and the Soviet Union, the gold standard would end the speculation in gold.

The results of international monetary reform would be dramatic. By pinning down the future price levels, it would create compelling incentives to channel savings away from short-term speculation into long-term capital markets. Long-term interest rates would fall, encouraging investment and creating worldwide demand for unemployed labor to man the new plant and equipment. Domestic and foreign debtors would service their debts at lower interest rates in expanding world markets. Federal budget deficits would become more manageable – because of lower interest rates and an expanding tax base – and be contained by the external discipline of a convertible currency and a sound but elastic monetary system. A balanced budget amendment amidst rapid economic growth would finish the job.

While the world would have many problems yet to solve, our legacy to future generations would be the least imperfect monetary system known to free peoples who live under the law. The truth is government-manipulated currencies today are the monetary equivalent of the unacceptable 19th century doctrine of Social Darwinism – the triumph of unrestrained competition over justice.

Here we should not be confused by those who sincerely but wrongly think that this represents an arbitrary "fixing" of the price of gold. On the contrary, free people voluntarily establish objective standards. Like the 36-inch yardstick, the gold monetary standard is an agreed-upon measuring rod of economic value. Who would give any board or governors authority to manipulate the value of the yardstick – to depreciate it to 30 inches one year, to augment its value to 40 inches another?

The gold monetary standard is both a symbol and a practical agent of justice because convertibility is a constitutional rule of equity to which all are bound. The First Amendment wisely prohibits government censorship (that is, the devaluation) of speech; the gold standard prohibits government devaluation (censorship) of money – the currency of honest labor.

*"The classical argument for free trade holds
perfectly true, but only when the indispensable
minimum international conditions for fair and rational
trading have been established."*

Chapter Thirteen

"AN EXORBITANT PRIVILEGE"

National Review, November 21, 1986

Two years ago, Congress began to assemble the most comprehensive protectionist legislation since the disastrous Smoot-Hawley Tariff of 1929-1930. Hundreds of new bills have been introduced, some calling for fair trade, others calling for quotas, "voluntary" and "orderly" marketing agreements, export subsidies, selective import fees, countervailing duties, and manipulation of foreign-exchange rates. Such measures signal real danger for the free world trading order, so laboriously constructed after World War II upon the foundations of the Bretton Woods Monetary Agreement of 1944 and the General Agreement of Tariffs and Trade (GATT) of 1948.

The overvalued dollar of 1985, combined with slow growth for the past two years, has brought about consensus for some form of U.S. protection. The cries for relief from declining unions and wounded industries will not be stilled by Administration rhetoric. In August 1986, Congress came within eight votes of overriding the President's veto of the textile, apparel, and shoe protection bill. With mines, farms, and industrial plants shut down all over America, what congressman could fail to be moved by the pleas from unemployed workers and underemployed manufacturers? The numbers are staggering. The merchandise trade deficit grew from $40 billion in 1981 to $123 billion in 1984 to $150 billion in 1985; at present rates it will wind up at approximately $170 billion for 1986. More than 400,000 jobs in the manufacturing sector have been lost in the last 24 months. Since 1980, almost three million skilled manufacturing jobs have been lost. Net of offsetting gains, two million well-paid industrial jobs have disappeared. While more than nine million jobs have been added to the U.S. economy since 1980, it does no injustice to point out that nearly 60 percent are in "miscellaneous services," where the average wage is 25 percent above the poverty level if it supports a family of four. Another 30 percent have been added in retail, where the average wage is 82 percent of the poverty level if it supports a family of four.

Some economists have correctly pointed out that the very strength of the Reagan recovery has inflated the merchandise-trade-deficit figures. When the United States leads a world economic recovery, its import growth tends to outpace its export growth. In that sense a modest trade deficit can be an indicator of economic expansion. But since 1983, when Reagan growth- and productivity-oriented economic policies took hold, imports have risen 60 percent while exports have risen 6 percent. And the most recent trade-deficit figures come on top of eight quarters of low (2 percent) growth. Even those economists and politicians who look to German and Japanese expansion to augment U.S. growth should remember that offsetting the U.S. trade deficit would require an implausible 50 percent increase in German and Japanese imports from the United States.

In 1985 and 1986, trade in advanced technology, the symbol of American entrepreneurship, has turned from surplus to deficit. Farm trade has been in deficit – June, July, and August 1986 – for the first time in a generation. I pinpoint farming and technology because the U.S. farm sector has been an historical exporter and U.S. technology a competitive advantage. The charge that American industry is not dynamic cannot apply to semiconductors, where 10.7 percent of industry revenues goes to research and development. Similarly, the American textile industry has been one of the most significant investors in capital per worker in the world, and nevertheless has lost 350,000 jobs since 1981. Many Americans wonder, in the light of these statistics, if the American trade problem is partly due to unfair or predatory trade practices, as suggested by the widely publicized Hitachi memorandum directing the company's sales force to quote 10 percent below American semiconductor prices, regardless of cost.

One need not subscribe to the mercantilist fallacies of economic nationalism to be alarmed by these events and statistics. Even if one disagrees with their policies, one must give the protectionist politicians credit for coming to grips with the problem. The defenders of "free trade," meanwhile, with their shopworn slogans, have been on the defensive for two years. The classical and endlessly repeated argument for free trade – that a free market moves nations into industries in which they are competitive, and out of those in which they could not hope to compete, for the benefit of all – is undeniable. But even those who accept its wisdom may be excused for questioning its relevance, when they see their nation being outstripped in so many of the most promising industries, especially those in which it seems to have a clear natural advantage. It is a contemporary paradox that nearly all academic economists, liberal or conservative, monetarist or Keynesian, agree on free trade as they agree on almost nothing else, and yet on this one point on which they are agreed, much of the political, business, and labor communities dissents.

Like all good paradoxes, this one contains hidden wisdom. The classical argument for free trade holds perfectly true, but only when the indispensable minimum international conditions for fair and rational trading have been established. The simple problem we face is that with nearly as much unanimity as they endorse free trade, most establishment economists have rejected – and convinced heads of state and monetary authorities to reject – the essential pre-condition of international free trade: a workable international monetary standard that would both guarantee reasonably stable future values for national currencies and guarantee that those currencies would be exchanged for each other at fixed and stable rates. The classical model of international free trade describes an elegant and precise mechanism for world prosperity; trying to run that mechanism without stable money is like trying to run the New York Stock Exchange on a barter system.

It is of little use to drop explicit tariffs and quotas, which distort relative prices, if relative prices are even more distorted by wild gyrations, or even deliberate manipulations, of the rates at which national currencies are exchanged. Yet such gyrations are the inevitable result of two decisions: abolishing even the remnants of an international gold standard and replacing it, de facto, with an international fiat dollar standard; and abolishing fixed-exchange rates based on convertible national currencies and substituting the current floating system based on manipulated currencies.

Modern mercantilism – generally ignored by economists and politicians alike during the past 15 years – has been practiced circuitously through the smokescreen of unrestrained monetary policies. This ruthless monetary struggle takes the form of a competitive depreciation of currency values similar to that which led us from the Depression of the 1930s into the nightmare of World War II. Managed floating-exchange rates have become the hidden proxies for explicit tariffs, quotas, and export subsidies. The new exchange-rate wars provoke protectionist trade retaliation in response, dangerously retarding world economic growth.

The past 15 years of financial history show this to be true, the economic disorders of today being part of an unmistakable pattern. From 1971 – when President Nixon formally suspended the international convertibility of the dollar and thus ended the Bretton Woods exchange-rate agreement – until 1974, America endured four phases of wage and price controls. Then came the "energy crisis"; an "era of limits" resource crisis; sustained double-digit inflation rates, unprecedented in the entire peacetime history of the Republic; back-to-back recessions, in 1980 and 1981-1982, that set records for suddenness and severity; Treasury interest rates topping 15 percent (twice the level that prevailed during the Civil War, when the Union had collapsed); total economic disarray in the farm belt, the mining industry, and the heavy-industry sector; a domestic and international banking crisis under way since 1982 (with failure rates of all banks now running higher than in any year since the Depression); a budgetary crisis pushing federal deficits to record levels in a conservative Administration; and currency fluctuations that defy seasoned money managers, who successively warn that the dollar "must come down," "may never come down," and, most recently, "may come crashing down."

The formal switch to today's floating system occurred in 1973, when the last vestiges of international currency stability were swept away. Under a system of floating-exchange rates, which rules out a common international currency and encourages all nations to faithlessly manipulate the value of their currencies in order to gain temporary advantage by reducing real wages, the world gradually reverts to a system of barter. The true and necessary functions of money are progressively undermined, as currency becomes a vehicle of speculation instead of a fixed standard, a known unit of account, a reliable store of value, a stable medium of exchange against goods and services.

It seems difficult to believe today, but floating-exchange rates were actively desired by a majority of a whole generation of economists, both monetarist and Keynesian. In the late 1960s, both schools believed that stable exchange rates stood in the way of their economic policy objectives: for the Keynesians, full employment through budget deficits and Federal Reserve credit expansion; for the monetarists, price stability through targeting the domestic money supply. The irony, of course, is that the United States achieved neither full employment nor price stability under floating-exchange rates. Instead, we suffered "stagflation," only partly ameliorated by Reagan reforms in the fiscal arena.

The neo-Keynesians of the 1960s blamed fixed-exchange rates for an overvalued dollar. John Maynard Keynes had, in part, built his economic theory on the assumption that prices and wages are rigid. He proposed "demand management" – central-bank manipulation of deficit spending – to stimulate investment and employment, essentially by reducing real wages through inflation. Keynes's followers, grafting onto his model net exports as another source of demand, argued that devaluation of the exchange rate could stimulate exports and thus employment – once again, by reducing real wages at home to gain a competitive advantage abroad. Monetarists dispute this effect because in their frictionless model of the economy, everyone adjusts quickly to changes in the value of the currency: Neither workers nor consumers nor importers can be tricked into accepting lower real value in exchange for their money or services. But the real world falls somewhere between Keynesian wage rigidity and the quick-adjusting monetarist model. In the real world, producers and consumers are hemmed in by previous commitments. Steelworkers in a steel town may not be willing either to move or to strike, and thus will accept for a time the lower real wages that result from inflation or devaluation. It is precisely because Keynesian manipulations of the exchange rate are not ineffectual in the short run that they are dangerous tools of policy. It is the elusive promise of a free lunch that tempts nations to competitive currency manipulations.

But manipulation and counter-manipulation create currency chaos, guaranteeing economic havoc and protectionist retaliation.

The monetarists – more classical in their views of wage and price flexibility – pointed out the inflationary bias in Keynesian domestic economic policy. But, curiously enough, they were prepared to accept the neo-Keynesian float for purposes of international exchange. In the monetarists' view, stable exchange rates stood in the way of their prescription for stable domestic prices and output: controlling the domestic money supply. As the monetarists recognized, it is impossible to target both the price of a currency (the exchange rate) and its quantity (the money supply) at the same time. If the exchange rate must be X, then possible manipulations of the money supply are severely limited.

But in freeing exchange rates to allow targeting of the domestic money supply, the monetarists unhinged their own theory. Monetarist strategies depend almost entirely on the assumption that the demand to hold cash balances is stable. If the demand to hold cash balances becomes unstable, the monetarists become like Archimedes trying to move the earth without a place to stand. If the demand for cash fluctuates, it becomes impossible for the Federal Reserve Board to predict what effect its monetarist operations will have on the supply and the price level of money. Now, the monetarists, in establishing their theory, had gathered compelling empirical evidence that the demand for cash balances is fairly stable. Their evidence, however, came substantially from periods of fixed-exchange rates based on gold convertibility. But if nations unhinge exchange rates (the first monetarist step) and switch to government-managed paper money, then the demand for cash balances will fluctuate as wildly as predictions of the currency's future value.

There is another well-known explanation for today's financial turmoil: the "twin-deficit theory," which argues that the U.S. trade deficit is caused by the federal budget deficit and that the budget deficit has nothing to do with floating-exchange rates. The theory argues that a budget deficit financed by federal borrowing will cause interest rates to be higher than they otherwise would be, thus leading to volatile international capital movements and fluctuating exchange rates. Therefore, it is argued that if nations end their budget deficits, a system of fixed rates based on gold convertibility is superfluous; and, on the other hand, if nations do not balance their budgets, the system of currency convertibility – the classical gold standard – will become useless anyway.

In truth, the twin deficits *are* at the heart of the world's fundamental economic problem. As a practical matter, however, the causation is substantially the reverse of the twin-deficit theory. The twin deficits – in U.S. trade and the federal budget – are as much the symptoms as the causes of monetary disorder, both in the United States and in the international economy.

To get at this point, first consider classical monetary policy. Under the classical gold standard, central-bank reserves consisted largely of gold. That is to say, gold was the common coin among different national currencies, all directly convertible to gold at fixed rates. The monetary base in each country was backed by both gold and liquid financial assets denominated in the domestic currency, e.g., secured commercial paper. "Fixed-exchange rates" were merely another way of saying that all national currencies were linked directly to the gold standard at fixed parities. Thus, all currencies shared a common monetary standard – gold – rather like the fact that the bank deposits for the 12 regional Federal Reserve Banks are linked by a common currency, the dollar.

It is of the utmost importance to grasp that neither Bretton Woods nor the fixed-rate system of the 1920s and 1930s, which collapsed into the Great Depression, was a classical gold standard. Rather, in those eras the world monetary system was based on "reserve-currency" systems. Under a reserve-currency system, central-bank reserves consist not only of gold and domestic currency claims but also of the currencies of the major foreign powers. In the 1920s, the dollar and the pound sterling were the reserve currencies; under Bretton Woods, the dollar became the official reserve currency. It remains the dominant official reserve currency even today. Under the Bretton Woods rules, for example, other major currencies were convertible into dollars, but only dollars were officially convertible into gold. The American banking system, under the Federal Reserve, became in effect the world's central bank. The credit of other nations was leveraged upon U.S. credit, which, in turn, was leveraged upon declining U.S. gold reserves. Our banking system and money markets accepted on deposit the

117

dollar reserves of foreign central banks and re-lent them to private or public borrowers, these foreign dollar reserves having been accumulated through sustained U.S. balance-of-payments deficits.

The reserve-currency system made a certain sense during the 1950s, when the United States was all-powerful and the other industrial nations were virtually prostrate. But once reconstruction was substantially advanced and the European currencies became externally convertible into one another in 1958-1959, the Bretton Woods system lasted only 12 more years, collapsing in 1971.

The dollar's official-reserve-currency status conferred an obvious benefit upon the United States. Charles de Gaulle called it an "exorbitant privilege." Jacques Rueff, the French economist chiefly responsible for the French recovery of the early 1960s, spoke of "deficits without tears." They meant that under the reserve-currency system, Federal Reserve credit expansion and American balance-of-payments deficits were automatically financed by the voluntary or coerced buildup of dollar balances abroad; and these official foreign dollar reserves were naturally invested directly or indirectly in the market for U.S. securities, thus returning to the United States the purchasing power lost abroad as a result of the persistent U.S. balance-of-payments deficit. But the exorbitant privilege has its price: The reserve-currency role placed increasing burdens on the American economy, because the foreign demand for dollar reserves gradually led to an overvalued dollar, to overpriced tradable U.S. goods, and, of course, to calls for protection.

Thus, fixed rates alone will not lead to free and fair international trade if they are based on a reserve currency rather than on an independent monetary standard, a non-national common currency. Under fixed-exchange rates based on a true international gold standard, even during periods of very rapid growth – as during the first century and a half of the Industrial Revolution – global financial balance is maintained by virtue of the fact that total international reserves increase through increased gold production, not increased dollar (or other reserve-currency) debt. Also, under the classical gold standard, as one country loses reserves, another country gains them, thus stabilizing the general price level among countries. When, in one country, a rising price level or a too-easy domestic money market leads to a private-capital outflow or an excess of imports, the balance-of-payments deficit to be settled abroad must lead to increased exports or, in their place, a loss (export) of gold reserves.

But when one country's currency, the world reserve currency, is used to settle international payments – as today with the dollar – the balance-of-payments adjustment mechanism will be jammed for that country, and for the world. The extra demand for the dollar as the world's official reserve currency tends to keep its value higher than it otherwise would be. Normally an excess of dollars abroad would be cleared (returned to the United States) by an increased demand for U.S. exports (including gold if necessary). But under a reserve-currency system, foreign central banks accumulate these excess dollars to augment their reserves, so rather than being released to buy U.S. exports the dollars are held as foreign official reserves. Of course they are invested, in large part, in short-term financial instruments on the U.S. dollar market. Thus the United States experiences a short-term capital inflow just when it should be experiencing an export outflow – a trade surplus. U.S. export prices also remain higher than they otherwise would, in the first place because of the dollar's higher value, but also because of the concurrent domestic budget deficit, financed and encouraged by those foreign reserves invested here. The budget deficit intensifies the disorder by "bidding" for goods that could be exported. For some time at least, the process is self-perpetuating: The excess demand for the dollar caused by its use as a reserve currency tends to keep its value up, thus making foreign banks more willing to let their dollar reserves climb.

Everything proceeds as if there were no budget or current-account deficit. The foreign dollar reserves are used in the United States, the official-reserve-currency country, to finance the budget deficit, to purchase more imports, and to finance domestic consumption of goods that could otherwise be exported at competitive prices to re-establish equilibrium in the international balance-of-payments. In the absence of deliberately tight Federal Reserve policy (which tends toward deflation, as in 1984), the reserve-currency system thus finances, or subsidizes, demand within the United State for foreign goods, leads to a dollar exchange rate above what it would be under a true gold standard, and in the short run permits real wage rates and production costs for tradable goods to rise higher than they would under a convertible-currency system. Steadily, the trade balance of the reserve-currency country declines, along with its international competitiveness.

Ultimately, this process is not sustainable. The foreign demand for the reserve currency has a limit, and when it is clearly surpassed, foreign holders will unload that currency, and it will begin to fall rapidly. The reserve-currency country will then be faced, as the United States is today, with the choice between propping up interest rates and deflating the domestic economy, or else repudiating all or part of its debts (by ending convertibility as in 1973, or by devaluating under the float as in 1986).

It is essential to understand these defects of a reserve-currency system because the dollar's reserve-currency role did not end with the breakdown of Bretton Woods. In fact, with gold immobilized, the dollar's role expanded. Demand for the dollar as a reserve currency continued or increased. Thus, it is no accident that since 1974 – the year of our last nearly balanced budget – the twin deficits of the United States have mushroomed.

I do not argue that, under a properly functioning international monetary system, a trade surplus is good and a trade deficit bad; that argument is an all-time fallacy. In fact, a trade deficit leading to greater investment and output is a good thing. The point is that under the present floating system the increased foreign official dollar reserves – redeposited, say, in New York – permit the United States to sustain increased current consumption in excess of real income, for example by financing the budget deficit. In addition, the dollar's reserve-currency status alters, and at times jams, the natural adjustment mechanism of world payments, prices, and trade – whether exchange rates are fixed or floating.

We seem to be dealing here with what insurance companies call "moral hazard." The late Professor Wilson E. Schmidt once wrote a paper called "The Moral Hazard of IMF Lending" in which he argued that the offer of large loans to troubled borrowers tends to increase the number of troubled borrowers. Similarly, the reality behind the twin deficits is this: The greater and more permanent the facilities for financing the budget and trade deficits, as is the case under an official-reserve-currency system, the greater will be the deficits, or the subsequent devaluation. This principle helps to explain the total collapse of the congressional budget process and U.S. trade policy, not to mention the increasingly wild, coercive, and ineffectual attempts to correct them. Such administrative and statutory attempts to end the deficits will be futile until the crucial underlying monetary deficit is remedied.

A new international monetary system should not only adopt the strengths but also remedy the defects of Bretton Woods. It should also solve the institutional problems of today's managed floating-exchange rates. The way to do this is to make the dollar convertible to gold domestically, as it was not under Bretton Woods; and, by law, to substitute gold, self-liquidating Treasury bills, and secured commercial paper as the backing for U.S. currency. In addition, as part of a new Group of Five (or Seven) understanding, all governments would agree to rule out further accumulation of any national currency as an official reserve currency.

My fundamental argument is that only gold, an objective non-national monetary standard, an independent reference point, not subject to creation by sovereign governments, can be the stable underlying reserve currency – the common currency linking all the nations. This is true for two reasons: First, the reserve-currency problem requires as a solution that all nations share a common monetary standard separate and apart from any national currency. Second, the protectionist, or mercantilist, temptation inherent in floating rates requires that all currencies be directly convertible into this monetary standard at fixed parities. Practically speaking, this leaves us the following choice: We can return to multilateral currency convertibility into gold (we could keep saying, "or some other commodity," but monetary authorities for millennia have accumulated and still hold more than a billion ounces of gold, not pork bellies or platinum or baskets of commodities). Or, instead, we could create another supranational institution, a world central bank, whose credit would serve as reserves for all central banks, including the Federal Reserve. The latter choice is not only impractical; in the light of decades of experience of failure at the United Nations and the International Monetary Fund, it is undesirable and unworkable.

No other proposal offers a serious, lasting solution. The only significant criticism of the gold standard used to be that the supply of gold is "too inelastic"; but the facts of history show this to be untrue. Economic statistics show that gold production for centuries has grown directly in proportion to the average rate of world economic growth. Indeed, the major criticism of a world central bank is precisely that the supply of paper money in its hands would be too elastic. This is not to say that gold convertibility is a perfect solution – there is no such thing in an imperfect world. But fixed-exchange rates, based on multilateral currency convertibility, constitute the least imperfect monetary system known to history – if our goals are a trustworthy money, low long-term interest rates, a reasonably stable price level, and steady economic growth toward full employment.

If such a system is ever reinstituted, the results will be dramatic. The immediate effect of pinning down the future price level will be to curb wild currency speculation and inflation hedging and diminish the preference for short-term investments, thus channeling immense amounts of savings into long-term financial markets and production. Falling long-term interest rates will increase the demand for investment capital, and with increased capital investment will come demand for currently unemployed labor to work the new plant and equipment. As long-term interest rates fall to their historical levels (under convertible-currency systems) of 3-4 percent, the debtor nations of the Third World, now effectively bankrupt in all but the fantasies of Western bankers, will be able to service their debts and release their people from the pressure of IMF-imposed austerity.

The benefits of truly free and fair trade would be much greater than the returns most nations realize from an arbitrary sovereign power to manipulate the value of money. It is by giving up the autonomy to drive on the left side of the road that we gain the freedom to drive safely. By the same token, a new commitment to an international monetary order substantially free of arbitrary government manipulation will deprive national leaders of the license to change currency values in order to conduct covert protectionist warfare. As in all true exercises of financial statecraft, this is a reform from which all nations would gain more than they lose.

"Because of the unique monopoly status of the dollar in the international system, the United States alone can finance its deficits by issuing its own money – a reserve-currency role the dollar has maintained despite the end of its official position under Bretton Woods."

Chapter Fourteen

TRADE WAR OR MONETARY REFORM

The Wall Street Journal, January 28, 1987

The "twin deficits" and the protectionist effects of floating-exchange rates are now out of the financial section and on the front pages of the national print media. The present budget and trade crises cannot be exaggerated, even if their elusive monetary causes may now lead to mistaken tariff and quota policies. Indeed, after 25 years of fruitless debate over international monetary reform, recent signs of a steep inflation in the value of financial assets suggest the world may be in for yet another round of shocks, even while the conventional price indexes appear stable.

Now as before, the dollar reserve-currency system – which leads the world's trading nations to use their dollar holdings as a monetary base – lies at the root of the problem. This judgment is confirmed not only by the direct evidence of foreign-exchange markets during the past few months, but also by those who participated both in the collapse of Bretton Woods (1968-1973) and in the growing problems of floating-exchange rates (1973-1986).

For only one example, Helmut Schlesinger, vice chairman of the Bundesbank, has written and spoken of his experience during 1972-1973, the final days of Bretton Woods, when the Bundesbank and the Swiss and Japanese central banks had to buy billions of unwanted depreciating dollars in exchange for newly issued Deutsche marks, Swiss francs and yen – thereby creating excess liquidity in all major currency markets, leading directly to the oil-price mutation of the early 1970s and also to "imported" inflation in Europe, Japan and the Far East. He and his central-bank colleagues also have described how the very same thing occurred amid the collapse of the dollar and the disarray of the managed float in 1978-1979, leading to a second oil-price explosion, the organization of the European Monetary System, and to the appointment of Paul Volcker as chairman of the Federal Reserve.

Take Leadership of Own Currency

This time, the world's central bankers and finance ministers are staring into a new kind of black hole into which undesired dollars the world over seem to be disappearing. The flight from the dollar takes the form of a flight to financial assets, as stock prices explode around the globe, while the world's premier currency grows shakier in the hands of those who would use it as a weapon in an incipient trade war. We should not be surprised that the United States has joined in the cutthroat currency competition, for under floating-exchange rates since 1973, mercantilist nations, young and old, have used undervalued currencies as battering rams to aggrandize world trade. It is this neo-mercantilism of manipulated exchange rates that has set ominous protectionist forces in motion.

In these circumstances, the United States has no choice but to take the leadership of its own currency. Once issued and accepted as foreign monetary reserves, these dollars only appear to be held by foreign official institutions abroad. They actually wind up invested in the global dollar market that has its center in New York. Moreover, much of the active, foreign official dollar reserves are invested directly in U.S. Treasury securities. For example, foreign official institutions own $40 billion more of U.S. Treasury securities in January 1987 than a year earlier – a 30 percent increase of these reserves in one year. And these are only their officially reported holdings.

Because of the unique monopoly status of the dollar in the international system, the United States alone can finance its deficits by issuing its own money – a reserve-currency role the dollar has maintained despite the end of its official position under Bretton Woods. As a result, everything goes on in the United States as if there were no budget deficit. Indeed, for a time earlier in the 1980s when monetary conditions were tight, the dollar reserve-currency system engendered a sort of hidden worldwide demand for U.S. budget deficits. Now, after two years of Fed looseness, deficit-bred reserves have reached a crisis point.

We are seeing in the financial markets the results of this condition. The Germans and the Japanese, for example, buy the Fed's newly created dollars in order to protect their export industries and to ensure the value of their own dollar holdings at the core of their monetary base. But the marks and yen, newly issued in order to hold up the dollar, are not completely "sterilized" (mitigated by domestic monetary tightness in those countries); they, thus provide new liquidity in the yen and mark area, and tend to lift financial markets abroad. Moreover, the dollars bought up by central banks are then invested in short-term financial instruments in New York. This in turn tends to hold down U.S. short-term interest rates below where they otherwise would be. Together with a declining currency, the low yields discourage the holding of long-term fixed-rate U.S. instruments and help to make equities here relatively more attractive. In foreign countries, the increase in liquidity – at a time of stable, tradable-goods prices after six years of commodity surplus – has similar effects in financial markets. Excess liquidity now goes to equities, not to commodities.

To end this financial disorder and the worldwide trend to protectionism, we face the following choice: either fixed-exchange rates based on key currencies convertible directly to gold, a true international gold standard or, as some propose, we could entrust our fate to a World Central Bank – a monetary United Nations – whose credit would serve as reserves for all national central banks, including the Federal Reserve.

If, however, we stipulate that a new world monetary system be neither inflationary nor deflationary over the long run, history shows that, in the real world, there is no effective alternative to unrestricted domestic and international convertibility at fixed rates into gold.

Thus, the specific minimum elements of a lasting monetary reform are these:

- First, as a follow-up to the G-5 agreement of September 1985, President Reagan should direct the Treasury to cooperate formally with the Group of Five to stabilize the value of the dollar and G-5 currencies at a level consistent with mutually balanced, longer-term purchasing-power parities. (This measurement is the quantity of various currencies required to buy, say, a constant basket of standardized manufactured goods and services in each country. Indexes to measure this value can be agreed upon in conference.)
- Second, the President should promptly send legislation to Congress to restore gold as the monetary standard of the United States to take effect at a fixed date after currency stabilization, say one year from now. At that date, the gold value of the dollar would be fixed. This convertibility price should provide for a steady output of gold, the new international monetary standard, consistent with long-term world economic growth. In the interest of equity, the gold price should be at a level to avoid any decline in the average level of nominal wages. The optimum gold parity thus would reflect a gold price proportional to its marginal cost of production in America under full employment conditions.

(This pricing technique would avoid the mistake made in Britain during the 1920s. Winston Churchill, Chancellor of the Exchequer, undervalued gold and overvalued the pound at the pre-war parity, thus raising labor-intensive export prices and simultaneously lowering import prices. Underemployment in Britain was the result, and statist remedies were adopted.)

I estimate that the gold parity should be about $500 an ounce under existing world-market conditions. However, if we wait, a deflationary world economy over the next five years could bring the price down as low as $200, while an inflationary five years could bring about a price even higher than $1,000.

The same congressional statute fixing the dollar's gold value also should contain a provision restricting the monetization of U.S. government debt, thus restoring the internal budget discipline of the original Federal Reserve Act of 1913.

- Third, the existing official dollar reserves owned by foreign governments could and should be consolidated and refunded – not unlike the great Hamiltonian refunding at the birth of the American republic. These dollar debts would be reimbursed by the United States in part through immediate gold redemption, and gradually by means of amortization of long-term treasury debt – all brought about via the rise in the value of U.S. gold reserves to $500 from their last official valuation of $42.22.

- Fourth, the President should convene an international monetary conference of the principal industrialized democracies, in order to stabilize the reciprocal values of all major currencies, and proceed to general convertibility of these currencies directly to gold – and thus to international fixed-exchange rates. The new system would automatically, therefore, rule out any official national reserve currency.

- Fifth, following the international monetary agreement by the major nations of the free world, the conference agenda should be expanded to include trade discussions to dismantle quotas and tariffs and other barriers to trade.

Some argue that there are always weaknesses in any exchange-rate system. And they are, of course, correct. But currency convertibility is the least imperfect, stable exchange-rate system known to human history. Recent experience has shown again that international free trade without stable exchange rates is a fantasy.

As in the past, the results of currency convertibility would be dramatic. With the future price level pinned down, which only convertibility can guarantee on a long-term basis, funds would be channeled gradually from speculation and hedging into long-term investment markets. This monetary reform is the true and enduring road to financial stability, low long-term interest rates and full employment.

"We are again witnessing increasingly wild and ineffectual attempts to stem the deficits. But presidential and congressional attempts to end the deficits by raising taxes are futile. They do nothing to remedy the most fundamental defect of our monetary and fiscal system: managed floating-exchange rates based on the reserve currency role of the dollar."

Chapter Fifteen
THE CURSE OF THE PAPER DOLLAR

The Wall Street Journal, November 6, 1990

The dollar is once again bouncing around its all-time lows of 1980 and 1987, as it is driven down by Washington's deliberate depreciation of the currency. Why the dollar bashing? The answer is that contemporary mercantilism is practiced behind a smokescreen of unrestrained monetary policies. Managed exchange rates are exploited to subsidize exports and tax imports in very much the same style as the Smoot-Hawley tariffs of yesteryear.

Under floating-exchange rates, the U.S. economy has suffered unprecedented financial instability for nearly 20 years. Between 1971 (when President Nixon destroyed the Bretton Woods exchange-rate agreement) and 1974, Americans endured four phases of wage and price controls, while the free-floating dollar plunged in value. Then came the "energy crisis": sustained double-digit inflation and interest rates on Treasury securities that topped 15 percent – double the level that prevailed during the Civil War when it wasn't clear that there would be a United States for very much longer. International banking has been in turmoil since 1982, and the banking crisis of 1990 is only the latest consequence of Federal Reserve sponsorship of profligate U.S. banking practices.

Financial Disorders

Many observers blame the world's present financial disorders not on floating-exchange rates, but on the U.S. budget and trade deficits. The U.S. budget deficit and trade deficit are indeed at the heart of the world's fundamental economic problems. But the deficits in the federal budget and in U.S. trade are the symptoms, not the causes, of monetary disorder.

It has been so long since the world has enjoyed stable money that we have forgotten what it looks like. Neither the post-war Bretton Woods system nor the fixed-rate system of the 1920s and 1930s were stable exchange-rate systems based on an independent monetary standard. Rather, they were international monetary systems largely based on "reserve currencies," the pound sterling and the dollar. Under a reserve-currency system, central bank reserves consist not only of gold and domestic claims but also of claims in the currency of the major financial power.

These reserve currencies become international money and lead to over-extension of their issuers' domestic banking systems. In the 1920s, the dollar and the pound sterling were reserve currencies; under Bretton Woods, the dollar alone. The dollar remains the dominant official reserve currency today, making the Federal Reserve in effect the world's central bank.

This sort of exchange-rate system faces one big risk: What if the country issuing the reserve currency decides to inflate its money? As the reserve currency – in this case, the dollar – floods onto international markets, the world's central banks at some point must purchase and hold these excess dollars. If they don't, the value of the dollars decline, making the other countries' exports costlier in the United States. It was this feature of the reserve-currency system that helped to cause the collapse of the interwar financial system in 1930-1932 and also of the Bretton Woods regime in 1971.

After the collapse of Bretton Woods foreign central banks continued buying dollars. For the most part, they have been left to lie at the Fed in the form of Treasury securities. Last month these reserves exceeded $250 billion. The long decline of the dollar against the yen and other major currencies has coincided with the rise of official dollar reserves held by foreign central banks.

There is no adequate adjustment mechanism to discipline a reserve currency. As the dollar declines, rising foreign dollar reserves are redeposited in the Eurodollar market and in the United States, where they finance the budget deficit, or finance more imports or finance domestic consumption of goods that would otherwise be exported at competitive prices to re-establish equilibrium in the international balance-of-payments.

But the inflation of the reserve currency is not ultimately sustainable. The foreign demand for the reserve currency has a limit. When that limit is surpassed, foreign holders will unload the dollar, and it will begin to fall rapidly. The reserve-currency country will then be faced, as the United States is today, with pressure to raise interest rates to stabilize the currency at the very moment that the real economy is weak.

It seems difficult to believe today, but floating-exchange rates were actively desired by a majority of a whole generation of economists and investment experts, both monetarist and Keynesian. In the late 1960s, both schools believed that stable exchange rates stood in the way of their economic policy objectives: Full employment via budget deficits and Federal Reserve credit expansion for the Keynesians; price stability through control of the domestic money supply for the monetarists.

The Keynesians complained that the system of fixed-exchange rates that prevailed until 1971 overvalued the dollar. They argued that devaluation of the exchange rate, by reducing the real value of U.S. wages, could stimulate exports and thus employment. And they insisted that "fine-tuning" of fiscal and Federal Reserve policy could control whatever inflation resulted from devaluation.

The monetarists prophetically pointed out the inflationary bias in Keynesian domestic economic policy. But, curiously enough, they were, for reasons of their own, prepared to accept floating rates. Fixed-exchange rates stood in the way of the monetarist prescription (or stable domestic prices and output – control of the domestic money supply. It is impossible to target both the price of a currency (the exchange rate) and its quantity (the money supply) at the same time. If the exchange rate is fixed, then manipulation of the money supply is constrained.

But in freeing exchange rates, the monetarists unhinged their own theory. This is because monetarist strategies depend on the assumption that the demand for cash is more or less stable. If the demand for cash becomes unstable, the monetarists, like Archimedes, are left trying to move the earth without a place to stand: It becomes impossible for the Federal Reserve Board to predict what effect open-market operations will have on the supply of money and the price level.

True, the monetarists had gathered compelling empirical evidence that the demand for cash balances is fairly stable. But this evidence came substantially from periods of fixed-exchange rates based on gold convertibility. A theory based on a world of gold convertibility ceases to apply in a world of floating currencies.

Under a properly functioning exchange rate mechanism, anchored by currency convertibility, a trade surplus is not necessarily good and a trade deficit is not necessarily bad. But under the present floating-exchange rate system, rising official dollar reserves abroad permit the United States to sustain increased consumption in excess of real income at the expense of foreigners and at the risk of a catastrophic eventual collapse in the dollar.

Thus in the short run the reserve currency system permits the reserve country to finance very large budget and trade deficits. And the greater and more permanent the facilities for financing the budget and trade deficits, the bigger those deficits will be – and the bigger the subsequent devaluation. This principle helps to explain the "bipartisan," 30-year depreciation of the dollar and the total collapse of the congressional budget process as well as of U.S. trade policy.

As a result, financial disorder becomes perennial. We are again witnessing increasingly wild and ineffectual attempts to stem the deficits. But presidential and congressional attempts to end the deficits by raising taxes are futile. They do nothing to remedy the most fundamental defect of our monetary and fiscal system: managed floating-exchange rates based on the reserve currency role of the dollar.

Bretton Woods's Flaws

A reformed international monetary system would remedy this situation. Reform must, however, not only adopt the strengths but also remedy the flaws of Bretton Woods. The way to do this is to make the world's major currencies directly convertible to gold, as they were not under Bretton Woods. Then, the United States must use gold, self-liquidating treasury bills, and secured commercial paper as the backing for the U.S. currency. In addition, as part of a new Group of Seven understanding, all governments would agree to rule out any further accumulation in their central banks of any national currency in the form of official reserves. This agreement would restore discipline to the dollar.

The results of such a reform would be dramatic. The immediate effect of such a pinning down of the future price level and establishing a limit on the financing of the deficit would be the curbing of wild currency speculation. The reform would diminish investors' preference for short-term investments, and therefore channel savings into long-term financial markets and new production. Falling long-term interest rates would increase the demand for investment capital. With increased capital investment would come demand for currently unemployed labor to work the new plant and equipment. As full employment was approached, tax revenues would rise and, along with spending restraint and much lower debt service costs, bridge the budget deficit gap.

This same policy would also remedy the domestic and international banking crisis. As long-term interest rates fell to 3 to 4 percent, their average historical level in the United States (in the days when the currency was backed by gold), the debtor nations of the Third World, now in the austere grip of the IMF, and the commercial banks of the West, now the wards of their governments, would be able to refinance and service their liabilities on the sound foundation of reliquefied assets and low interest rates.

"For other countries to increase their foreign exchange reserves, the reserve currency country must purchase more wealth abroad than it sells – i.e., run a balance-of-payments deficit. This demand for wealth without a matching supply causes inflation of either goods or securities prices – usually both in succession."

Chapter Sixteen

THE CURSE OF BEING A RESERVE CURRENCY

The Wall Street Journal, January 4, 1993
With John D. Mueller

The European monetary system is breaking down for the same reason the gold-exchange standard in 1931 and the Bretton Woods system in 1971 collapsed: the use of domestic currencies as international reserves.

Germany inhabits within Europe today roughly the same position the United States did in the world of the 1950s. In the 1950s there was a lot of hand-wringing about a supposedly structural "dollar shortage." But this dollar shortage was essentially a superabundance of European currencies. Once European countries curbed the issuing of money to cover budget deficits and "hardened" their international payments in 1958, the dollar shortage turned overnight into a dollar glut.

Now theories are put forward asserting a structural shortage of Deutsche marks. Some say that stable exchange rates are not possible in Europe because of the task of rebuilding eastern Germany. But they do not explain why the much larger task of rebuilding West Germany after World War II was accomplished under stable exchange rates.

Some also argue that Europe's being tied to the mark during reunification imposed "deflation" on other countries. But they do not explain how countries with inflation rates of 4 percent to 6 percent a year, like Italy and Britain, were suffering deflation. Still others argue that the European monetary system somehow requires a perverse convergence or interest rates but not inflation rates. They do not explain why, say, Italy's interest rates are seldom less than three percentage points higher than Germany's.

The Weakest Currencies

Just as with the dollar shortage of the 1950s, the apparent dearth of marks is partly a plethora of pounds (and lira and francs). The balance sheets of Europe's central banks reveal that the weakest currencies are almost invariably those whose central banks "monetize" – that is, purchase – government debt on a large scale: the lira, the pound, the peseta and even, lately, the French franc. By contrast, the mark and those currencies that have had no problem remaining tied to the mark – for example, the Belgian franc and the Dutch guilder – have central banks that don't monetize government debt in significant amounts.

Yet, also like the United States under Bretton Woods, Germany is still suffering from inflation caused by the rapid recent expansion of its reserve currency role. (U.S. inflation has been much higher since the end of dollar-gold convertibility, but U.S. consumer and producer prices both doubled under Bretton Woods.)

To describe the problem simply: For other countries to increase their foreign-exchange reserves, the reserve currency country must purchase more wealth abroad than it sells – i.e., run a balance-of-payments deficit. This demand for wealth without a matching supply causes inflation of either goods or securities prices – usually both in succession.

Any other country would be forced to correct such an imbalance, or else lose all of its international reserves and devalue. But the reserve currency country's loss of reserves takes the form of IOUs to foreign central banks, so its net reserves can be negative without any absolute limit. The inflationary pressure is therefore unchecked, and it quickly spreads to other countries through the reserve currency country's purchases of foreign wealth. Instead of making repeated small corrections to keep its prices, costs and payments in balance with the rest of the world, the reserve currency country piles up an ever-larger imbalance.

When the reserve currency country does apply the monetary brakes, however, the result can be a deflation potentially as large as the previous inflation (as from 1928 to 1932, when virtually all the world's official foreign-exchange reserves were wiped out, and prices declined to pre-World War I levels). The only alternative is a large devaluation of the reserve currency (Britain in 1931, 1949 and 1967, and the United States in the 1970s and late 1980s). The danger is magnified because central banks do not track the actual inflationary or deflationary forces at work. With reserve currencies, domestic money supply growth alone gives false signals, because the inflationary or deflationary potential also includes any change in holdings of the reserve currency by foreign central banks.

Using a similar analysis, Jacques Rueff correctly warned of the collapse of the 1920s gold-exchange standard. And in the 1960s, Professor Rueff and Robert Triffin accurately predicted the breakdown of the gold-dollar Bretton Woods system. In the past few years, we have extended the analysis to show that the waves of worldwide inflation since Bretton Woods are also largely due to the dollars' continued status as the world's chief reserve currency. For over half a century, major changes in U.S. inflation including the 1989-1991 episode – have been preceded by commensurate changes in what our firm has called the "World Dollar Base." The World Dollar Base consists of U.S. currency and bank reserves plus foreign official dollar reserves.

The same process is now at work in Germany, thanks to the mark's role as the regional reserve currency of Europe. According to the International Monetary Fund, foreign central banks held about DM200 billion at the end of 1991 – more than $125 billion. The rapid expansion of foreign mark reserves accompanied a tremendous simultaneous expansion of credit in the German banking system, which under Europe's stable exchange rate system would otherwise have exhausted Germany's international reserves.

Comprehensive data for mark reserves do not go as far back as for dollar and sterling reserves. But they strongly indicate that what we call the World Deutsche Mark Base – the sum of German currency and bank reserves plus foreign mark reserves – has about the same impact on mark inflation as the World Dollar Base has on dollar inflation.

For the United States, we chose the producer price index to measure inflation. For Germany, we used the gross national product index. The reason for the difference is that the World Dollar Base affects commodity inflation worldwide, because the commodity markets are conducted in dollars, while the World Deutsche Mark Base mostly affects the price of German output. Germany imports some inflation from the dollar-based commodity markets, which is not fully offset by mark appreciation against the dollar. But Germany's inflation is now higher than in the United States – not because of German reunification, but because reunification has been partly financed through the mark's reserve currency status.

To curb the inflation, the Bundesbank has tried to bring about, all at once, a correction of inflationary pressures that had built up for years. The adjustment has been dramatic. We know from published statistics that between the end of 1991 and September 1992, Germany's net reserve position increased by a staggering DM94 billion (about $60 billion) – probably much more. Yet the essence of the reserve currency system is that the net reserve increases of other countries depend on the net reserve losses and balance-of-payments deficits of the reserve currency country. Thus, the $60 billion increase in German net reserves in nine months was necessarily mirrored by equal net reserve losses – and balance-of-payments deficits – of other countries. This put impossible strains on the exchange rate mechanism.

The fault does not lie with the Bundesbank, but with the reserve currency system, which was chosen by the other central banks. Faced with a domestic recession after its earlier boom, the Bundesbank has begun to lower interest rates. Continuing to do so would also allow other European countries to cut interest rates and rebuild their foreign-exchange reserves. But a renewed increase in mark reserves would renew the German balance-of-payments deficit and restart domestic German inflation. There is no way, within the current system, to escape this dilemma. Either Germany must get used to chronic inflation – punctuated by draconian yet ultimately futile interest-rate hikes to bring it under control – or else the mark must stop being a reserve currency.

Some will say that all this is a good argument for a European Central Bank. The proposed Federal Reserve System of Europe would forbid the monetization of national budget deficits and end the reserve currency role of national currencies like the mark. But have proponents of a European Central Bank thought far enough? Since a new European currency would be used as a reserve currency by other countries, all of Europe would suffer the same reserve-currency inflation we have seen in the United States and now in Germany. This would be true even if the European Central Bank did not compound the problem by monetizing the deficits of a Federal European government.

Moreover, Europe will still import some commodity inflation from the dollar area as long as the dollar's worldwide reserve currency role continues. And there is another worldwide problem. With inflation down for now, or coming down, as the result of past monetary squeezing, how do we deal with the burden of debt built up during the period of inflation? Trying to "stimulate" the economy with still more debt or more inflation would be self-defeating, because it would require a still larger adjustment later on. What is needed is to make the world financial system more liquid – to increase the ratio of money to debt – without triggering significant inflation or deflation.

The Most Effective Solution

An effective solution would need to cover a number of details, but the essential condition is clear: International money must be one country's asset without being another country's liability. Central banks already have such an asset: gold. The simplest and most effective solution would be one proposed but not adopted in the 1920s and 1960s. Central banks should revalue their gold reserves from the still official price of $42.22 an ounce, and use the resulting increase in monetary reserves – which would be augmented by private dishoarding and new gold production – to replace foreign exchange as official international reserves. (Some foreign currency reserves could be retired by swaps of offsetting claims or amortized with government-to-government debt.)

The two requirements of a modern international gold standard – ending the monetization of government debt and reserve currencies – are the same as for any country joining the proposed European currency union. But only such a reform, by sharply increasing the net reserves of the world as a whole, would also sharply lower interest rates, stimulate investment, increase employment, and facilitate the repayment of existing debt – without engendering significant inflation or deflation. Absent such a plan it is clear that, while improvements can be made in individual countries, there will be no lasting economic stability in Europe – or anywhere else – as long as the international monetary system is based on reserve currencies.

"Gold itself stabilizes. Under an international gold standard, the supply of gold coins or bullion responds to the level of prices generally. For an individual country, a rise or fall in prices relative to other gold standard countries leads to an outflow or inflow of gold money."

Chapter Seventeen

REDEEM US WITH A CROSS OF GOLD

The Wall Street Journal, July 8, 1994
With John D. Mueller

Fifty years ago this month, the Allied nations met at Bretton Woods, New Hampshire, to create the post-war monetary system. Bretton Woods re-established international convertibility of the major currencies into gold or gold-convertible dollars. The system lasted until Aug. 15, 1971, when President Nixon suspended gold payments to foreign governments.

Measured against the period since 1971, Bretton Woods seems almost a golden age. Consumer prices more than doubled between 1944 and 1971, an average annual rise of 3.2 percent; but after the Korean War the average rise was 2.3 percent. By contrast, since 1971 prices have multiplied 3.5 times, an average annual rise of 6 percent.

In broader historical perspective, however, Bretton Woods is a distant second best. The record of price stability under the classical gold standard, from 1834 to 1862 and 1879 to 1913, is without parallel. U.S. consumer prices varied in a 26 percent range in those 62 years, and stood at almost exactly the same level at the beginning and end of both periods. Average inflation was zero, while the average annual variation of prices in either direction was 2.2 percent. From 1879 to 1913, when the U.S. and most other major nations shared the gold standard, U.S. consumer prices ranged only 17 percent in 34 years. Average inflation was again zero, and the average annual variation of prices, up or down, was 1.3 percent. This stands in sharp contrast to the average price gyrations during and after the Civil War (6.2 percent), the period from World War I to Bretton Woods (5.6 percent) and the period since Bretton Woods (6 percent).

After the Breakdown

What accounts for the difference? The level of consumer prices has always mirrored a measure we have named the World Dollar Base – the sum of "high-powered money" including U.S. currency, bank reserves and foreign official dollar reserves. In our chart, the World Dollar Base is shown relative to growth (for our calculations we used an annual trend of 1.9 percent growth per capita, the average growth rate of real income as far back as we have records). The supply of dollars exploded after the breakdown of Bretton Woods.

Dollar Explosion
World dollar base and consumer prices

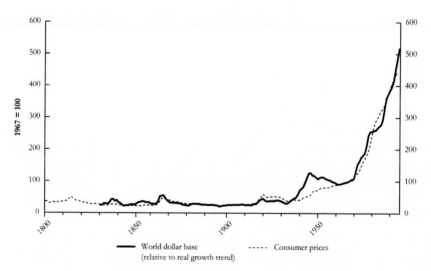

Source: Consumer prices, BLS; World Dollar Base: Lehrman Bell Mueller Cannon, Inc.

Let's take a moment to review the reasons for this change. The fluctuations in the chart reflect changes in the standards by which money is issued. High-powered money is simply the standard (gold or paper) money in circulation, plus any official monies convertible into standard money. Before 1914, high-powered money meant metal and paper currency held by banks and the public. In 1914, the Federal Reserve system added a new form of high-powered money – bank deposits at the Fed, which substitute for vault cash. Then, after World War I, foreign central banks created a third category of U.S. high-powered money when they began to accept foreign exchange – chiefly dollar or sterling assets – in lieu of gold.

This "gold-exchange standard" was formalized in the Bretton Woods agreement. Since 1971, official reserves have mostly been in foreign exchange. It might seem that this would not affect the high-powered money of a reserve-currency country like the U.S. Foreign central banks typically convert their dollar holdings in U.S. Treasury securities. But this is the whole point – just like bank deposits at the Federal Reserve, these dollar reserves substitute for official payment in standard money. They behave as a form of U.S. high-powered money, and fuel the kind of growth the chart reflects.

Gold itself stabilizes. Under an international gold standard, the supply of gold coins or bullion responds to the level of prices generally. For an individual country, a rise or fall in prices relative to other gold standard countries leads to an outflow or inflow of gold money. A worldwide rise in wages and prices discouraged gold production (it raised mining costs), while a fall in prices stimulated gold production. So, absent sharp expansions or contractions of credit, the price level varied within narrow limits.

Gold convertibility also regulates the supply of paper money. But swings in credit permit sharper price fluctuations than would otherwise have been possible. Without convertibility, this constraint is removed altogether. A detailed analysis shows that all major inflations and deflations, under every U.S. monetary standard, have involved credit. They have been driven by variation in the "fiduciary" part of the World Dollar Base, the part based on credit rather than precious metals.

In fact, the Bretton Woods system contained the seeds of its own destruction. Like the interwar gold-exchange standard, Bretton Woods differed from the gold standard in one essential respect: the use of foreign exchange along with gold as international reserves. And this turned out to be its fatal flaw. Steady expansion of dollar reserves contributed to rising prices, and rising prices steadily diminished the supply of new gold. In 1960, Jacques Rueff and Robert Triffin, economist-statesmen, predicted the eventual run on the dollar. This would lead to either deflation or suspension of gold payments and continued inflation.

The world had stumbled into deflation under similar circumstances in the 1930s, with foreign exchange playing a key role. From negligible levels in 1913, official sterling and dollar reserves mushroomed to more than 60 percent of the value of world gold reserves in 1928. From 1929 to 1932, during runs first on sterling and then on the dollar, almost all these foreign-exchange reserves were liquidated, sucking prices down toward their pre-war levels. A surge of gold money, which accelerated to a flood after the dollar's devaluation in 1934, was what stopped the deflation.

Yet in 1971, the United States chose to suspend dollar-gold convertibility, and the world moved onto today's loose "dollar standard." This was not merely throwing the baby out with the bathwater – it was a case of throwing out the baby and keeping the bath water. Gold was always the element of price stability and foreign-exchange reserves the element of instability in the international monetary system. We kept foreign-exchange reserves and got rid of gold.

A stable system could have been re-established – and still could be – if the major countries restored a gold standard without foreign-exchange reserves. This would be, basically, Bretton Woods minus dollar reserves. Of course, the gold value of convertible currencies must be properly chosen to avoid any deflation. The proposal was in fact made in the 1920s and 1960s but rejected. The experts had other ideas. Yet over the years, all the arguments against returning to gold have withered and dropped like leaves in autumn.

It used to be claimed that inflation is necessary to keep unemployment down, but we have learned from bitter experience that this simply isn't true. It was said that the gold standard caused deflation, but as we have seen, all the major inflations and deflations were due to paper, not gold. It was said that adjustments under floating-exchange rates would be smooth and gradual, but this hasn't happened either.

There was also the celebrated prediction that if gold were delinked from money, its price would plunge to $6 an ounce from $35 – proving that paper money "supported" gold. Yet the dollar now trades for less than a tenth of its former gold value. Finally, it was argued that a return to gold was unthinkable because it would benefit the Soviet Union and South Africa; today, of course, we want to integrate both countries into the world trading system. It has been said – including on this page – that we could manage the current system just fine by targeting the money supply or commodity prices. But the quantity of foreign-dollar reserves cannot be targeted and commodity prices respond after a good two years – too late. There is no argument left against gold except "you can't turn back the clock."

Credit has continued to be the problem here. Since the Civil War, nearly all of the credit behind the World Dollar Base has gone to the U.S. Treasury. The nontechnical answer as to why prices have risen nearly fourfold since 1971 is that the (mutated) financial system has absorbed (monetized) over $2 trillion in Treasury debt since then. This is what has permitted ever-larger federal deficits.

Political Dangers

Some think this arrangement is just fine – financial and commodity speculators say so all the time. To judge by President Clinton's first appointments to the Fed, he, too, is partial to inflation. Yet, like President Bush, Mr. Clinton is about to learn the political dangers of monetary instability.

Back in 1988, we correctly predicted that U.S. consumer price inflation, then 4 percent, would peak between 6 and 7 percent in mid-1990, followed by a mild recession. That combination was enough to cost Mr. Bush re-election. Based on a similar analysis, we now predict a rise in consumer price inflation from 2.3 percent over the past 12 months to a peak of 4-5 percent by mid-1996. The rise of inflation should be associated with a slowdown of real economic growth, from almost 4 percent over the past year to near-zero in 1996. This may not, by itself, do in Mr. Clinton, but it will make the 1996 election interesting.

Perhaps one day even politicians, who made the wrong choice in 1971, will get fed up. They will reject the "cross of paper'" and return us to the only money that has worked: gold.

"...it must be emphasized that it was twelve years earlier, in 1922, at the little known but pivotal Monetary Conference of Genoa, that the unstable gold-exchange standard had been officially embraced by the European financial authorities. It was here that the dollar and the pound were first confirmed as official reserve currencies to supplement what was said to be a scarcity of gold."

Chapter Eighteen

JACQUES RUEFF, THE AGE OF INFLATION, AND THE TRUE GOLD STANDARD

Manuscript of Address at the Parliament of France (Assemblé Nationale), November 7, 1996
100th Anniversary of the Birth of Jacques Rueff

Distinguished Leaders of France:

In what I now say to you, I draw from the speeches, the writings, and the letters of the greatest economist of the 20th century. Your courtesy may require you to hear politely the words I now speak. But I beg you to believe me, that all the arguments I shall make in your presence are distilled from the wisdom of the master himself. The ideas I set before you originate in the proven genius of an extraordinary teacher, a selfless servant of the French people, and a peerless citizen of the world – in the words of General de Gaulle – un poète de finance."

I speak of Jacques Rueff.

As a soldier of France, no one knew better than Jacques Rueff that World War I had brought to an end the preeminence of the classical European states system; that it had decimated the flower of European youth; that it had destroyed the European continent's industrial productivity. No less ominously, on the eve of the Great War, the gold standard – the gyroscope of the Industrial Revolution, the proven guarantor of one hundred years of price stability, the common currency of the world trading system – this precious institution of commercial civilization was suspended by the belligerents.

The Age of Inflation was upon us.

The overthrow of the historic money of commercial civilization, the gold standard, led, during the next decade, to the great inflations in France, Germany, and Russia. The ensuing convulsions of the social order, the rise of the speculator class, the obliteration of the savings of the laboring and middle classes on fixed incomes, led directly to the rise of Bolshevism, Fascism, and Nazism – linked, as they were, to floating European currencies, perennial budgetary and balance-of-payments deficits, central bank money printing, currency wars and the neo-mercantilism they engendered.

Today, three quarters of a century later (1996), one observes – at home and abroad – the fluctuations of the floating dollar, the unpredictable effects of its variations, the abject failure to rehabilitate the dollar's declining reputation. Strange it is that an unhinged token, the paper dollar, is now the monetary standard of the most scientifically advanced global economy the world has ever known.

In America, the insidious destruction of its historic currency, the gold dollar, got underway in 1922 during the inter-war experiment with the gold-exchange standard and the dollar's new official reserve currency role. It must be remembered that World War I had caused the price level almost to double. Britain and America tried to maintain the pre-war dollar-gold, sterling-gold parities. The official reserve currency roles of the convertible pound and dollar, born of the gold-exchange standard, collapsed in the Great Depression and so did the official foreign-exchange reserves of the developed world – which helped to cause and to intensify the Depression. Franklin Roosevelt in 1934 reduced the value of the dollar by raising the price of gold from $20 to $35 per ounce, believing the change to be a necessary adjustment to the post-World War I price level rise.

But it must be emphasized that it was twelve years earlier, in 1922, at the little known but pivotal Monetary Conference of Genoa, that the unstable gold-exchange standard had been officially embraced by the European financial authorities. It was here that the dollar and the pound were first confirmed as official reserve currencies to supplement what was said to be a scarcity of gold. For those of you who remember his writings, Jacques Rueff warned in the 1920s of the dangers of the Genoa gold-exchange system and, again, predicted in 1960-1961 that the Bretton Woods system, a post-World War II gold-exchange standard, flawed as it was by the same official reserve currency contagion of the 1920s, would soon groan under the flood weight of excess American dollars going abroad. Rueff in the 1950s and 1960s forecast permanent U.S. balance-of-payments deficits and the tendency to constant budget deficits, and ultimate suspension of dollar convertibility to gold.

After World War II, he saw that because the United States was the undisputed hegemonic military and economic power of the free world, foreign governments and central banks, in exchange for these military services and other subsidies rendered, would for a while continue to purchase, (sometimes to protect their export industries) excess dollars on the foreign exchanges against the creation of their own monies. This was the inevitable result of the dollar's official reserve currency status. But these dollars, originating in the U.S. balance-of-payments and budget deficits, were then redeposited by foreign governments in the New York dollar market which led to inflation in the United States, and inflation in its European and Asian protectorates which were absorbing the excess dollars. Incredibly, during this same period, the International Monetary Fund authorities had the audacity to advocate the creation of Special Drawing Rights, SDRs, so-called "paper gold," invented, as International Monetary Fund officials said, to avoid a "potential liquidity shortage." At that very moment, the world was awash in dollars, in the midst of perennial dollar and exchange rate crises. Jacques Rueff casually remarked to *Le Monde* that the fabrication of these SDRs by the International Monetary Fund would be as gratuitous as "irrigation plans implemented during the flood."

The dénouement of post-war financial history came at the Ides of March, in 1968, when President Johnson suspended the London Gold Pool and, mercifully, abdicated his candidacy for reelection. And so after a few more disabling years, Bretton Woods expired on August 15, 1971. The truth is that monetarists and Keynesians sought not to reform Bretton Woods, as the gold standard reform of President de Gaulle and Jacques Rueff did, but rather to demolish it. The true gold standard, indeed any metallic currency basis, was passé among the cognoscenti. I shall give you just one example of the obtuseness of the political class, which happened at the height of a major dollar crisis. A friend of Jacques Rueff, the renowned banking expert and policy intellectual, Henry Reuss, chairman of the Banking and Currency Committee of the U.S. House of Representatives, went so far as to predict in *The New York Times*, with great confidence and even greater fanfare, that when gold was demonetized, it would fall from $35 to $6 per ounce.

President Nixon, a self-described conservative, succeeded President Johnson and was gradually converted to Keynesian economics by so-called conservative academic advisers, led by Professor Herbert Stein. Mr. Nixon had also absorbed some of the teachings of the Monetarist School from his friend Milton Friedman – who embraced the expediency of floating exchange rates and central bank manipulation and targeting of the money stock. Thus it was no accident that the exchange rate crises continued, and on August 15, 1971, after one more major dollar crisis, Nixon defaulted at the gold window of the western world, declaring that "we are all Keynesians now." In 1972, Nixon, a Republican, so-called free market President, imposed the first peacetime wage and price controls in American history – encouraged by some of the famous "conservative" advisers of the era.

In President Nixon's decision of August 1971, the last vestige of monetary convertibility to gold, the final trace of an international common currency, binding together the civilized nations of the West, had been unilaterally abrogated by the military leader of the free world.

Ten years later at the peak of another inflation crisis, the gold price touched $850. At the time, Paul Volcker, chairman of the Federal Reserve, declared that the gold market was going its own way and had little to do with the Fed's monetary policies. The gold market is but "a side show," added Professor Wallich, a prominent Federal Reserve governor. Secretary of the Treasury William Miller, who had been selling U.S. gold at about $200 in 1978, announced solemnly that the Treasury would now no longer sell American gold. Presumably Secretary Miller, an aerospace executive, meant that whereas, more than one-half the vast American gold stock had been a clever sale, liquidated at prices ranging between $35 and $250 per ounce – now, in the manner of the trend follower, Secretary of the Treasury Miller earnestly suggested that gold was a "strong hold" at $800 per ounce.

On January 18, 1980, Henry Wallich, a former Yale economics professor, explained Federal Reserve monetarist policies in an article appearing in the *Journal of Commerce*:

"The core of Federal Reserve….measures," basing "control upon the supply of bank reserves," he said, "gives the Federal Reserve a firmer grip on the growth of monetary aggregates…"

As subsequent events showed, the Federal Reserve promptly lost control of the monetary aggregates. The bank prime rate rose to 21 percent. As all of Jacques Rueff's experience as a central banker had taught him, what his monetary theory and his econometrics demonstrated was, in fact, that no central bank, not even the mighty Federal Reserve, can determine the quantity of bank reserves or the quantity of money in circulation – all conceits to the contrary notwithstanding. The central bank may influence indirectly the money stock; but the central bank cannot determine its amount. In a free society, only the money users – consumers and producers in the market – can determine the money they desire to hold. It is consumers and producers in the market who desire and decide to hold and to vary the currency and bank deposits they wish to keep; it is central banks and commercial banks which supply them.

During the past twenty-five years, the important links between central bank policies, the rate of inflation, and the variations in the money stock have caused much debate among the experts. It is still generally agreed by neo-Keynesian and some monetarist economists and central bankers that the quantity of money in circulation, and economic growth, and the rate of inflation can be directly coordinated by central bank credit policy. But the economists at the Federal Reserve have been required to accommodate to a reality in which, for example, during 1978, the quantity of money in Switzerland grew approximately 30 percent while the price level rose only 1 percent. Indeed in 1979, the quantity of money, M-1, grew about 5 percent in the United States while the inflation rate rose 13 percent.

If then, a central bank cannot determine the quantity of money in circulation, what, in Rueffian monetary policy, can a central bank realistically do? To conduct operations of the central bank, there must be a target. If the target is both price stability and the quantity of money in circulation, one must know, among other things, not only the magnitude of the desired supply of money, but also the precise volume of the future demand for money in the market – such that the twain shall meet. It is true that commercial banks supply cash balances, but individuals and businesses – the users of money – generate the decisions to hold and spend these cash balances. Thus, the Federal Reserve must have providential omniscience to calculate correctly, on a daily or weekly basis, the total demand for money – assuming the Fed could gather totally reliable statistical information – which it cannot; and even if the Fed's definitions of the monetary aggregates were constant – which they are not.

Jacques Rueff, himself the Deputy Governor of the Bank of France, clarified this fundamental problem in the form of an axiom: Because the money stock cannot be determined by the Federal Reserve Bank, nor can it determine a constant rate of inflation, the monetary policy of the central bank must not be to target the money supply or the rate of inflation. The Federal Reserve Bank simply cannot determine accurately the manifold decisions to hold money for individual and corporate purposes in order to make necessary payments and to hold precautionary balances. Neither, may I say, with respect, can the leaders of the great Bundesbank; nor even the geniuses at the Banque de France.

But, if the true goal of the central bank were long-run stability of the general price level, the operating target of monetary policy at the central bank must be simply to influence the supply of cash balances in the market, such that they tend to equal the level of desired cash balances in the market. To attain this goal, the central bank must abandon open market operations and simply hold the discount rate, or the rediscount rate, above the market rate – when, for example, the price level is rising – providing money and credit only at an interest rate which is not an incentive to create new credit and money. Indeed, if the target of monetary policy is long-run price stability, the central bank must supply bank reserves and currency only in the amount which is equal to the desire to hold them in the market. For if the supply of cash balances is approximately equal to the demand for them, the price level must tend toward stability. If there are no excess cash balances, there can be no excess demand, and, thus, there can be no inflation.

Professor Rueff shows in *L'ordre social* why an effective central bank policy must reject open market operations. He shows further that, in order to rule out inflation, and unlimited government spending, the government Treasury must be required by law to finance its cash needs, including a sometimes limited Treasury deficit, in the market for savings, away from the banks. That is, a government Treasury, in deficit, must be denied the privilege of access to new money and credit at the central bank and commercial banks, in order also to deny the government the pernicious privilege of making a demand in the market without making a supply – the ultimate cause of inflation. This exorbitant privilege is a necessary cause of persistent inflation. It is also a necessary cause of unlimited budget deficits and bloated big government.

You can see that the monetary theory and policy of Jacques Rueff finally does come to grips with, indeed it modifies, the famous Law of Markets of Jean Baptiste Say, building of course on Say's insights, but perfecting the flawed Quantity Theory of Money. Jacques Rueff reformulated the quantity theory of money, definitively, in the following proposition: aggregate demand is equal to the value of aggregate supply, augmented (+/-) by the difference between the variations, during the same market period, in the quantity of money in circulation and the aggregate cash balances desired. This is a central theorem of Rueffian monetary economics. Rueff demonstrated that Say's law does work, namely, that supply tends to equal demand, provided, however, that the market for cash balances must tend toward equilibrium. Any monetary system, any central bank, which does not reinforce this tendency toward equilibrium in the market for cash balances destroys the first law of markets, namely, overall balance between supply and demand, the necessary condition for limiting inflation and deflation.

Now it is conventional wisdom that Milton Friedman and the monetarists try to regulate the growth of the total quantity of money through a so-called money stock rule designed to constrain the central bank monopoly over the currency issue. In practice, the central bank has failed and will fail to succeed with such a flawed, academic, and impractical rule. But the much simpler, more reliable, market-biased technique, proven in the laboratory of history, as Professor Rueff demonstrated, would be to make the value of a unit of money equal to a weight unit of gold, in order to regulate, according to market rules, the same central bank monopoly. But academics have argued for a century that a monetary "regulator," such as gold money, absorbs too much real resources – by virtue of the laborious process of gold production – and is therefore, in social and economic terms, too costly.

Whatever the minor incremental economic cost of a convertible currency, it is a superior stabilizer, as all occidental history shows. The empirical data also show that it is a more efficient regulator of price stability in the long run. This is no accident. The gold standard was no mere symbol. It was an elegantly designed monetary mechanism – carefully orchestrated over centuries by wise men of great purpose – who developed convertibility into a supple and subtle set of integrated financial institutions organized to facilitate rapid growth and a stable price level guiding free economic institutions. Thus did the international gold standard become a gyroscope of rapid economic growth during the industrial revolution. Who can deny that a generation of floating exchange rates, and discretionary central banking, have burdened the world with immense inflation costs, orders of magnitude greater than the comparatively modest cost of mining gold?

Therefore, in order to bring about international price stability and long-run stability in the global market for cash balances, the dollar and other key currencies should be defined in law as equal to a weight unit of gold – at a statutory convertibility rate which insures that nominal wage rates do not fall. Indeed, nothing but gold convertibility will yield a real fiduciary currency, *un vrai droit*, as Professor Rueff called it.

As we approach the millennium, the world requires, indeed it is begging, world leaders to create a real monetary standard to deal with the monetary disorder of undervalued, pegged, currencies and manipulated floating exchange rates – the diabolical agents of an invisible, predatory mercantilism. Despite all denials, the currency depreciations of today, are, without a doubt, designed to transfer unemployment to one's neighbor and, by means of undervalued currency, to gain share of market in manufactured, labor intensive, value-added, world traded goods. If these depreciations and undervaluations are sustained, floating exchange rates will, at regular intervals, blow up the world trading system. Great booms and busts, inflation and deflation must ensue.

To head off the mercantilism of present floating exchange rates, and the exchange rate disorders caused by official dollar reserves, an international monetary conference is indispensable. The present high rates of unemployment and perverse trade effects, associated with floating exchange rates, require an efficient and lasting international monetary reform. A European Monetary Union may be necessary; but it is not sufficient.

Now we see clearly, what before we saw in a glass darkly – the dollar's official reserve-currency status still gives an exorbitant privilege to the United States. Jacques Rueff spoke of American "deficits without tears," because the American budget deficit and balance-of-payments deficits were – they still are – almost automatically financed by the Federal Reserve and the reserve-currency system – through the voluntary (or coerced) buildup of dollar balances in the official reserves of foreign governments. These official dollar reserves were, and still are, immediately invested by foreign authorities, directly or indirectly, in the dollar market for U.S. securities, thus giving back to the United States, at subsidized rates, the dollars previously sent abroad as a result of the persistent U.S. balance-of-payments deficit and budget deficits. To describe this awesome absurdity, Jacques Rueff invoked the metaphor of an overworked tailor to the King, yoked permanently to fictitious credit payments by His Majesty's unrequited promissory notes.

There is not sufficient time to dwell on all the intricacies of the superior efficacy of the balance-of-payments adjustment mechanism grounded in domestic and international convertibility to gold. But it can, I think, be shown that, in all cases, currency convertibility to gold is the least imperfect monetary mechanism, both in theory and in practice, by which to maintain global trade and financial balance, a reasonably stable price level, and to insure budgetary equilibrium. This proposition has been proven in the only laboratory by which to test monetary theory – namely, the general history of monetary policy under paper and metallic regimes, and, in particular, the history of the international gold standard, 1813-1914.

Whereas, by contrast, when one country's currency – the dollar reserve currency of today – is used to settle international payments, the international adjustment and settlement mechanism is jammed – for that country and for the world. This is no abstract notion. During the past 12 months alone, 100 billion dollars of foreign-exchange reserves have been accumulated by foreign governments which have been directly invested in U.S. Treasury securities held in custody at the New York Federal Reserve Bank – thus financing the U.S. current account and U.S. budget deficits.

It is essential to understand the nature of this ongoing process of currency degradation – because the dollar's reserve-currency role in financing the U.S. budget and balance-of-payments deficits did not end with the breakdown of Bretton Woods in 1971.

The anomaly of perennial U.S. budget and balance-of-payments deficits still persist because there is, today, no efficient international monetary mechanism to forestall the U.S. deficits. Indeed, Professor Rueff argued over and over that if the official reserve role of the dollar, i.e., the dollar standard, were abolished, and convertibility restored, the immense U.S. budget and current account deficits must end – a blessing not only for the U.S., but for the whole world.

The reality behind the "twin deficits" is simply this: the greater and more permanent the official reserve currency facilities for financing the U.S. budget and trade deficits, the greater will be the deficits and the growth of the U.S. Federal government. All administrative and statutory attempts to end the U.S. deficits have proved futile, and will prove futile, until the crucial underlying flaw – namely the absence of an efficient international monetary mechanism – is remedied by international monetary reform and a new international gold standard.

That is why Professor Rueff and President de Gaulle, in the 1960s, called for a new international monetary system which we now need, above all, to solve the additional problems of manipulated floating exchange rates inaugurated in 1971-1973.

Broadly speaking, three essential steps toward convertibility could be taken by French, American and other great power authorities.

1) President Jacques Chirac should request the Bank of France to cooperate with, say, the Group of Five to stabilize the value of key currencies at levels consistent with balanced international trade among national currency areas. That is to say, exchange rates

should be stabilized at approximately their longer term purchasing power parities, based largely upon comparative unit labor costs of standardized world traded goods. To do this, indexes of purchasing power can be agreed upon within the Group of Five and, thus, an optimum and fair value determined for convertibility of national currencies. But how should the value of the gold monetary standard be determined? The optimum value of the gold parity should reflect a gold price correctly positioned within the hierarchy of all prices; that is, a price proportional to its underlying cost of production. This dollar price of gold, or more properly, the defined gold weight of the monetary standard, must be set above the average of the marginal costs of production of gold mines operating throughout the world. This price would provide for steady output of the gold monetary base (about an average of 1.5 percent increase per year over a long run, as two centuries of available monetary statistics show). Such a gold price would also prevent any decline in the average level of nominal wages – avoiding, for example, the British problem of gratuitous underemployment in the 1920s caused by an overvalued pound. Under existing conditions, during the present market period, I have estimated, based on empirical data, that the optimum convertibility price of gold is not less than $600 per ounce (1996).

2) President Chirac should recommend to the Group of Ten, that convertibility regimes take effect at a fixed date in the future, perhaps three years from now, just after the European Monetary Union is created. The gold dollar and the European gold currencies should become the monetary standards of Europe, of the United States, of the world, just as the gold standard should again become the common money of world trade and finance.

To simplify, if the U.S. government creates too many or too few dollars, under conditions of gold convertibility, it will be forced in a relatively short period to change, because market participants will exchange paper dollars for gold, or gold for paper, to bring the quantity of money in circulation into balance with the desire to hold these dollar cash balances.

Moreover, domestic monetary reform in the United States, France, and elsewhere, would also mean that only gold and domestic, non-government, short-term, self-liquidating securities, convertible at maturity to gold, could serve as collateral or backing for new currency issues such as Federal Reserve notes or French banknotes. Gold coins, minted according to the statutory standard, should be generally circulated in the market to be held by all working people, so as to guarantee that neither the monetary standard, nor the wages and savings of working people, will be arbitrarily abridged by inflationary governments. Such a regime, among other purposes, eliminates the advantage of clever speculators over middle-income people and those on fixed incomes.

3) The new international monetary system would rule out, by treaty, the official reserve currencies which so plagued the entire financial history of the 20th century. Existing official dollar reserves could be consolidated and refunded and then gradually amortized over the long term, even to a certain extent refunded through the rise of the U.S. official value of gold above the last official revaluation ($42.22 per ounce).

This was and is the Rueff plan, brought up to date to deal with the exigencies of 1996. May I say it is an intellectual scandal that such a solution is today regarded as impractical – even unrespectable. For if we and our former adversary, Russia, can share capsules in space, why can the United States and its trading partners not agree to restore monetary convertibility, the indispensable condition for stable currencies, world economic growth, and free trade?

By pinning down the future price level by gold convertibility, the immediate effect of international monetary reform will be to end currency speculation in floating currencies, and terminate the immense costs of inflation hedging, thus channeling immense new savings out of financial arbitrage and speculation, into long-term financial markets (and, incidentally, ending the predatory reign of speculators, and Federal Reserve dealers, with inside knowledge of Treasury and central bank operations.)

Increased long-term investment, improvements in world productivity will surely follow, as investment capital moves out of unproductive hedges and speculation, seeking new and productive outlets. Naturally, the investment capital available at long term will mushroom, inspired by restored confidence in convertibility because the long-run stability of the price level will be pinned down by gold convertibility – as history shows to be the case in some previous, well-executed monetary reforms of the past two hundred years. Along with increased capital investment will come sustained demand for unemployed labor to work the new plant and equipment.

Indeed, domestic and international monetary reform, i.e., the gold standard – a common, neutral, non-national currency, is the only true and lasting road to full employment. This is the reform plan set out for us by Jacques Rueff two generations ago. It is the outcome he looked forward to in his *Combat pour l'ordre financier*.

"Fondly do we hope, fervently do we pray" that some great statesman – will arise to lead the free world toward the age of financial order, clearly set out for us long ago by a great statesman of France, Jacques Rueff.

PART III. MONETARY DISORDERS OF THE TWENTY-FIRST CENTURY

The twin American deficits – in the balance-of-payments and the federal budget – are the symptoms rather than the causes of monetary disorder in the United States and in the international economy. When one country's currency – the reserve currency – is used to settle international payments, as with the dollar, the adjustment mechanism is jammed for that country – and for the world. In a word, the reserve currency role of the dollar duplicates purchasing power, unassociated with the production of new goods and services. In the reserve-currency country, an inflationary outflow of capital or a growing expenditure on imports – as it accumulates in foreign central banks – is promptly reinvested in the reserve currency (dollar) market, primarily in the U.S. Treasury securities sold to finance the U.S. budget deficit. Everything proceeds as if there were no deficit. The process accentuates easy money-market conditions and long-term inflation.

This monetary process in the reserve currency country tends to absorb domestic goods which otherwise would be available for export to reestablish equilibrium in the overall balance-of-payments. The reserve-currency system also accommodates and finances excess demand in the United States, and especially under fixed-exchange rates, tends to overvalue the dollar, permitting real wage rates and production costs for tradable goods to rise higher than they would under a multilateral gold standard. Of course, the trade balance of the reserve-currency country declines as a result, along with its international competitiveness.

161

Even a dollar-depreciation policy does not change the current account imbalance.

Ultimately, this process is not sustainable – as the world learned in the Great Recession of 2007-2009. Increased foreign official dollar reserves permit the United States either to increase current consumption in excess of income – for example by financing the budget deficit; or to acquire foreign assets, or both. Over time, there is a ratchet effect in the magnitudes of both the U.S. budget deficit and the U.S. current account deficit. The reality behind the twin deficits is simply this: the greater and more permanent the facilities for financing the budget and trade deficits, as is the case under an official reserve currency system, the greater will be the deficits. Everything goes on in the reserve currency country as if there were no deficit. This principle helps to explain the total collapse of the congressional budget process, and the many ineffectual attempts to correct it for two generations. Such administrative and statutory attempts to end the deficits will be futile until the crucial underlying flaw – namely the reserve currency role of the dollar– is remedied by restoration of the true gold standard without reserve currencies.

Chapter Nineteen	Go for the Gold – How to Lift the Reserve Currency Curse, *National Review*, December 15, 2008.
Chapter Twenty	Fiat Money, Fiat Inflation, *The Weekly Standard*, March 21, 2011.
Chapter Twenty-one	Forward to a Modernized Gold Standard, *Grant's Interest Rate Observer* Spring Conference, March 29, 2011.

"The dollar's reserve-currency status provides
short-term political advantages to U.S. congressmen seeking
reelection, but these are far outweighed by the
perennial disruptions it has caused to the world and
U.S. economy and to financial markets."

Chapter Nineteen

GO FOR THE GOLD – HOW TO LIFT THE RESERVE CURRENCY CURSE

National Review, December 15, 2008
with John D. Mueller

The most disturbing aspect of the current financial crisis is that no U.S. official has correctly identified its primary cause. Experts variously attribute the economic reverses to subprime lending, derivative trading, excessive leverage, and regulation that was either too lax or too strict (take your pick), but these are symptoms rather than causes. Ignored is the main culprit: the dollar's role as the world's main official reserve currency. Though he almost certainly doesn't realize it yet, President-elect Barack Obama will either set the dollar's reserve-currency status on the path to extinction or risk becoming the next victim of what we call "the reserve-currency curse."

Official reserves are money held by governments and central banks for the settlement of international payments. A Spanish bank may not want to accept Indian rupees, and it might be inconvenient for Qatar Petroleum to accept Mexican pesos for a million barrels of oil. An official reserve currency is also one everybody agrees to accept, and right now that currency is the dollar. But foreign-exchange reserves are commonly held in the form of government debts of the nation that issued the currency. In the case of the United States, that includes all those government bonds piling up in China and elsewhere. The problem is that, unlike gold, official dollar reserves increase the money supply in one country without decreasing it in another. When reserves are being increased, the effect is inflation. When reserves are liquidated, the effect is deflation – potentially dangerous deflation.

To understand how the dollar's reserve-currency role helped cause the recent bubbles, and the ensuing crisis in the world financial system, we must apply the analysis of the great French economist and central banker Jacques Rueff, who was the first to explain the process. As a financial attaché in London in the early 1930s, Rueff witnessed the collapse of the post-World War I monetary system. He correctly diagnosed the stock-market boom of the 1920s, and the subsequent crash and price deflation, as the result of massive official accumulation – and subsequent liquidation – of foreign-exchange reserves. Foreign countries' dollar reserves were certainly not the only factor involved, but before and during the Depression they were large enough to play a decisive role.

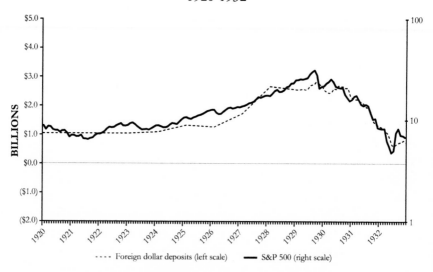

Foreign Dollar Deposits & U.S. Stock Market
1920-1932

Source: Federal Reserve, Monetary and Banking Statistics, 1914-41; Standard & Poor's 500 (Cowles Commission before 1926).

Foreign Dollar Deposits & U.S. Consumer Prices
1929-1948

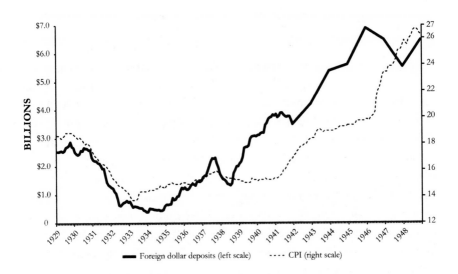

Foreign dollar deposits (left scale)   - - - - CPI (right scale)

Source: Federal Reserve, BLS

Many years later, in the 1960s, Rueff correctly predicted (and tried to prevent) the breakdown of the dollar-based Bretton Woods system. This 1944 agreement made the gold-convertible U.S. dollar the official reserve currency of the world monetary regime; it also fixed-exchange rates within narrow limits. When the United States abandoned gold convertibility in 1971, thereby eliminating fixed-exchange rates, the dollar's reserve-currency role expanded sharply; other countries may not have liked it, but without gold there was no practical alternative. Rueff died in 1978, but today's international monetary system – based on the paper dollar, which is backed by nothing but faith in the American economy – has the same potentially fatal flaw that he pointed out in two earlier gold-exchange standards. As was true in the 1920s and the 1960s, the dollar's reserve-currency role has led to the main pathologies that now plague the world economy: the speculative "hot money" flows that first inflated and then deflated stock, bond, and real-estate prices; the sharp rise and fall of commodity prices, especially of oil and other energy commodities; Congress's apparently incorrigible fiscal irresponsibility; and the mushrooming U.S. deficit in international trade and payments.

The key difference between a reserve-currency system and the gold standard is that foreign-exchange reserves, in the form of government bonds, are not only assets of the national authority that holds them, as gold was; they are also (unlike gold) debts of the country that issues them. Thus, when foreign monetary authorities acquire U.S. debt securities as reserves, U.S. monetary authorities are, in effect, borrowing the same amount.

We all hold our wealth in one of three forms: money, goods (including services), or securities (which are in effect claims on future goods). It is therefore a fundamental truth of accounting that the net international payments for official reserves (money), current account (trade in goods and services), and private-capital account (securities) must equal zero: That is a surplus or deficit in one account requires an offsetting surplus or deficit in the other two combined. Simply put, if you trade $100 in currency for $50 in goods and $50 in securities, somebody else has traded $50 in goods and $50 in securities for $100 in currency. Payments have to balance out. When foreign countries increase their dollar reserves, it means that U.S. residents buy that much more foreign wealth than they have sold. The result is a net outflow of capital known as "hot money" because it is highly mobile, speculative, and very sensitive to fluctuations in interest and exchange rates.

"A nimble financial class, in possession of cheap credit, is able both to enrich itself and to protect itself against inflation. But middle-income professionals and workers, on salaries and wages, and those on fixed incomes and pensions, are impoverished by the very same inflationary process that subsidizes speculators and bankers."

Chapter Twenty

FIAT MONEY, FIAT INFLATION

The Weekly Standard, March 21, 2011

Since the beginning of 2009, oil prices have almost tripled, gasoline prices are up about 50 percent, and basic food prices, such as corn, soybeans, and wheat, have almost doubled around the world. Cotton and copper prices have reached all time highs; major rises in sugar, spice, and wheat prices have been creating food riots in poor countries, where basic goods inflation is rampant. That inflation is in part financed by the flood abroad of excess dollars created over the last couple of years by the Federal Reserve.

Those dollars also made possible the emerging market equity boom of 2009-2010. But foreign authorities are now raising interest rates as growth shifts to the United States and Europe. The years 2011-2012 will witness a Fed-fueled expansion in the United States. Unless there is a major oil spike from here, growth for 2011 in the United States will be above the new consensus of 3.5 percent – perhaps as high as 5 percent this year, with about 8 percent unemployment at year-end.

At first, the enormous Fed credit creation of 2008-2010 could not be fully absorbed by a U.S. economy in recession. But much of this new Fed credit has flooded stocks, bonds, and commodities. The excess credit went abroad, too, causing a fall in the dollar and creating bull markets and booming economies in the developing world. At the same time, inflation intensified, with riots and political turmoil as a result.

There is little new in this latest post-war boom cycle, associated as it is with the world dollar standard we have been living under since the end of gold convertibility, and the Bretton Woods monetary system in 1971. With expansive credit policy and Fed financing of the U.S. government deficit, every boom and bust cycle has been enabled by the Fed. At this moment, we are witnessing in the U.S. equity market, and once again in the decline of the dollar, the predictable effects of Federal Reserve money and credit creation. This latest Fed credit boom has begun with commodity inflation. The extraordinary Treasury deficit, financed by the Fed at home, is financed abroad by the official reserve currency status of the dollar. For example, in addition to the Fed purchases of U.S. government securities, foreign financial authorities have absorbed at least $4 trillion of U.S. government securities, against which foreign central banks have created their own domestic money. And the U.S. budget deficit can continue to expand so long as there is undisciplined Fed and foreign credit to finance it.

To finance the government deficit, the Treasury now sells bills and bonds at a rate of about $120 billion a month, or about $1.5 trillion per year. But this new Fed-created money, which finances the government deficit, is not associated with any production of new goods and services. Thus, total monetary demand, or purchasing power, exceeds the existing supply of goods, equities, and services at prevailing prices, with the predictable result that prices rise. But some of the excess dollars go abroad, creating booms and inflation in emerging markets. As prices rise faster than wages, profits rise. Production increases. A boom is underway.

But it's a boom that turns into a bubble. And there are social effects, not only financial effects. This insidious international monetary and fiscal arrangement has been a primary cause of the increasing inequality of wealth in American society. At home, bankers and speculators have been and are the first in line, along with the Treasury, to get zero interest money and credit from the Fed. They are first to get bailed out. Then with new money, they finance stocks, bonds, and commodities, anticipating, as in the past, a Fed-created boom.

Prices rise first for the most volatile goods, especially stocks, commodities, and financial claims, because they are relatively liquid vehicles for speculators and banks. This is the story of the past two years, with stocks and commodities advancing amidst a sluggish U.S. economy. This is also the story of post-war Fed-created booms. Each cycle experiences an inflation boom, often in different assets, e.g., internet stocks in the late 1990s and real estate in the last boom and bust.

Inflation at the consumer level has been muted by high unemployment and unused production facilities. But the social effects are already discernible. The near-zero interest rates maintained by the Fed have primarily benefited the large banks and their speculator clients. A nimble financial class, in possession of cheap credit, is able both to enrich itself and to protect itself against inflation.

But middle-income professionals and workers, on salaries and wages, and those on fixed incomes and pensions, are impoverished by the very same inflationary process that subsidizes speculators and bankers. Those on fixed incomes will likely earn very little or even a negative return on their savings. Thus, they save less. New investment then depends increasingly on bank debt, leverage, and speculation. The unequal access to Fed credit was everywhere apparent during the government bailout of favored brokers and bankers in 2008 and 2009, while millions of not so nimble citizens were forced into bankruptcy. This ugly chapter is only the most recent in the book of sixty years of financial disorder.

The inequality of wealth and privilege in American society is intensified by the Fed-induced inflationary process. The subsidized banking and financial community, along with the chaos of floating-exchange rates and an overvalued dollar, underwritten by China and other undervalued currencies, has submerged the American manufacturing sector, dependent as it is on goods traded in a competitive world market. In a word, the government deficit and the Federal Reserve work hand in hand, perhaps unintentionally, to undermine the essential equity and comity necessary in a democratic society. Equal opportunity and the harmony of the American community cannot survive perennial inflation.

If the defect is inflation and an unstable dollar, what is the remedy?

A dollar convertible to gold would provide the necessary discipline to secure the long-term value of middle-income savings, to backstop the drive for a balanced budget, and to end the dollar standard and the special access of the government and the financial class to limitless cheap Fed money.

And the world trading community would benefit from a common currency, a non-national, neutral, monetary standard that cannot be manipulated and created at will by the government of any one country.

That is to say, dollar convertibility to gold, a non-national common currency, should be restored. And dollar convertibility to gold should become a cooperative project of the major powers. This historic common currency of civilization was, during the Industrial Revolution and until recent times, the indispensable guarantee of stable purchasing power, necessary for both long-term savings and long-term investment, not to mention its utility for preserving the long-term purchasing power of working people and pensioners. In a word, the gold standard puts control of the supply of money into the hands of the people, because excess creation of credit and paper money can be redeemed for gold at the fixed statutory price. The monetary authorities are thus required to limit the creation of new credit in order to preserve the legally guaranteed value of the currency.

To accomplish this reform, the United States can lead, first, by announcing future convertibility, on a date certain, of the U.S. dollar, to be defined in statute as a weight unit of gold, as the Constitution suggests; second, by convening a new Bretton Woods conference to establish mutual gold convertibility of the currencies of the major powers.

A dollar as good as gold is the way out. It is the way to restore real American savings and competitiveness. It is the way to restore economic growth and full employment without inflation. It is the way to restore America's financial self-respect, and to regain its needful role as the legitimate and beneficent leader of the world.

"These floating-exchange rates have caused huge upward and downward currency moves, which reprice abruptly the entire productive machinery of all nations subject to the float, rendering whole economic sectors unprofitable, and thus steady long-term investment and output very difficult."

Chapter Twenty-one

FORWARD TO A MODERNIZED GOLD STANDARD

Grant's Interest Rate Observer Spring Conference, March 29, 2011

Between 2009 and 2010 we have experienced a major, emerging market equity and economic boom – but at the very same time, sluggish growth in the United States. Foreign authorities are now reacting to inflation, raising interest rates, just as relative growth shifts to America. I believe we will witness during this year, a Fed-fueled economic expansion, above consensus, in the United States. Why such a sluggish, then quickening sequence in the United States? Because, at first, the vast Fed credit creation of 2008 to 2010 could not be fully absorbed by the U.S. economy – coming as it did after wild panic and deep recession. However, the unparalleled Fed credit expansion, beginning in late 2008, did flood into U.S. stocks, bonds, and commodities. But the excess credit also went abroad, causing not only a fall in the dollar, but also the emerging market financial boom – because the financial authorities abroad purchased the incoming flood of excess dollars against the creation of their local currencies – the new money being put to work promptly, creating a rise in almost all financial claims in the developing world.

Today I should like to argue that there is little new in this latest, four-year panic-bust-new boom cycle, associated as all of these cycles have been, with

the unstable post-war Bretton Woods monetary system, followed in 1971 by
the termination of the last vestige of gold convertibility. After 1971, the rise
of the world dollar standard engirdled the globe.

Expansive Fed credit policy – above all, Federal Reserve and foreign
financing of the U.S. balance-of-payments deficit and the *government
budget deficit* – has been behind almost every boom and bust cycle since
the end of World War II – engineered often unwittingly by the combined
operations of the Fed, foreign central banks, and the opaque workings of
the official reserve currency system. First came the post-war Bretton Woods
gold-exchange system, then after 1971, the disorder of floating-pegged
exchange rates, both leading to an overvalued dollar and the diminution
of our dominant manufacturing sector. These floating-exchange rates have
caused *huge upward* and *downward* currency moves, which *reprice abruptly*
the entire productive machinery of all nations subject to the float, rendering
whole economic sectors unprofitable, and thus steady long-term investment
and output very difficult. Such underinvestment leads unavoidably to
scarcity booms, fueled at the beginning by Fed subsidized credit to the bank
and the Treasury. But many countries have pegged their currencies to an
overvalued dollar in order to subsidize and sustain their export production
machines – the ancient practice of mercantilism.

It is obvious that *this* current Fed credit cycle, coming out of the bust,
did quicken to life a major equity and commodity boom. But who will
reasonably doubt that the ultimate source of the equity and commodity
inflation is the Fed monetization of insolvent U.S. mortgage-backed
securities and the Treasury deficit. This outpouring of Federal Reserve credit
at home then leaks abroad, to be absorbed by foreign governments, and
monetized as *official* foreign-exchange reserves. These foreign official dollar
reserves are recycled into the market for U.S. Treasury securities, whereby
they finance the perennial balance-of-payments deficit and the rising budget
deficit. For example, in addition to the planned Fed purchases of 600
billion dollars of U.S. government securities in a mere eight months, *foreign*
financial authorities have to date purchased, in total, at least $3.5 trillion
dollars of U.S. government securities, against which these foreign central
banks created *new domestic money* and *credit* – the penultimate trigger of
past booms and busts in their home countries. This foreign credit financing

of the U.S. Treasury deficit comes in addition to the more than one trillion dollars of government securities purchased by the Fed against the issuance of new money and credit. With limitless financing available, we can foresee that the Treasury deficit will continue to expand – so long as there is unrestrained Fed and foreign credit available. This is the infamous "deficit without tears."

However, all of us must observe that U.S. economic policy causes not only financial effects, but also unstable and inequitable social effects. In a word, the monetary system has been a primary cause of the increasing inequality of wealth in American society. But first, let us ask what is the mechanism of Federal Reserve open-market operations which, I believe, is at the epicenter of this social disorder – inflation, speculation, boom, bust, and their consequences. Simplified, and focusing on today only, this is the sequence. In order to finance the government deficit, the Treasury now sells bills and bonds at a rate of about $120 billion a month, that is, about $1.5 trillion per year – about equal to the present annual Treasury deficit. The Federal Reserve, the banking system, and foreign central banks purchase these Treasury bills and bonds against the issue of new money and credit. But, *during this same market period*, the newly created money to finance the U.S. government deficit is *not* associated with the production, by the Treasury, of any new goods, new services, new equities. Thus, *during the market period* in which the Treasury spends the newly issued money, total monetary demand, or purchasing power, exceeds, in the same market period, the total value of the supply of goods, equities and services – at prevailing prices. Prices *must* rise – in the most recent period, for equities and commodities. But some of the Fed-created excess dollars go abroad, creating a boom in financial claims in emerging economies. However, if there is unemployed labor, prices will rise faster than wages. Then, of course, profits rise. Then new production kicks in. That is where we are now.

The cyclical expansion, financed by the Fed and the world dollar standard, is now underway. But the long-term inflationary process can take a decade or more to produce its full general price level effects. For example, the booms and busts of the decade of the 1970s followed from the explosive central bank and official reserve currency policies of the decade of the 1960s. With them came the euphoria of suppressed U.S. inflation in the

1960s. Then, despair in the 1970s.

Let us return to the markets of this very day.

In this inflationary process, bankers and speculators have been, and are, the first in line, along with the Treasury, to get the near-zero interest credit from the Federal Reserve. They are, also, first to get bailed out with new Fed money. Then with the new money, as we have observed, they finance depressed stocks, bonds and commodities – front running, as in the past, an *advertised* Fed-created financial boom. For example, the Fed's most recent *marketing* plan *to raise equity prices*, with QE2, appeared late last year in the *Washington Post*. In each boom cycle, prices rise first for scarce and volatile goods, this time especially stocks, commodities, and financial claims, not least because they are relatively liquid vehicles for speculators, brokers, and banks. The bulls congratulate themselves. The lost tribe of the bears is decapitated. But as in other credit cycles, the excess Fed-created money will move into real estate, or internet stocks, or emerging market equities, or, into whichever sector, scarcity and romance entices investors and speculators with cheap, new Fed credit.

The gradual and insidious process of inflation is hidden *at first* from the vast majority of working people – at home and abroad. For example, inflation is muted in the United States, at the consumer price level, by high unemployment and unused production facilities – both inherited from the last panic and bust – also caused by monetary policy. Combined with falling real incomes of the average American household, consumer prices will be sticky in the present market period.

But over many inflation cycles, the social effects of financial disorder and undervalued currencies have brought about increasing inequality. The near-zero interest rates, now maintained by the Fed, have primarily benefitted preferred banks and their financial clients. A nimble financial class, in possession of cheap credit, can maneuver to protect itself against inflation. Euphoria, born of incipient inflation and credit-fueled bull markets, takes over in the financial sector. Then it is advertised, worldwide, by bubble-vision.

Monetary reform is again put on the shelf. But the vast population of middle-income professionals and workers, on salaries and wages, and those on fixed incomes and pensions, are impoverished by this very same volatile, inflationary process. Worse yet, average American savers, those on fixed or stable nominal incomes, will earn a negative return on their savings. Thus, they save less. Thus, new investment will once again come to depend increasingly on bank debt, leverage, and speculation. Inequitable access to cheap Fed credit was everywhere apparent during the government bailout of favored brokers and bankers in 2008 and 2009, while millions of not so nimble citizens were forced into bankruptcy. This ugly chapter is only the most recent in a very long century of disruption of the international monetary system.

Our era of financial disorder was actually inaugurated in 1914 by the onset of World War I. The Great War, as it was called, had brought to an end the preeminence of the classical European states system. It had decimated the flower of European youth. It had destroyed the European continent's industrial primacy. On the eve of the Great War came the end of the gold standard – the monetary gyroscope of the Industrial Revolution and its extraordinary economic growth, the proven guarantor, also, of one hundred years of price stability. The general price level, almost literally, wound up at the same level in 1914, as it was, one century before.

With the onset of World War I, the Age of Inflation was upon us.

Strange it is *today* that an unhinged token, the *paper* dollar, is now the monetary standard of the most scientifically advanced global economy the world has ever known anchored as it is by global standards, for example, global telecommunications and accounting standards.

How and when did the international economy start down this road to the paper dollar standard? It was in 1922, at the little known, but pivotal, post-World War I Monetary Conference of Genoa, that the gold-exchange standard had been officially embraced by the academic and political elites. It was here that the *dollar and the pound* were confirmed as *official* reserve currencies, that they might substitute for what was said to be a scarcity of gold. But there was no true scarcity, only overvalued national currencies – overvaluation maintained despite the doubling of the general price level during World War I. Professor Jacques Rueff warned in the 1920s of the dangers of this flawed, official reserve currency system, designed "in camera" by the experts supposedly to economize the true gold standard. The former central banker warned of the coming collapse of this newly rigged monetary system. It did collapse, in 1929-1931, with catastrophic effects. Rueff again predicted in 1960-1961 that the Bretton Woods jerry-rigged dollar system, a post-World War II form of the *official reserve currency system*, would collapse. In newspapers and books, Rueff predicted that the world would groan under the *flood-weight* of excess American dollars going abroad. During the 1950s and 1960s, he said that Federal Reserve credit policy, combined with the official reserve currency status of the dollar, would cause permanent U.S. balance-of-payments deficits and the tendency to constant Federal budget deficits. For, under the world dollar standard, these twin deficits would be financed, at home and abroad, by new central bank money and credit. In April of 1961, in *Fortune* magazine, he foretold the coming end of gold convertibility of the dollar – *unless* there were a reform of the monetary system. His prescience was confirmed by President Nixon's suspension of convertibility in August of 1971.

Now, let us go for a moment to the booms and busts of the 1970s – subsequent to the 1971 suspension of convertibility. It is in this period, we can see the future, in a glass darkly. In 1980 at the peak of a double-digit inflation crisis, the gold price touched $850. At that time, Paul Volcker, chairman of the Federal Reserve, in similar words to the present Fed chairman, declared that the gold market had little to do with the Fed's monetary policies. But unlike his predecessors, Volcker did act. Volcker engineered a draconian credit contraction, a 20 percent Fed Funds rate, 15 percent long-term U.S. Treasury rates, leading to near 11 percent national unemployment and a decline in inflation.

During this entire period, the important links between central bank policies, the rate of inflation, the variations in the money stock, and economic growth caused much debate among economists and experts. It is still generally thought by some neo-Keynesian and monetarist economists, *and* central bankers, that the quantity of money in circulation, the economic growth rate, and a stable price level can be directly coordinated by the commissars of central bank credit policy.

In sum, the inflation rate, the rate of economic growth, and the growth of the money stock, cannot be precisely coordinated by Federal Reserve manipulation of the money supply. What a central bank is not able to do, it must not try.

So, if the problem of the post-war monetary system has been extreme booms and busts – an unstable world reserve currency, inflation and deflation, and incipient currency wars – what is the solution? The historical and empirical data show that gold convertibility is the least imperfect regulator of general price stability in the long run. In monetary and economic policy, there is only one laboratory for experiments, the laboratory of empirical evidence in human economic history. Perfect stability is, of course, unattainable in human affairs – except in a university classroom. But *blackboards* at the University of Chicago and at Cambridge University will not do, to sustain the social and economic order. The gold standard was no blackboard exercise, no mere mathematical symbol on the blackboard. It was an elegantly designed institutional set of monetary mechanisms – carefully orchestrated over centuries of experience by merchants and bankers of great purpose – who developed monetary convertibility into a supple and subtle set of integrated financial and credit institutions – organized to facilitate economic growth, job creation for an increasing population, a rising standard of living, and a stable price level – above all, to maintain a certain social stability, amidst the hurly-burly of free economic institutions. These free market institutions were designed to mobilize the free price mechanism and the international monetary system in order to act as the balance wheels of rapid economic growth of an increasingly integrated world economy. International trade among different cultures, different national currencies, competitive nations, was firmly grounded, despite all culture and language differences, on a common monetary standard. All countries traded according to one, objective yardstick of value. Under the rules, no one should arbitrarily depreciate the yardstick, to 29 inches.

The world now tries to embrace global standards in accounting, telecommunications, and computers. For an even greater purpose, who will reasonably deny the world needs a common, monetary standard?

Therefore, in order to restore long-term international price stability, and a sustainable and equitable market for growing world trade, the dollar and other key currencies must again be defined in law as a precise weight unit of gold – at a statutory convertibility rate which insures that nominal wage rates do not fall – this stipulation necessary to avoid the unwitting deflations ensuing after World War I. Indeed, *nothing but gold convertibility, a true gold standard without official reserve currencies, will yield a real fiduciary monetary standard* for the integrated world economy. Such a true fiduciary standard provides simultaneously all the necessary functions of money – domestic and international – that is, to say, a long-term store of value for saving, the stable means of exchange for trading, and the stable unit of measure by which to compare all other articles of wealth in the market. Like every standard of measurement – the yardstick, the meter, the liter – the monetary standard must be constant in order to maintain an equitable and growing economic order.

Only such a common, non-national monetary standard can rule out manipulated floating-exchange rates – themselves the diabolical agents of predatory mercantilism. Despite all denials, undervalued currencies and currency depreciations of today are, without a doubt, designed to subsidize exports, and to transfer unemployment to other nations, to beggar thy neighbor, and, by means of an undervalued currency, to gain share of market in manufactured, labor intensive, value-added, world traded goods. If these competitive depreciations and undervaluations are sustained, floating-exchange rates, combined with the twin budget and trade deficits will, at regular intervals, blow up the world trading system. *The gradual diminution of property rights will follow.*

Unlike the paper dollar, created at will by the authorities of one country at zero marginal cost, the gold standard effectively puts control of the supply of money into the hands of a democratic people, because central bank excess creation of credit and paper money can be redeemed for gold by free people and businesses, both at home and abroad, at the fixed statutory convertibility price. If today we know that excess cash balances are the necessary cause of inflation, the monetary authorities under the gold standard are required by law to limit the creation of excess credit in order to preserve the guaranteed value of the currency. Such a straightforward but subtle mechanism causes the banking systems to bring the quantity of money in circulation into balance with the desire to hold it and to use it for productive purposes. Under the gold standard, there can be no sustained, extreme surfeit of excess cash balances. Thus, there can be no sustained, extreme inflation and deflation of the general price level. Wars may interrupt the constancy of the gold standard. But resumption is always availing.

In a few words, dollar convertibility to gold, a proven non-national global standard, is the solution. But dollar convertibility to gold must become a cooperative project of the major powers.

To accomplish this reform, the U.S. must lead: *first*, to announce future convertibility, on a date certain, of the U.S. dollar – the dollar itself to be defined in statute as a weight unit of gold.

My research suggests that the convertibility price, during the present market interval, given the hierarchy of relative prices and the all-in costs of gold production, should approximate $2,000 per ounce. Any substantial delay will occasion a different estimate of the sustainable, convertibility price. Second, a new Bretton Woods conference must be convened to establish mutual gold convertibility of the currencies of the major powers. Third, the curse of official reserve currencies must be ruled out, while at the same time a consolidation of official dollar reserves must be organized – into long-term debt, to be funded in the way Alexander Hamilton funded the volatile national and state debts at the birth of the American republic.

I believe a dollar as good as gold is the way out of this monetary maze. This is also the road to restoration of real and substantial American savings, the indispensable means to global competitiveness, without inflation. The gold standard is, above all, the global standard by which to restore America's financial self-respect, to regain its needful role as the equilibrium leader of a growing world economy.

"So long as the Treasury deficit can be financed with discretionary money and credit – newly created by the Federal Reserve, by the banking system, and by foreign central banks–the federal budget deficit will persist."

Chapter Twenty-two

MONETARY REFORM: THE KEY TO SPENDING RESTRAINT

The Wall Street Journal, April 26, 2011

Paul Ryan's plan won't succeed without legislation to prevent the Federal Reserve from monetizing the national debt.

No man in America is a match for House Budget Committee Chairman Paul Ryan on the Federal budget. No congressman in my lifetime has been more determined to cut government spending. No one is better informed for the task he has set himself. Nor has anyone developed a more comprehensive plan to reduce, and ultimately eliminate, the Federal budget deficit than the House Budget Resolution submitted by Mr. Ryan on April 5.

But experience and the operations of the Federal Reserve System compel me to predict that Mr. Ryan's heroic efforts to balance the budget by 2015 without raising taxes will not end in success – even with a Republican majority in both Houses and a Republican President in 2012.

Why? Because the House Budget Resolution fails to reform the Federal Reserve System that supplies the new money and credit to finance both the budget deficit and the balance-of-payments deficit. So long as the Treasury deficit can be financed with discretionary money and credit, newly created by the Federal Reserve, by the banking system, and by foreign central banks – the federal budget deficit will persist.

It is true that federal deficits will rise more or less with the business cycle, leading previous deficit hawks such as Senators Phil Gramm and Warren

Rudman to believe that if we just reined in federal spending and increased economic growth we would have a balanced budget. Indeed, for two generations, fiscal conservatives and Democratic and Republican presidents alike have pledged to balance the budget and bring an end to ever-rising government spending.

They, too, were informed, determined, and sincere leaders. But they did not succeed because of institutional defects in the monetary system that have never been remedied.

President Reagan was aware of the need to reform the monetary system in the 1980s, but circumstances and time permitted only tax-rate reform, deregulation efforts, and rebuilding a strong defense. And so the monetary problem remains.

The problem is simple. Because of the official reserve currency status of the dollar, combined with discretionary new Federal Reserve and foreign central bank credit, the Federal government is always able to finance the Treasury deficit, even though net national savings are insufficient for the purpose.

What persistent debtor could resist permanent credit financing? For a government, an individual or an enterprise, "a deficit without tears" leads to the corrupt euphoria of limitless spending. For example, with new credit, the Fed will have bought $600 billion of U.S. Treasurys between November 2010 and June 2011, a rate of purchase that approximates the annualized budget deficit. Commodity, equity and emerging-market inflation are only a few of the volatile consequences of this Fed credit policy.

The solution to the problem is equally simple. First, in order to limit Fed discretion, the dollar must be made convertible to a weight unit of gold by congressional statute at a price that preserves the level of nominal wages in order to avoid the threat of deflation. Second, the government must at the same time be prohibited from financing its deficit at the Fed or in the banks both at home or abroad. Third, only in the free market for true savings – undisguised by inflationary new Federal Reserve money and banking system credit – will interest rates signal to voters the consequences of growing federal government deficits.

Unrestricted convertibility of the dollar to gold at the statutory price restricts Federal Reserve creation of excess dollars and the inflation caused by Fed financing of the deficit. This is so because excess dollars in the financial markets, at home or abroad, would lead to redemption of the undesired dollars into gold at the statutory parity price, thus requiring the Fed to reduce the expansion of credit in order to preserve the lawful convertibility parity of the dollar-gold relationship, thereby reducing the threat of inflation.

This monetary reform would provide an indispensable restraint, not only on the Federal Reserve, but also on the global banking system-based as the system now is on the dollar standard and foreign official dollar reserves. Establishing dollar convertibility to a weight unit of gold, and ending the dollar's reserve currency role, constitute the dual institutional mechanisms by which sustained, systemic inflation is ruled out of the integrated world trading system. It would also prevent access to unlimited Fed credit by which to finance ever-growing government.

By adding these monetary reforms to his House Budget Resolution, Mr. Ryan has a chance to succeed where previous deficit hawks have failed. As today's stalwart of a balanced budget, he must now become a monetary-reform statesman if he is to attain his admirable goal of balancing the federal budget by 2015 without raising taxes.

"The purchasing power of a dollar saved in 1971 under Nixon has today fallen to 18 pennies. Nixon's new economic policy sowed chaos for a decade. The nation and the world reaped the whirlwind."

Chapter Twenty-three

THE NIXON SHOCK HEARD 'ROUND THE WORLD'

The Wall Street Journal, August 15, 2011

On the afternoon of Friday, August 13, 1971, high-ranking White House and Treasury Department officials gathered secretly in President Richard Nixon's lodge at Camp David. Treasury Secretary John Connally, on the job for just seven months, was seated to Nixon's right. During that momentous afternoon, however, newcomer Connally was front and center, put there by a solicitous President. Nixon, gossiped his staff, was smitten by the big, self-confident Texan whom the President had charged with bringing order into his administration's bumbling economic policies.

In the past, Nixon had expressed economic views that tended toward "conservative" platitudes about free enterprise and free markets. But the President loved histrionic gestures that grabbed the public's attention. He and Connally were determined to present a comprehensive package of dramatic measures to deal with the nation's huge balance-of-payments deficit, its anemic economic growth, and inflation.

Dramatic indeed: They decided to break up the post-war Bretton Woods monetary system, to devalue the dollar, to raise tariffs, and to impose the first peacetime wage and price controls in American history. And they were going to do it on the weekend – heralding this astonishing news with a Nixon speech before the markets opened on Monday.

The cast of characters gathered at Camp David was impressive. It included future Treasury Secretary George Shultz, then director of the Office of Management and Budget, and future Federal Reserve Chairman Paul Volcker, then undersecretary for monetary affairs at Treasury. At the meeting that afternoon Nixon reminded everyone of the importance of secrecy. They were forbidden even to tell their wives where they were. Then Nixon let Connally take over the meeting.

The most dramatic Connally initiative was to "close the gold window," whereby foreign nations had been able to exchange U.S. dollars for U.S. gold – an exchange guaranteed under the monetary system set up under American leadership at Bretton Woods, New Hampshire, in July 1944. Recently the markets had panicked. Great Britain had tried to redeem $3 billion for American gold. So large were the official dollar debts in the hands of foreign authorities that America's gold stock would be insufficient to meet the swelling official demand for American gold at the convertibility price of $35 per ounce.

On Thursday, Connally had rushed to Washington from a Texas vacation. He and Nixon hurriedly decided to act unilaterally, not only to suspend convertibility of the dollar to gold, but also to impose wage and price controls. Nixon's speechwriter William Safire attended the conference in order to prepare the President's speech to the nation. In his book *Before the Fall*, Safire recalled being told on the way to Camp David that closing the gold window was a possibility. Despite the many international ramifications of what the administration would do, no officials from the State Department or the National Security Council were invited to Camp David.

The President had little patience or understanding of the disputes among his economic team members. He found wearisome the mumbo-jumbo from Federal Reserve Chairman Arthur Burns. But the President had determined he would have a unified economic team and a unified economic policy, no matter what the consequences. So the White House dutifully leaked stories designed to undermine and humiliate Burns, as Connally waited in the wings with his "New Economic Policy."

At Camp David, Connally argued: "It's clear that we have to move in the international field, to close the gold window, not change the price of gold, and encourage the dollar to float." Burns timidly objected but was easily flattered by the President. By the evening of August 15, Burns was on board with terminating the last vestige of dollar convertibility to gold, depreciating the dollar on the foreign exchanges, imposing higher tariffs, and ultimately ordering price and wage controls.

Nixon and Safire put together a speech to be televised Sunday night. It had taken only a few hours during that August 1971 weekend for Nixon to decide to sever the nation's last tenuous link to the historic American gold standard, a monetary standard that had been the constitutional bedrock (Article I, Sections 8 and 10) of the American dollar and of America's economic prosperity for much of the previous two centuries.

At least one Camp David participant, Paul Volcker, regretted what transpired that weekend. The "Nixon Shock" was followed by a decade of one of the worst inflations of American history and the most stagnant economy since the Great Depression. The price of gold rose to $800 from $35.

The purchasing power of a dollar saved in 1971 under Nixon has today fallen to 18 pennies. Nixon's new economic policy sowed chaos for a decade. The nation and the world reaped the whirlwind.

"China has been financially colonized by the United States.
But why is this a fact? Simply because China has chained itself
to the world dollar standard at a pegged undervalued exchange
rate, choosing therefore to hold the foreign-exchange value
of its trade surplus – that is, its official national savings –
in U.S. dollar securities."

Chapter Twenty-four

CHINA: AMERICAN FINANCIAL COLONY OR MERCANTILIST PREDATOR?

The American Spectator, September 2011

China is an important trading partner of America. But it may also be
a mortal threat. And not for the conventional reasons usually cited in the
press. Ironically, it is a threat because China is in fact a financial colony
of the United States, a colony subsidized and sustained by the pegged,
undervalued, yuan-dollar exchange rate. Neither the United States nor
its economic colony seems to understand the long-term destructive
consequences of the dollarization not only of the Chinese economy but
also of the world monetary system. While the Chinese financial system has
been corrupted primarily by tyranny, deceit, and reckless expansionism, it is
also destabilized by the workings of the world dollar standard. Neither the
United States nor China has come to grips with the perverse effects of the
world dollar standard.

The social and economic pathology of 19th century colonialism is well
studied, but the monetary pathology of its successor, the neo-colonial
reserve currency system of the dollar, is less transparent. In order to remedy
this pathological defect, the United States must rid itself of its enormous
Chinese financial colony, whose exports are subsidized by the undervalued
yuan in return for Chinese financing of the U.S. twin deficits. Both

China and the United States must also free themselves from the increasing malignancy of the dollar reserve currency system, the primary cause of inflation in both China and the United States.

In the end, only monetary reform, including an end to the reserve currency system, can permanently separate the dollar host from its yuan colony. Without monetary reform, the perverse effects of the dollar reserve currency system will surely metastasize into one financial and political crisis after another – even on the scale of the 2007-2009 crisis.

It is, of course, a counterintuitive fact that China has been financially colonized by the United States. But why is this a fact? Simply because China has chained itself to the world dollar standard at a pegged undervalued exchange rate, choosing therefore to hold the foreign-exchange value of its trade surplus – that is, its official national savings – in U.S. dollar securities. It is true that the dollar-yuan strategy of America's Chinese colony has helped to finance a generation of extraordinary Chinese growth. But China now holds more than 3 trillion dollars of official reserves and more than a trillion dollars in U.S. government securities. These Chinese dollar reserves directly finance the deficits of the American colonial center. This arrangement clearly resembles the imperial system of the late 19th century. The value of a British colony's reserves were often held in the currency of the imperial center, then invested in the London money market. Thus, the colony's reserves were entirely dependent on the stability of the currency of the colonial center. While China is America's largest financial colony, most other developing countries are also bound to neo-colonial status within the reserve currency hegemony of the dollarized world trading system.

China's dollarized monetary system reminds us of nothing so much as the historic colonial financial arrangements imposed by the later British Empire on India before World War I – India actually remaining a financial colony of England long after its independence in 1947. How did the sterling financial empire work? The imperial colony of India, beginning in the late 19th century, held its official Indian currency reserves (savings) in British pounds deposited in the English money market; independent developed nations at that time, like France and Germany, held their reserves in gold. That is, France, Germany, and the United States settled their international payment imbalances in gold – a non-national, common, monetary standard – holding their official reserves, too, in gold. But the London-based reserves of colonial India were held not primarily in gold, but in British currency, helping to finance not only the imperial economic system, but also the imperial banking system, imperial debts, imperial wars, and British welfare programs. Eventually, as we know, both the debt-burdened British Empire and its official reserve currency system collapsed.

For more than a generation now, a similar process has been at work in China. China is America's chief colonial appendage. The Chinese work hard and produce goods. Subsidized by an undervalued yuan, they export much of their surplus production to America. But, like the Indians who were paid in sterling, the exports of Chinese colonials are substantially paid in dollars, not yuan – because bilateral and world trade, and the world commodities market have been dollarized. And thus it may be said that the world financial system is today an unstable, neo-colonial appendage of the unstable dollar.

China, like its predecessor the British colony of India, has chosen to hold a significant fraction of what it is paid in the form of official dollar reserves (or savings). These dollars are promptly redeposited in the U.S. dollar market, where they are used to finance U.S. deficits. Every Thursday night, the Federal Reserve publishes its balance sheet, and there we now read that more than $2.5 trillion of U.S. government securities are held in custody for foreign monetary authorities, 40 percent of which is held for the account of America's chief financial colony, Communist China. It is clear that without financial colonies to finance and sustain the immense U.S. balance-of-payments and budget deficits, the U.S. paper dollar standard and the growth of U.S. government spending would be unsustainable.

It is often overlooked that these enormous official dollar reserves held by China are a massive mortgage on the work and income of present and future American private citizens. This Chinese mortgage on the American economy has grown rapidly since the suspension of dollar convertibility to gold in 1971. China – poor and undeveloped in 1971 – was at that time very jealous of its sovereign independence, sufficiently so to reject its alliance with the Soviet Union – even earlier to attack U.S. armies on the Chinese border during the Korean War. In an ironic twist of fate, China surrendered its former independence and, as a U.S. financial colony, joined the dollar-dominated world financial system. China's monetary policy is anything but independent. It is determined primarily by the Federal Reserve Board in America, the pegged yuan-dollar exchange rate serving as the transmission mechanism of Fed-created excess dollars pouring into the Chinese economic system. Perennial U.S. balance-of-payments deficits send the dollar flood not only into China but also into all emerging countries. The Chinese central bank buys up these excess dollars by issuing new yuan, thereby holding up the overvalued dollar, and holding down the undervalued yuan. Much of these Chinese official dollar purchases are then invested in U.S. government debt securities. So even though America exports excess dollars to China, China sends them back to finance the U.S. budget deficit – much like marionettes walking off one side of the stage, merely to reappear unchanged on the other side.

This is the little-understood arbitrage mechanism of the pegged-exchange rate system by which Fed-created excess dollars are bought and held as reserves by the Chinese central bank, in exchange for which newly created yuan are issued, thereby supercharging inflation in China. The Chinese dollar reserves, which are reinvested in the United States, help to ignite inflation in America. It is clear that the workings of the official dollar reserve currency system cause purchasing power to be multiplied, or at least doubled, in both countries. But these central bank issues of new money are unassociated with the production of new goods and services during the same market period. Thus total spending, or purchasing power, exceeds the total value of goods and services at prevailing prices. When total demand exceeds total supply, the price level must rise.

But just as the subservient, colonial Indians were constrained not to sell their sterling reserves too quickly, so the Chinese are constrained – by politics, diplomacy, and self-interest – not to dump their depreciating American dollars. The Indians had to consult their imperial bankers, even though the English were debtors to their Indian colony, because the Indians did not wish to anger the colonial center, nor to precipitate a sterling crisis. From time immemorial, creditors with too large a stake in an over-sized debtor often beg leave of their debtor to get their money back.

China is frustrated by circumstances similar to those of a colony of imperial Britain. Hostility has arisen in the debtor – the United States. Fear of setting off a dollar slide haunts the hostile creditor, China. The difficulty of finding a suitable portfolio of alternatives for a trillion dollars in U.S. government debt annoys the outspoken Chinese financial colony, as it calls for a new world monetary system. But there seems to be no genuine alternative to the very liquid dollar market. De facto illiquidity of official Chinese dollar reserves is enforced by political sensitivities, not by market salability. The debtor, as the saying goes, is "too big to fail." Thus arises an unstable stalemate – a yuan-dollar, pegged-exchange rate regime constantly on the edge of a crisis.

The "exorbitant privilege" of the dollar is matched by the insupportable burden of America's overvalued reserve currency role, which has tended to deindustrialize the colonizer, gradually increasing social inequality by reducing the standard of living of lower- and middle-income American families. The reserve currency country then feels compelled, as the Fed does today, to depreciate the dollar in the vain hope of eliminating the trade deficit and the balance-of-payments deficit – by becoming more competitive abroad as it becomes poorer at home. The perversity of the official reserve currency system is endless as China now endures high inflation engendered by its colonial status in the world dollar system.

The floating, pegged-exchange rate system based on the dollar has been slowly decaying since the end of World War II. But the dollar-based reserve currency system, because of the unmatched scale and liquidity of the dollar markets, could last another generation. When it will collapse cannot be predicted. That it will collapse, without systemic reform, I think inevitable. Few predicted the timing of the collapse of the pegged-dollar system of Bretton Woods. But it did collapse in August of 1971, followed by America's worst decade since the Great Depression.

Ultimately America, the leader of the unstable world financial system, must choose between two options:

1) The United States can wait for the eventual demise of the world dollar standard under chaotic conditions, similar to the final sterling collapse and the subsequent collapse of Bretton Woods in 1971.

2) Or, America could take the lead in reforming the official reserve currency system based on the dollar. Such a monetary reform

program would entail a careful windup, by agreement, of the world
dollar standard. At the same time America would reestablish by
statute a dollar convertible to gold, i.e., a dollar defined in law as a
weight unit of gold. Gold would replace the dollar as the world's
reserve currency.

The reform would, first and foremost, establish a tested, non-national,
neutral monetary standard as the basis of a stable dollar – one which
reasonable sovereign trading partners could accept. Gold would become the
international settlements currency and thus would replace the dollar as the
basis of world trade and finance. Inasmuch as monetary history shows that
no unstable national currency can permanently serve as the crucial world
reserve currency, it follows that neither can an unstable basket of national
currencies, nor can a fiction such as the SDR – the reserve asset created by
the International Monetary Fund to supplement member countries' reserves.

But we are left with the question: what does the evidence of American
history suggest as the basis for a stable dollar?

The stability of the U.S. dollar has varied widely in its history. This
variation is explained by two factors: the monetary standard chosen for
the dollar, and whether other countries have simultaneously used cash and
securities payable in dollars as their own reserves, even as their monetary
standard itself (i.e., official reserve currencies in place of gold).

After the failures of several generations of unhinged paper currencies,
pegged and floating-exchange rates, America should embrace a stable
monetary system tested in the laboratory of human history – the
cornerstone of which the elites have rejected for a century. It is now
time to restore that cornerstone – the true gold standard, shorn of the
economic pathology of official reserve currencies. Now is the time to
restore the American monetary standard authorized by the Founders in the
Constitution – Article I, Sections 8 and 10. Now is the historical moment
for America to take the lead and again give the world a real money, the
Founders' gold dollar of the Coinage Act of 1792. What the Founders
learned from the paper money inflation of the Revolution, the recent past
has taught us again. America and the world need a monetary standard
which, unlike the paper-credit dollar, cannot be created at zero marginal

cost with which to dispossess the prudent and to subsidize the U.S. government and insolvent financial institutions at near-zero interest rates.

For America to establish the gold standard would provide the least imperfect monetary solution to the problems of a century of financial disorder – engendered over and over by central bank-manipulated paper money, official reserve currencies, and floating-pegged exchange rates. Only a stable dollar, a dollar defined by statute as a weight unit of gold, can pin down the long-term price level, restoring the incentive to save and ruling out extreme inflation and deflation. Such a dollar convertible to gold would reopen the road to confidence in the long-term value of the U.S. monetary standard. This is the durable road to economic growth and prosperity – financed by increased long-term savings, increased long-term investment, and rising demand for labor at rising real wages.

*"...post-war free trade leadership and the dollar's reserve
currency status inadvertently made the U.S. open market a target
for foreign export machines – using, among other strategies,
undervalued currencies as their battering rams. Moreover,
as countries abroad gained dollar reserves, the counterpart
of those reserves was ignored – namely, ever increasing foreign
held U.S. Treasury debt – the form in which foreign countries
hold the bulk of their official reserves."*

Chapter Twenty-five

THE TRUE GOLD STANDARD:
A MONETARY REFORM PLAN

Cato Institute Seminar and Luncheon, October 28, 2011

We are gathered in this quiet hall, still focused on the world outside,
engulfed as it is by gradual financial disintegration. Today, the economic
crisis we endure is only the latest chapter in the century-long struggle to
restore financial order – the success (or failure) of which is inextricably
bound up with American prosperity and the promise of the American way
of life.

As we think through the consequences of financial disorder, the historical
causes of the great world wars of the 20th century come to mind. They
compel us to remember that floating-exchange rates and competitive
currency wars became the occasion for violent social disorder and
revolutionary civil strife abroad. It is well to recall that natural resource
rivalry, monetary depreciations, mercantilism, and *war clouds* have appeared
together from time immemorial. As a result, American national security
risks are today high and rising.

But, let us now reflect upon how we got *here* – into the maelstrom – and
then, how we get from here to *there* – that is, to a stable monetary and fiscal
order. (This is the theme of my new book.) Between 2009 and 2011, all of

you know we experienced an emerging market equity and economic boom – but at the very same time, sluggish growth in the United States. Why such a sluggish sequence in the United States, despite 3.5 trillion dollars of Treasury and Federal Reserve subsidies to the banking cartel and favored corporations? The answer is because the vast Fed credit creation of 2008 to 2011 could not be fully absorbed by the U.S. economy – coming as it did after wild panic, deep recession, and deflation – economic growth having been preempted by the drive for solvency and debt repayment.

It is too easy to forget that the newly created money by the Fed flooded primarily into U.S. stocks, bonds, and the dollarized world of commodities. But excess Federal Reserve credit also cascaded offshore, igniting not only a fall in the dollar, but the superboom in emerging markets. The transmission mechanism in both cases is the role of the dollar as the world's primary reserve currency.

What is the reserve currency monetary mechanism which links unrestrained Fed credit expansion and a falling dollar to emerging market financial and economic booms?

It is simply this: the financial authorities in the emerging countries – usually their central banks – issue immense new quantities of their local currencies in order to purchase the incoming flood of Fed-created excess dollars. This they do to keep their currencies from rising, to subsidize their exports, and to accumulate dollar reserves. But the new issues of local money in the emerging markets are then put to work there – first, of course, in liquid assets, creating a boom in all financial instruments and commodities, and then a boom in the local economy. This is an ineluctable arbitrage – born of the reserve currency system based on the dollar.

After the catastrophe of World War I, the system of official reserve currencies was *first* adopted by the Great Powers in order to suppress the classical pre-war gold standard. The new system was known as the gold-exchange standard – a perverse and profoundly flawed corruption of the true gold standard prior to World War I. Thus, during the interwar period, the pound sterling and the dollar became the official reserve currencies – used to settle payment imbalances – in place of gold.

Equally perverse, a similar, dollar-based Bretton Woods gold-exchange system was adopted in 1944 – fully in effect but two decades.

After Nixon's destruction of the last vestige of convertibility in 1971 came the much-heralded floating-pegged exchange rate arrangements – which envelop the world to this very day. The key financial point is that both the Bretton Woods system and its successor, the world paper dollar standard, have created excess demand for the dollar to carry out international transactions, *and* to accumulate official dollar reserves in foreign central banks in the form of ever-rising U.S. debt. Excess demand for the dollar, the dominant world currency – composing 65 percent of the world's currency reserves; used in 85 percent of commodity and currency trading, and 65 percent of export invoicing – *this excess demand* kept the value of the dollar higher than it would otherwise have been in world trade. Thus, it was that post-war free trade leadership and the dollar's reserve currency status inadvertently made the U.S. open market a target for foreign export machines – using, among other strategies, undervalued currencies as their battering rams. Moreover, as countries abroad gained dollar reserves, the counterpart of those reserves was ignored – namely, ever increasing foreign held U.S. Treasury debt – the form in which foreign countries hold the bulk of their official reserves.

Thus, the exorbitant privilege of the world reserve currency gradually became, as it is today, an insupportable burden. For example, the dollar's official-reserve currency role has eroded U.S. international competitiveness. In 1980, U.S. residents owned net investments in the rest of the world equal to about 10 percent, but by 2009 had become net debtors equal to about 20 percent, of U.S. GDP. Meanwhile U.S. net official monetary assets – official monetary assets minus foreign liabilities – declined by almost exactly the same amount, while the books of the rest of American residents remained in balance or showed a slight surplus. This comparison proves that the entire decline in the U.S. net investment position has been due to federal borrowing from foreign monetary authorities; and ending the dollar's role as chief official reserve currency is necessary to end chronic U.S. payments deficits and restore U.S. international competitiveness.

The reserve currency role of the dollar and unrestrained Federal Reserve credit policy cause manifold perverse financial effects. Above all, they permit the United States to finance its budget and balance-of-payments deficits by issuing, without limit, its own currency. This so-called exorbitant privilege has caused the twin deficits to be perennial. And these deficits will continue in the absence of profound monetary and fiscal reform.

So let us now inquire into the precise financial mechanisms set in motion by hyperactive Federal Reserve open market operations and the international settlement procedures under the reserve currency system. Both are at the epicenter of permanent balance-of-payments deficits and budget deficits – engendering alternating inflation and deflation – speculation, boom, bust, and their consequences.

Simplified, and focusing on QE1 and QE2, this is the sequence: In order to finance the government deficit, the Treasury sold bills and bonds at a rate of about $120 billion a month, that is, about $1.5 trillion per year – as you can see, about equal to the annual budget deficit. But the Federal Reserve System, the world banking system, and foreign central banks purchase these Treasury bills and bonds – against the issue of *new* money, or *newly created domestic credit*. Since 2008, the Fed has added over two trillions of U.S. government and mortgage-related securities to its portfolio. Foreign central banks now own at least $3.5 trillion of U.S. government securities, held in custody at the Federal Reserve. Now, consider the fact that the Fed and foreign central bank purchases of U.S. government securities reduce their supply in the market, while at the same time increasing the quantity of money in circulation. But, the Fed created money – used to finance the U.S. government deficit – combined with the new money issued by central banks abroad to purchase excess dollars in their banking systems – is not associated in the same market period with the equal production of new goods and services.

Thus, during the global market period in which the Treasury and foreigners spend the newly issued central bank credit and money, total spending, or purchasing power, must exceed, in that same market period, the total value of available goods and services – at prevailing prices. Of course, prices must rise when total demand exceeds the total value of supply. The result is secular inflation, punctuated by bouts of debt deflation.

This insidious process of monetary inflation is hidden from the vast majority of working people – at home and abroad – not least by a fictitious Consumer Price Index. But, the social and economic effects of inflation, financial volatility, and the overvalued dollar have intensified inequality in America. The near-zero interest rates, maintained by the Fed today, subsidize the banker class and their financial clients. And so it is, that a nimble financial class, in possession of cheap credit, and close proximity to the Fed and Treasury, can maneuver to protect itself against inflation – as well as to mitigate the subsequent effects of deflation. But the vast population of middle-income professionals and workers – on very lagging salaries and wages, as well as those on fixed incomes and pensions – are impoverished by the very same volatile, inflationary, and deflationary markets. Civil strife, born of resentment, was all but inevitable.

The same inflationary process goes on abroad – igniting revolutionary social movements on every continent. Worse yet, sensible and careful American workers and savers, especially those on fixed incomes, earn today a negative return on their meager savings. The prudent are dispossessed. The reckless are bailed out. Thereupon the tea party arrives, born of injustice.

Without a comprehensive financial reform to end inflation and to increase true savings, new investment will once again come to depend increasingly on bank debt, leverage, and speculation – with similar consequences.

Ours is but the latest ugly chapter in a century of financial disorder. Where did the first chapter of the Age of Inflation and of *official* reserve currency systems begin?

The age of inflation was inaugurated in 1914 by the onset of World War I. The Great War, as it was called, had brought to an end the preeminence of the European states system. It had decimated the flower of European youth. It had destroyed the European continent's industrial primacy. All the belligerents in World War I had suspended the classical international gold standard.

This action was surely the unmistakable herald of a century of monetary and financial disorder. Indeed, the classical gold standard had been the monetary gyroscope of the Industrial Revolution, the pilot of its extraordinary, economic growth – marked by almost one hundred years of general price stability. For example, under the classical gold standard the general price level in America wound up at the very same level in 1914 as in 1879, even at the same level it was in 1834.

Compare this to the 40-year period since 1971, the year President Nixon suspended dollar convertibility to gold. Adjusted for the CPI, the dollar has in fact lost about 85 percent of its purchasing power since 1971, 98 percent of its purchasing power in gold prices – gold prices having a mere 3,000-year history to recommend them.

Strange it is today that an unhinged token, the paper dollar, is now the unstable monetary standard of the most scientifically advanced global economy the world has ever known, a world increasingly dependent on *reliable* and *trustworthy standards* – in technology, telecommunications, and accounting.

It was in 1922, at the post-World War I Monetary Conference at Genoa that the gold-exchange standard – the first modern *official* reserve currency system – was *officially* embraced by the Great Powers – and by the international academic, banker, and political elites. It was at Genoa that the dollar and the pound were confirmed as *official reserve currencies* – in order that these national currencies might substitute for gold as the means to settle residual balance-of-payments deficits; and that managed currencies might take the place of a free monetary order. There was said to be a scarcity of gold. But there was no true gold scarcity, only overvalued national currencies relative to the pre-war gold price. For example, British currency overvaluation was maintained after World War I despite the vast rise of the general price level in national currencies during the Great War. The result was the deindustrialization of England, financial disorder, and during 1930 to 1931, the collapse of the official reserve currency system – a primary cause of the Great Depression.

Let us now travel quickly to World War II. Under the Bretton Woods System, after World War II, the U.S. financial authorities – now backed up by 50 percent of world output – embraced the Fischer-Keynesian theoretical conceits of a managed currency and a hyperactive fiscal policy. Now, it was said, the important links between central bank money, the rate of inflation, the variations in the money stock, and economic growth could be manipulated successfully by the mandarins at the central bank and the Treasury.

In fact, it is *still generally thought* by academics and central bankers, and by neo-Keynesian and some monetarist economists, that the quantity of money in circulation, the economic growth rate, the level of employment, and a stable price level can be controlled by the commissars of the central bank. Long ago their theories were falsified by a reality in which, for example, during 1978, the quantity of money in Switzerland grew approximately 30 percent, while the price level was stable. In the United States, the quantity of money, M-1, grew in 1979 about 5 percent while the inflation rate rose 13 percent and the economy stagnated.

In a word, the empirical evidence shows that the inflation rate, the rate of economic growth, and the growth of the money stock, cannot be centrally controlled by Federal Reserve manipulation of the money supply. What a central bank cannot do, it must not try; or social distemper is the unavoidable consequence. So, if the problem is the reserve currency system, combined with an unconstrained fiscal and Federal Reserve credit policy – what is the solution?

The historical and empirical data show that currency convertibility to gold, *without reserve currencies*, is the *least imperfect* regulator of economic growth and general price stability in the long run. In monetary and economic policy, there is only one laboratory for experiment, the laboratory of empirical evidence in human economic history.

The classical gold standard of the Industrial Revolution – that is, *the true gold standard* fully integrated with, and guiding, the modern credit super-structure – was no blackboard exercise, no mere mathematical symbol drawn from a university monograph. The international gold standard was an elegantly designed set of institutional monetary and credit mechanisms. Carefully orchestrated during centuries of experience, merchants and bankers of great purpose integrated national currency convertibility to gold with a supple and subtle set of market-based credit institutions. During the Industrial Revolution, these gold-based credit institutions facilitated price level stability and secular economic growth, different in scope and duration from any previous period of economic history. During the 19th century, the U.S. economy grew at the average annual rate of 4 percent.

Above all, in order to protect the least among us, to insure a certain social stability amidst the hurly-burly of free economic institutions, the gold standard stabilized the value of wages of working people. The gold standard established a dollar of stable purchasing power over the long run, not only to enhance saving and investment, but especially to provide for a family's future needs and for retirement. The endurance of the gold standard was reinforced by balanced budgets. So, if a stable dollar is the issue, what does the evidence tell us about the stability of the dollar throughout American history?

Let us summarize the data from my book and that of my colleague John Mueller. Applying two criteria divides the monetary history of the United States into distinct phases. We can compare the stability of different monetary regimes by examining the variation in the Consumer Price Index (as reconstructed back to 1800), using two simple measures: long-term CPI stability (measured by the annual average change from the beginning to the end of the period of each monetary standard) and short-term CPI volatility (measured by the standard deviation of annual CPI changes during the full period). What do we conclude?

Weighting these two criteria equally, the classical gold standard from 1879-1914 provided the most stable dollar of all U.S. monetary regimes (as John Mueller's table shows in my Congressional testimony of March 17, 2011).

So, how *do* we get from *here* – namely, the volatile paper dollar standard, the anarchy of floating-exchange rates, and a perverse official reserve currency system – to *there*, that is a stable dollar and stable exchange rates?

First, may I be so bold to recommend my book for this purpose? Even its straightforward, five-step program? (Not twelve steps, only five.)

To restore long-term price stability, stable exchange rates, and global economic growth, surely the United States must lead.

The dollar must again be defined in law as a precise weight unit of gold – at a statutory convertibility rate which insures that nominal wage rates do not fall – this latter stipulation necessary in order to avoid the deflations ensuing after World War I.

Indeed, *nothing* but gold convertibility, a true gold standard *without official reserve currencies*, will yield a stable monetary standard for an integrated, growing, world economy – based as it must be on stable exchange rates. Without strong global growth, nations will falter in succession, or succumb to beggar-thy-neighbor policies. For two generations, policy makers have ignored at their peril the proposition that free trade, without stable exchange rates, is at first a fantasy, then a nightmare.

Thus, the United States *must* be the *leader* of monetary reform by convening an international monetary conference to restore stable exchange rates.

Only stable exchange rates, based on a common, impartial, international monetary standard, can rule out manipulated, floating-exchange rates and unconstrained central banks – the agents of predatory mercantilism. Despite all political denials, undervalued currencies and currency depreciations of today, are, without a doubt, designed to subsidize exports, and to transfer unemployment to other nations, to beggar thy neighbor, and, by means of an undervalued currency to gain share of market in manufactured, labor intensive, value-added, world traded goods. If competitive depreciations and undervaluations continue, floating-exchange rates, combined with the U.S. twin budget and balance-of-payments deficits, will at regular intervals blow up the world financial system.

It is, I believe, incontestable that all the celebrated monetary gods of the 20th century have failed. Originating in the conceits of 20th century academics, bankers, economists, and politicians, these monetary gods have sowed chaos. Now we reap the whirlwind. But the proven monetary gyroscope of the extraordinary Industrial Revolution still awaits its moment to be remobilized.

In my book, *The True Gold Standard: A Monetary Reform Plan without Official Reserve Currencies* (2012), I chart a road to get from *here* – a world of financial disorder, to *there* – the remobilization of the gold standard. But I do emphasize that if the United States takes the lead to re-establish dollar convertibility to gold, the project should become a cooperative effort of the major powers.

To accomplish such a reform, *first* the United States announces future convertibility of the U.S. dollar – the dollar itself to be defined in statute, on a date certain, as a weight unit of gold. *Second*, a new Bretton Woods conference must be convened to establish mutual gold convertibility of the currencies of the major powers – the U.S., if necessary, proceeding to convertibility unilaterally. *Third*, the curse of official reserve currencies born of the 1922 Genoa and 1944 Bretton Woods agreements must be ruled out – gold alone designated to settle residual balance of payment deficits. At the same time, a consolidation of official dollar reserves must be organized into long-term debt – to be funded in the very way the Founders funded the volatile national and state debts at the birth of the American republic.

A sound and stable dollar – the historic American monetary standard – is the way out of the financial maze into which we have ensnared ourselves. If we have eyes to see and ears to hear, we know that where there is no vision, the people perish. The American Founders did give us, in the Constitution, the necessary vision. Theirs was a sound doctrine. Article I, Section 8 of the U.S. Constitution ordains that Congress has the power "to coin money", to regulate foreign money, and to fix the standard of weights and measures, including thereby the monetary standard.

The U.S. Constitution in Article I, Section 10 further ordains that the states shall make *nothing* but gold and silver coin a legal tender. The founders intended that the constitutional American monetary standard should be a standard weight and measure of gold (or silver), gold having proved itself over a long testing period as the least imperfect monetary standard. The Coinage Act of 1792 is the irrefutable evidence. It defined the dollar as a weight unit of gold and silver.

In this crisis of economic policy, to restore the gold standard *is the one needful thing*: It was not only the *cornerstone* of American financial integrity and balanced budgets.

It was also the trusted monetary standard by which America rose from 13 impoverished colonies by the sea to the leadership of the world. There is an imperishable truth in our American saga. And it is this… as with individuals, so it is with nations…. character is the all-decisive factor. With the restoration of American financial integrity, we can restore American prosperity, and we can restore American leadership.

It is a great lesson of American history that the classical, or the true gold standard – a dollar defined as a weight unit of precious metal – is in fact the constitutional American monetary standard. Let us uphold the Constitution and thereby inaugurate a new industrial revolution, rebuild America's self- respect, and with our constitutional monetary standard, restore American leadership in the global economy.

*"First, the discipline of convertibility would automatically
set the limit on Treasury access to its Federal Reserve credit card.
If the Federal Reserve created more money than participants
in the market wanted to hold, people would get rid of the
inflationary excess by promptly exchanging paper
and credit money for the gold equivalent."*

Chapter Twenty-six

BUDGET COLLAPSE:
TOO MUCH FREE MONEY

The American Spectator blog, December 29, 2011

The super-committee of Congress is the latest group to confess abject defeat by the Treasury budget deficit. Who can be surprised by this total failure? During the past generation, Congress has made as many as fifteen legislative attempts to control government spending – aimed ultimately at a balanced budget. The most notable efforts were those sponsored by the all-time budget hawk, Senator Phil Gramm of Texas. But every administrative and legislative effort by the authorities, no matter how well intentioned, has collapsed. Why is this so?

Nobel economist Milton Friedman believed the solution to the budget deficit problem was to deny Congress tax revenues. So he advised congressmen and presidents to oppose all tax increases – thereby denying bloated government the funds with which to increase spending. But Friedman's advice has failed, too. We know this because marginal tax rates have been reduced from as high as 70 percent in 1964 to 15-20-39 percent in 2011 – depending on the type of income. But congressional spending has nevertheless increased every year – such that, today, only 60 percent of the Federal budget is financed by taxes, the remainder by Treasury debt. Total direct Federal debt is now about equal to total U.S. output.

The intractable budget deficit and the inexorable rise of government spending has a simpler explanation. Congress and the Treasury are in possession of several open-ended charge accounts – "permanent credit card financing" – with no limits. With its charge cards the Treasury can borrow new credit (money) from the banking system – much of what it needs every year to finance the ever-rising budget deficit.

A look at the current Federal Reserve balance sheet shows that the Fed has created about $1.7 trillion of *new* credit (money) with which to purchase Treasury debt. Foreign central banks have created about $2.7 trillion of new credit to purchase U.S. Treasury bonds. This global, electronic, money-printing exercise has financed almost 30 percent of the total direct debt of the U.S. Treasury. In 2002, Ben Bernanke, now chairman of the Fed, did not mince words to describe this process: "[U]nder a fiat (that is, paper) money system, a government (in practice, the central bank in cooperation with other agencies) should always be able to generate increased nominal spending and inflation, even when the short-term nominal interest rate is at zero.... [T]he U.S. government has a technology, called a printing press (or, today, its electronic equivalent), that allows it to produce as many U.S. dollars as it wishes at essentially no cost."

He might have added that these "no cost" dollars, printed by the Fed, are the enablers of the perennial U.S. budget deficit.

But the Fed is not the only credit card used by the Treasury to finance the budget deficit. Because the dollar is the world's reserve currency, foreign central banks also finance U.S. budget deficits (as the custody account of the Fed balance sheet shows). Domestic and foreign commercial banks, too, supply vast amounts of new credit to the U.S. Treasury because domestic, foreign, and international bank regulators, such as the Basel authorities, define U.S. sovereign bonds as high quality assets for which bank reserves are not necessary. Therefore financial institutions can qualify their overleveraged balance sheets by loading up on Treasury securities. Indeed, only 10-20 percent of the total direct debt of the U.S. Treasury is now owned by the non-bank, non-government private market. In a word, given the reserve currency role of the dollar, the Federal Reserve and foreign central banks have been given every institutional incentive to finance the U.S. budget deficit. Beginning with World War I, every monetary discipline has been removed by domestic and international authorities, such that runaway government spending everywhere relies on the ultimate credit card – newly created money in the banking system.

The simplest solution to the government spending problem in Congress is "to tear up" its credit cards. The way to do this is not with ad hoc and unavailing administrative patchworks, all of which are nullified by world banking system credit made available to the U.S. Treasury. Instead, the effective democratic solution is authorized by the United States Constitution – in Article I, Sections 8 and 10 – whereby the control of the supply of dollars is entrusted to the hands of the people – where it stayed for most of American history, especially from 1792 to 1914. This was America's longest period of rapid, non-inflationary, economic growth – almost 4 percent annually, with the budget under control except wartime.

Congress need only mobilize its unique, Article I, constitutional power "to coin money and regulate the value thereof." From 1792 to 1971 Congress defined by law the gold value of the currency such that paper dollars and bank demand deposits were convertible to their gold equivalent – by the people (1792-1914) and/or by governments (1933-1971). Congress should exercise this constitutional power to restore dollar-gold convertibility, because of the proven budgetary and economic growth benefits of a dollar as good as gold.

First, the discipline of convertibility would automatically set the limit on Treasury access to its Federal Reserve credit card. If the Federal Reserve created more money than participants in the market wanted to hold, people would get rid of the inflationary excess by promptly exchanging paper and credit money for the gold equivalent. But under the true gold standard, the Fed and the commercial banks would be required by law to maintain dollar-gold convertibility at the statutory gold-dollar parity – or suffer insolvency. In order to maintain dollar convertibility to gold, the Fed and the commercial banks must reduce the quantity of money and credit, including credit to the Treasury – thus controlling government spending increases and inflation.

Second, the empirical evidence of American economic history also shows that convertibility to gold stabilizes the value of the dollar. The same evidence shows that a stable dollar also stabilizes the general price level over the long run. For example, under the gold standard, the price level in 1914 was at almost exactly the same level as it was in 1879 and in 1834. There was no long-term inflation, even over an 80-year period! But from 1971 – Nixon's termination of dollar-gold convertibility – until 2011, the purchasing power of the dollar (adjusted by the CPI) has fallen 85 percent in a 40-year period.

Third, gold convertibility of the dollar leads to a vast outpouring of savings from inflation hedges such as commodities, farmland, art, antiques – almost anything perceived to be a better store of value than depreciating paper currencies. Stable money also creates incentives to save from income. Combined with the global release of trillions of hoarded, inert, unproductive inflation hedges, convertibility triggers new savings which would pour into the productive investment market. The new investment would give rise to a general economic expansion – through new business, new products, new plant, and equipment – creating thereby a renewed demand for labor to work the expanding production facilities.

The restoration of a dollar worth its weight in gold provides not only a missing and necessary brake on government spending, but a stable dollar supplies the missing steering wheel by which to guide the immense, hoarded savings into long-term productive investment. Dollar convertibility to gold is the simple, institutional financial reform which terminates the fear of rapid inflation – thus transforming unproductive, store-of-value hedges into real investment capital with which to inaugurate a new American era of rapid economic and employment growth.

*"When the government or banks create excess
money to finance deficits, people do not have to hold the
excess money because they recognize the threat of inflation.
A free people will demand redemption of the excess currency
in gold in order to preserve the purchasing power
of their wages and savings."*

Chapter Twenty-seven

JOIN THE ALLIANCE FOR A SOUND DOLLAR

The New York Sun, January 30, 2012

At a recent presidential debate, the Republican candidates discussed a new
Gold Commission much like the one to which President Reagan appointed
Ron Paul and me in 1981. When asked, Jim Grant and I agreed to serve
as co-chairmen of a new gold commission – proposed by Newt Gingrich if
he were elected. Just weeks prior, Senator Rand Paul was reported by *The
Weekly Standard* as having called for just such a commission. We said at the
time that we would serve on a gold commission established by any President
seriously interested in monetary and Federal Reserve reform.

The next gold commission, however, must be different from the Reagan
Gold Commission, the majority of which endorsed the managed paper
dollar and floating-exchange rates. As the two dissenting minority members
of the 1981 commission, Ron Paul and I filed a minority report. We called
for the restoration of the gold standard – that is, a stable dollar defined by
law as a certain weight of gold. The minority report, entitled *The Case for
Gold*, was later republished in book form.

My views on monetary reform have not changed, except that my sense of
urgency is even greater. The Constitution in Article I, Sections 8 and 10,
makes clear that Congress has the full authority "to coin money" from gold
to be the monetary standard of the United States. Since 1792, Congress by
statute established a stable dollar, defined in law as a specific weight unit of

gold, but a 1971 executive order effectively changed that.

Was the original constitutional dollar stable? The fact is that the purchasing power of the convertible or redeemable dollar over an 80-year period under the true gold standard was constant – from 1834 until 1914, save for the Civil War wherein the nation's survival was at stake. This long-term stability of the general price level and of a stable dollar redeemable in gold are necessary results of the simple mechanisms by which the gold standard operates spontaneously.

When the government or banks create excess money to finance deficits, people do not have to hold the excess money because they recognize the threat of inflation. A free people will demand redemption of the excess currency in gold in order to preserve the purchasing power of their wages and savings. But the banks and the government under the gold standard are required by law to maintain the convertibility of the currency when they are losing gold in the process of redeeming the currency.

Thus the banks and the government must reduce the quantity of money and credit in circulation to a level which people and firms in the market desire to hold. Since only undesired excess money causes excess demand for goods which causes inflation, the process of redemption of excess currency for gold extinguishes the excess currency. So stability returns to the general price level. The perennial stability of a dollar convertible to gold also is secured.

Over the long run, all working people want the purchasing power of their savings to remain stable in order to educate their children, to retire in modest comfort, to pass on a modest legacy of stable value. But during the past 40 years of the Fed-managed paper dollar standard, the purchasing power of the dollar adjusted by the CPI has declined a shocking 85 percent.

Consider also that economic and employment growth, during the long American gold standard period, exceeded that of the present paper dollar era. If fully debated during a presidential campaign, the American people now have the economic facts by which to decide between the manipulated paper dollar and the gold-backed dollar.

It is clear that a Gold Commission II must not be an academic exercise, nor the means by which a paper money majority is enabled to deep-six serious consideration of the means by which to reestablish a stable dollar convertible to gold. The purpose of Gold Commission II should be to spell out a plan whereby Congress and the President are enabled, effectively and successfully, to restore the gold-backed dollar.

All relevant evidence and points of view must be considered, but the fundamental purpose of the Gold Commission II should be to render judgment on the era of the declining paper dollar – its consequences, and above all, the remedies for inflation.

Jim Grant and I have recommended that Gold Commission II should focus on the following agenda in order to show how a stable dollar engenders economic growth and tends toward full employment. The purpose of the agenda should be to demonstrate that a dollar convertible to gold is the missing link in presidential growth plans limited to deregulation, tax reform, and balanced budgets.

- American monetary and financial history, and its lessons for the present and the future;
- American monetary policy and the Federal Reserve System after the restoration of dollar convertibility to gold;
- A practical plan to restore convertibility of the dollar to gold; a timetable by which Congress defines the dollar in law as a certain weight unit of gold, to which bank notes and bank demand deposits would be convertible; a plan to include other major nations in a reformed international monetary system based on stable exchange rates in order to increase world trade.

When considering a practical plan to restore convertibility of the dollar to gold, we have recommended that Gold Commission II consider these specific issues:

1) The procedure and transition by which we get from here to there, i.e., from the current paper dollar to the once and future gold dollar.
2) The free market period of price discovery during the transition up to a date certain wherein convertibility of the dollar to gold becomes unrestricted. (Consideration of what happens during the run-up to gold convertibility.)
3) How to include the international community in order effectively to end the inflationary regime of reserve currencies and how best

to include other major nations in a modernized international gold standard? For example, how would America bring other countries into the new monetary system – one in which a non-national global monetary standard, namely gold (not the dollar) is the world's reserve currency?

4) Consideration of the methodology by which Congress and the President should determine the dollar convertibility price of gold (the gold-dollar parity). By using historical and empirical data, demonstrate that the existing world gold stock at the future convertibility price is more than sufficient to maintain the long-term convertibility of the dollar and of all other convertible currencies. (Show also that the zero marginal cost of producing a manipulated paper currency lead to long-run inflation, but the real costs of labor and capital required to produce the gold monetary standard leads to stability of the currency and long-run stability of the price level.)

5) Specify the timetable for restoring the convertibility of the dollar to gold at a value which should last for many generations, giving rise to a new international monetary system, free trade, and economic growth over the long run.

6) To ensure by law the freedom of Americans to use and to save in gold money. The resumption of gold as money in the private and public sector is warranted by the Constitution.

Only convertibility to gold can restore stability and confidence in the convenient use and holding of paper money and bank deposits without government subsidies.

Having served with Ron Paul on Reagan's Gold Commission in 1981 and having testified recently before his monetary subcommittee, I know firsthand what a hero Dr. Paul has been in the campaign for sound money. The entire nation now knows that Dr. Paul, as a presidential candidate, continues to make the case for the gold standard.

Newt Gingrich, to his credit, has added his voice to the alliance for sound money. Let us hope that Governor Mitt Romney and Senator Rick Santorum will join the alliance and help to incorporate a restoration of a sound dollar into the Republican Platform of 2012. Who knows? Even a gold Democrat might emerge to pick up the mantle of President Grover Cleveland, a famous gold Democrat, who emphasized the centrality of a sound, stable, constitutional gold dollar.

Recent polling suggests that the American people sense the need for a dollar as good as gold. Now the Republican candidates have the opportunity to fulfill that need, win the presidential election, and restore sound money and economic growth.

"American economic reconstruction, grounded by the true gold standard, would lead to a resurgence of rapid economic growth, empowered by renewed confidence born of market expectations of a stable long-term price level. With American leadership, other nations would follow."

Chapter Twenty-eight

FIGHT THE FIAT

The American Spectator, July-August 2012

The Consequences of Disorder

The economic crisis we endure today is only the latest chapter in the century-long struggle to restore financial order in world markets – a struggle whose outcome is inextricably bound up with U.S. prosperity and the promise of the American way of life.

As we think through the consequences of financial disorder, what come to mind are the economic heresies of fascism and bolshevism, and the catastrophic world wars of the 20th century. These historical episodes compel us to remember that floating-exchange rates and competitive currency wars became the occasion for violent social disorder and revolutionary civil strife in the first half of the 20th century. They remind us that natural resource rivalry, monetary depreciation, mercantilism, and war clouds have appeared together from time immemorial.

The monetary disorder and national currency wars of that era are now being repeated in our own time, and have again led to social disorder and pervasive civil strife. I cite only one example among legions. The recent "Arab spring," a revolutionary upheaval of the suppressed Islamic poor and middle class, was triggered by a vast food and fuel inflation, transmitted to the dollarized world commodity markets by hyper-expansive Federal Reserve monetary policy during 2008-2011. Huge price increases for necessities penetrated into the heart of all subsistence economies – in this case, North Africa. Because the dollar is the official reserve currency of the world trading system, when the Fed creates excess credit to bail out the banks and the U.S. government deficit, it exports some of the excess liquidity abroad, igniting basic commodity inflation and the social strife this engenders. At home, the same rising prices of food, fuel, and other basic needs impoverish those on fixed incomes. Moreover, they lower the standard of living of the middle class, held back by wages and salaries that always lag rising prices.

Even more ominous, the surge of contemporary mercantilism and competitive currency depreciations – initiated by monetary authorities worldwide – brings to mind the national rivalries among the Great Powers between World War I and World War II. Amidst financial disorder, floating-exchange rates, and beggar-thy-neighbor policies during the interwar period of 1918-1940, civilization witnessed the rise of imperial Japan, Mussolini, and Hitler. But the 1920s had begun with great hope, including overwhelming confidence in the primacy of central banking, led by Benjamin Strong of the Federal Reserve System and Montague Norman of the Bank of England. The unrestrained boom of the 1920s, rising on a flood tide of central bank credit – based on the reserve currency role of the dollar and the pound – led to the brief illusion of permanent prosperity. That "new era" ended in austerity, currency chaos, autarky, depression, and world war.

Thus, it becomes increasingly urgent, if we might learn from the past, to restore international monetary order now, with reforms to re-establish a stable dollar and stable exchange rates. The United States is still able to set the example for the world to emulate. Indeed, the major powers publicly endorse international monetary reform. All seem to sense that only with stable exchange rates can the world trading community rebuild global incentives for equitable, balanced, growing world trade – and, with these incentives, create the conditions for global growth and rising standards of living.

Now comes the perennial questions: How, precisely, does the United States once again establish a stable dollar? How do the United States and other countries get from "here" to "there" – that is, from the anarchy of floating-paper currencies to stable exchange rates based on an impartial, non-national monetary standard? These questions have been debated at crucial junctures over the last century: before and after the creation of the Federal Reserve System in 1913; after the catastrophe of World War I; after Franklin Roosevelt in 1933 expropriated and nationalized all American citizens' gold holdings; after Richard Nixon severed the last weak link between the dollar and its gold backing in 1971.

Recently, the same debate intensified after the Great Recession of 2007-2009, marked as it was by wild exchange rate and currency instability. But it was the vast, inequitable, financial subsidies – provided by the Federal Reserve System and the U.S. Treasury to an irresponsible, often insolvent, and cartelized world banking system – that sparked national outrage. In free markets, with responsible agents, insolvency should entail bankruptcy. Those who earn the profits in a free market must themselves endure the losses. Without the discipline of bankruptcy, crony capitalism must result – with the taxpayer providing the subsidies.

What lessons might we learn from American financial history? Consider the fact that from 1792 until 1971, the dollar was defined in law as a weight unit of gold (and/or silver). The last vestige of convertibility of the dollar into gold was abolished by President Nixon's executive order on August 15, 1971. Since then, the dollar has depreciated dramatically, to the point that it is now worth a mere 15 pennies, adjusted by the CPI. After generations of manipulated paper- or credit-based floating currencies – which ignite the currency wars of our own era – it has become increasingly clear that free trade without stable exchange rates is a fantasy.

It is true that the post-World War II, dollarized Bretton Woods system, inaugurated in 1944, gave rise to a new era of free trade; but it was free trade maintained and subsidized by the especially open market of the United States. After World War II, the United States controlled 50 percent of world output. Thus, the U.S. dollar became the sole acceptable reserve currency with which to conduct international trade – displacing gold by international agreement at Bretton Woods. The Bretton Woods system caused the dollar to become substantially overvalued as a result of worldwide excess dollar demand for transactions and foreign official reserve holdings. The overvaluation of the dollar was intensified by post-World War II currency depreciations and inflationary fiscal and monetary policies of other major countries.

The European currencies were finally stabilized and made convertible on current account in 1959 through the monetary reform of the European Payments Union. But the dollar remained overvalued as the sole official reserve currency of the Bretton Woods monetary regime (of 1944-1971). Overvaluation of the dollar was compounded by excessive Federal Reserve money expansion within the pegged currency system of Bretton Woods, thus systematically raising the cost and price level in America relative to other major currencies. This happens because the Federal Reserve creates money to purchase Treasury debt securities, a process which finances the U.S. budget deficit. But the newly created money on behalf of Treasury spending is not associated with the production of new goods. Thus total demand exceeds total supply at prevailing prices. Prices rise (inflation), followed by rising costs. American goods thereby become increasingly uncompetitive in world markets. After the collapse of the dollar-based Bretton Woods system, floating-pegged exchange rates ensued (1973-2012).

Compared to the United States, both developed and developing countries to this very day have aggressively protected their markets with undervalued currencies, quotas, high tariffs, and discriminatory regulations – China most egregiously in recent years, Japan earlier. This arrangement has characterized the world trading system not only under Bretton Woods but also amidst the floating-pegged currency arrangements of today. Successive American administrations, all committed to free trade, made the U.S. open market an easy target for mercantilist nations worldwide. The good intentions of American free traders have never been fully reciprocated. As a result, developing countries have mobilized undervalued currencies with which to build growing export machines, and without giving commensurate trade reciprocity to the United States – the General Agreement on Tariffs and Trade (GATT) and World Trade Organization (WTO) notwithstanding.

The World Dollar Standard
The dollar's role as an official reserve currency has enormously impacted the U.S. economy. Net U.S. investment abroad is the value of assets and claims held by U.S. residents and their government abroad, minus the assets and claims foreigners and their governments own in the United States. In

1980, net U.S. international investment was 10 percent of GDP. In 2010, it was negative 20 percent of GDP. The empirical data show that the entire shift from positive to negative is accounted for by the official, accumulated, U.S. balance-of-payments deficit.

In a nutshell, since World War II, free trade has often been at the expense of U.S. businesses, manufacturing, and labor. The problem of dollar overvaluation was compounded not only by the reserve currency role of the dollar, but also by the perennial U.S. budget deficit, increasingly financed by Federal Reserve money and credit creation. But the U.S. budget deficit is financed not only by the Federal Reserve and the banking system, but also by foreign government purchases of U.S. Treasury debt which is held as official national reserves. China and Japan, two major beneficiaries of U.S. trade and budget deficits, hold official reserves equal to approximately $2 trillion of U.S. government related debt. The authorities, mesmerized by neo-Keynesian mythology, do not understand that exponentially growing U.S. budget deficits absorb a huge fraction of domestic production, which would otherwise be available for export sales to the global market. Proceeds from these exports, growing faster than payments for imports, could then be used to settle U.S. balance-of-payments deficits, thereby reducing U.S. debt.

Let us remind ourselves that after World War I, the reserve currency system, based on the pound and the dollar, was liquidated in total panic (1929-1933), turning a cyclical recession into the Great Depression. Today we have relearned the lesson, as expansive Federal Reserve money creation has combined with the official reserve currency role of the dollar to cause massive credit, commodity, and general price inflation worldwide. (The purchasing power of the 1950 dollar adjusted by the CPI has declined over 90 percent.) But, like Banquo's ghost, deflation and unemployment still haunt us, despite the Greenspan-Bernanke era of quantitative easing (often known as money-printing). That is because as soon as Fed money printing slows down, prices tend to fall, with the threat of deflation and unemployment (2007-2012) coming to preoccupy the financial authorities. The inflation-deflation cycle is systemic, caused by perennial budget deficits and unhinged Federal Reserve stop-go monetary policies.

The scientific method and economic history teach us that under similar conditions, similar causes tend to produce similar effects. The saying makes the point: "History never repeats itself, but it often rhymes." We know that reserve currency systems have been tested by the market, and that they have failed in the past (e.g., Sterling in 1931; the Bretton Woods dollar in 1971). And the timing of their collapse cannot be accurately predicted. But now is the moment to prepare a program of monetary reform.

How, therefore, may America now lead other nations toward an equitable world trading system based on a balanced monetary order, a disciplined Federal Reserve, balanced budgets, stable exchange rates, and reciprocal free trade inuring to the mutual benefit of all? How do leading nations stage the resumption of a modernized true gold standard, ruling out the escalating debt and leverage engendered by the perversities of floating-exchange rates and official reserve currencies?

America at the Crossroads

For the purpose of true monetary reform, we have an example from the only available laboratory of monetary policy: human history (surely a better source than abstract equations imported from the blackboards of Princeton or the University of Chicago). The empirical data show that the classical gold standard (1879-1914) had its imperfections, but was the least imperfect monetary system of the last two centuries, perhaps even of the past millennium. At the end of the entire period (1879-1914), the general price level was almost exactly where it began. Overall economic growth was the equal of any period since the birth of the Republic.

Given the gravity of world financial disorder, America must take one of two divergent roads. She may persist on the road of soft indulgence afforded by the unstable dollar's official reserve currency role. It is true that the absolute dominance of the dollar has gradually diminished since World War II, given the rise of Asia and Europe. Still, the world dollar standard could continue for another generation because of the scale and liquidity of the dollarized markets across the globe. Consider the extraordinary fact that almost two-thirds of world trade, not including that of the United States, is still transacted in dollars. About 75 percent of world commodity markets are still settled primarily in dollars. U.S. dollar financial markets are the repositories for as much as 5 to 6 trillion of foreign reserves, not easily invested elsewhere. In the service of unrestrained U.S. politicians, the world reserve currency role of the dollar underwrites the twin budget and balance-of-payments deficits, as well as the exponential increase of U.S. debt – which must lead, in the absence of monetary reform, to national insolvency. This "exorbitant privilege" – that is, the dollar's role as the world's primary reserve currency – does mislead American authorities, policy makers, and academic economists to persist in rationalizing the reserve currency privilege of the dollar as a boon instead of a deadly economic malignancy.

On the other hand, far-seeing American leaders could acknowledge that the dollar's official reserve currency role is an insupportable burden instead of a privilege. It is a burden because 50 years of supplying official reserves to the world necessarily entails the uncontrolled increase of dollar debt, ultimately financed by Federal Reserve credit expansion, foreign central banks, and the global banking system as a whole. Moreover, dollar deficits, monetized by the Fed and foreign banking authorities, are the fundamental cause of 50 years of global inflation. Let me repeat that the purchasing power of the post-World War II dollar has shriveled to less than a dime. Finally, the steady dissipation of the U.S. international investment position – assets and claims in other countries owned by the United States, minus foreign liabilities – has led to the decline in American international competitiveness.

Recently, as much as 60 percent of the U.S. budget deficit has been financed by money and credit conjured into existence by the Federal Reserve. But these newly created dollars are not associated with new production of real goods and services. Under such market circumstances, total demand must exceed total supply, expressed by price increases in one sector of the world economy, such as oil and commodities (2003-2011), internet stocks (1995-2000), or real estate (2004-2007). Fed credit expansion unassociated with the production of new goods and services – that is, the creation of demand without supply – is the hidden inflationary mechanism behind the world dollar disease. However, when the Fed tightens credit abruptly and substantially, as in 2006, the process is reversed with deflationary consequences (2007-2009).

Moreover, some Fed-created excess dollars flood abroad, sustaining the perennial U.S. balance-of-payments deficit. But the excess dollars going abroad are not inert. They are purchased by foreign central banks against the issue of their newly created domestic money, most prominently today by China in the form of new yuan. Global purchasing power is thereby augmented in this case by new issues of yuan – also unassociated with the production of new goods. The Chinese and other foreign central banks promptly reinvest the accumulated dollar reserves in U.S. Treasurys, financing the U.S. budget deficit; these foreign dollar reserves also finance the U.S. balance-of-payments deficit and the inordinate personal consumption debt of U.S. residents.

Because of the official reserve currency role of the dollar, everything carries on as if there were no U.S. deficits. There is little compelling incentive for the U.S. government – or its congressional budget masters or the consumer holding the ubiquitous credit card – to adjust. In a word, the official reserve currency role of the dollar enables America to buy without paying. Worse yet, the necessary adjustment mechanism needed to rebalance world trade has been permanently jammed, immobilized.

If American leaders continue to choose rising debt and deficits financed by the Fed, and the reserve-currency dream world in the United States may carry on for many years before its collapse. But collapse is inevitable.

Monetary Reconstruction

The choice is ours. Indeed, this election may be our last chance. If American leaders embrace true monetary reform, they will reject the siren song of the reserve currency's exorbitant privilege. They will acknowledge the insupportable burden of the dollar's official reserve currency role. They will plan now for the termination and windup of the dollar's reserve currency role. They will plan to restore dollar convertibility, defining the dollar by statue as a certain weight of gold, and then propose gold as the missing and impartial, global balance wheel by which to settle residual balance-of-payments deficits among nations and currency areas. A balanced budget amendment to the U.S. Constitution should follow.

Moreover, such a monetary order, based on convertibility of the dollar to gold, free of government manipulation, provides an indispensable rule for the conduct of Federal Reserve System monetary policy – bringing to bear rule-based market discipline to stabilize the Fed's monetary policy. Domestically, the institutional discipline of dollar-convertibility would limit the Fed's unrestrained discretion to print money, finance the government budget deficit, and bail out the cartelized banking system. Under dollar convertibility, if the Fed creates too much money, causing inflation, the people are free to redeem currency for gold at a price set by law. Too great a loss of gold would threaten the solvency of the banks. Thus, the Fed and the banking system would be forced to reduce the growth of money and credit, thereby maintaining convertibility and containing inflation. Conversely, deflationary tendencies could be contained by Federal Reserve credit – made available at market rates on high-quality collateral – without threatening currency convertibility.

To choose true monetary reform and balanced budgets is to embrace not only the Constitution, but also the nation's historic financial policy that led to world leadership. Article I, Sections 8 and 10 of the United States Constitution enabled the monetary reconstruction of the American Republic at the founding on the bedrock of a gold dollar. The Constitution mandates that only Congress has the power "to coin money and regulate the value thereof." The Constitution prohibits the states from making anything but "gold and silver a legal tender." Shorn of the crushing weight of trade disadvantages caused by inflation and the accumulating debt and deficits – originating in budgetary excess and the reserve currency role of the dollar – America could again become Prometheus unbound.

American economic reconstruction, grounded by the true gold standard, would lead to a resurgence of rapid economic growth, empowered by renewed confidence born of market expectations of a stable long-term price level. With American leadership, other nations would follow. By re-establishing an effective and equitable international adjustment mechanism, international monetary convertibility to gold would end perennial deficits, manipulated currencies, and the threat of currency wars among the major nations.

The true gold standard – that is, a dollar convertible by statute to a specific weight of gold, joined to the windup of the official reserve currency role of the dollar – would make vast sums of money available for long-term productive investment. With a stable long-term price level, speculators worldwide would abandon unproductive inflation hedges. This dishoarding would yield immense, liquid savings productive investment in real goods and services. Equity and true capital investment would gradually displace debt and leverage. Under conditions of stable money and stable exchange rates, savings would be redeployed by entrepreneurs and investors in new and innovative plants, technology, and equipment – minimizing unemployment, as skilled and unskilled workers are hired to work the new facilities. The export production machine of the United States would be reoriented to produce for the world market, which would engage all the positive and equitable effects of economies of scale and free trade.

This is the true road of American monetary and economic reconstruction. Let us begin the great work before us.

"The most important economic and monetary issue before the Congress is how, through institutional reform of the Fed and the monetary system, to solve this Fed-created monetary problem of cyclical booms and busts – largely the results of unrestrained Fed interest rate manipulation and quantitative easing."

CODA

Testimony Prepared for U.S. House Subcommittee on Domestic Monetary Policy and Technology,
September 21, 2012

I. Preface: The Problem of Federal Reserve Manipulation of Interest Rates: What is the Solution?

The Federal Reserve System has in fact manipulated interest rates since the first year of Federal Reserve operations in 1914. Professor Allan Meltzer's magisterial, three-volume history of the Fed is the definitive witness to unrestrained Federal Reserve credit operations and their consequences. The problems created by Fed interest rate manipulation are very similar to the problems of government wage and price controls.

During the 1920s, the Federal Reserve collaborated with the Bank of England in suppressing interest rates, leading to the worldwide stock market boom and 1929 crash. Excessive Fed credit expansion and interest rate manipulation between 1996 and 1999 led to the wild tech-stock market boom during those years, and the subsequent collapse of the stock market between 2000 and 2002. The Fed suppression of interest rates between 2002 and 2005 led to the stock market, commodity, and real estate boom during those years; then the rise of interest rates, engineered by the Fed, causing an inverted yield curve; followed by the financial and economic collapse of 2008.

The extravagant and unprecedented Fed credit policy of quantitative easing, now intensified by QEIII announced Thursday, September 13, is one more extraordinary experiment in central bank interest rate and credit manipulation (money printing). These episodes of interest rate suppression and excessive Fed credit expansion – with effects similar to wage and price controls – have well-studied precedents in earlier economic and financial history. For example, the effects of the President Nixon-Arthur Burns (chairman of the Fed) credit expansion (1970-1973); and their wage and price controls of 1972 led to the collapse of financial markets in 1973 and 1974, and the worst economic decade in American history since the Great Depression. Indeed, during the late 1970s, the highest interest rates and inflation in American history were the ultimate result of previous Federal Reserve credit expansion, and government wage and price controls. The effects of substantial Fed interest rate suppression and credit expansion have, in the end, led to inflation of food prices – or oil, or natural resources, or real estate, or equities; or in the 1970s consumer price inflation – followed by a fall.

The most important economic and monetary issue before the Congress is how, through institutional reform of the Fed and the monetary system, to solve this Fed-created monetary problem of cyclical booms and busts – largely the results of unrestrained Fed interest rate manipulation and quantitative easing (money printing).

In my oral testimony and statement, I shall briefly focus on the problems caused by Federal Reserve interest rate manipulation and quantitative easing – more so on the solution to the problem. Herewith, in my longer, written testimony, I shall concentrate on a detailed solution to the problem.

II. Oral Statement for the Record

Mr. Chairman:

James Grant has described the consequences of Federal Reserve quantitative easing and interest rate suppression and manipulation. From Mr. Grant's analysis, one concludes that the Fed's unlimited power to purchase Treasury debt and financial market securities not only funds the Treasury deficit with newly printed money; but the Fed's market intervention process also makes of the financial class, a special interest group of privileged investors and speculators because of special access to near-zero interest rates at the Fed, while middle-income credit card users pay upwards of 20 percent. A well-connected financial class, subsidized by the Federal Reserve, is a crucial cause of increasing inequality of wealth in America. In this regard, I cite only one fact for the Monetary Subcommittee to contemplate: Since the termination of dollar convertibility to gold in 1971, the financial sector has doubled in size as a share of the American economy; but the manufacturing sector has been cut in half. Only a comprehensive reform of the Fed and termination of the reserve currency role of the dollar will arrest this trend.

In 2002, Mr. Bernanke described the Fed's extraordinary power to create new money and credit in our present financial regime of inconvertible paper money and inconvertible bank deposit money. I quote Bernanke:

> "Under a fiat (that is, paper) money system, a government (in practice, the central bank in cooperation with other agencies) should always be able to generate increased nominal spending and inflation, even when the short-term nominal interest rate is at zero. The U.S. government has a technology, Bernanke says called a printing press (or, today, its electronic equivalent), that allows it to produce as many U.S. dollars as it wishes at essentially no cost."

In effect, as James Grant wrote elsewhere, the Fed is not only the American central bank but, with this exalted power to print money, the Fed is now the government's central planner.

During the Volcker years from 1979 to 1987, Fed interest rate manipulation was justified as the means to end inflation. By 1994, employment as a Fed target had all but disappeared from the minutes of Fed meetings. Now in 2012, despite inflation being again on the rise, employment is, as a practical matter, the sole target of quantitative easing.

The Fed, and its apologists in the media and the academy, justify quantitative easing and its unlimited scope and duration, as the way to restore economic growth – surely an extraconstitutional form of fiscal spending through Federal Reserve capital allocation. But so soon as one examines the Fed balance sheet, which few politicians do, one sees that the Fed primarily buys Treasury securities and mortgage-backed securities, in effect a subsidy by which to finance the government deficit and to refinance bank balance sheets, that is to say, the promotion of more financial and consumption-sector growth. In a word, quantitative easing is the most pernicious form of "trickle-down economics".

The problem of the American economy is neither underconsumption, nor underbanking. The problem is the lack of rapidly growing investment in human capital, and in domestic production and manufacturing. Investment is the *necessary* means by which to enable our producers to lead in both domestic and global markets. It is rapidly increasing investment and production growth which begets employment growth, and with it, healthy, unsubsidized consumption growth – not transfer payments.

It is a truth of economic theory and practice that rising personal and family real income grows from increasing per capita investment in human capital, innovative businesses, new plant, and equipment. So, the question is in reforming the Fed, how can our runaway central bank be harnessed by the financial markets to target the goal of economic growth through increased productive investment, not the promotion of consumption and Treasury deficit funding by means of interest rate manipulation and quantitative easing? The answer is transparent – the Congress of the United States has the exclusive constitutional power (under Article I, Sections 8 and 10) not only to establish the definition of the dollar; but Congress also has the power to define by statute the eligible collateral that the Federal Reserve may buy and hold against the issue of new money and credit. Thus, a simple congressional statute – defining sound commercial loans as the primary eligible collateral for discounts and new credit from the Fed – would have two primary effects.

First, it should *rule out* Fed purchases of Treasuries, thus requiring the government to finance its deficits not with newly printed Fed money, but instead in the open market away from the banks. *Second*, the Fed would then become a growth-oriented central bank by which to finance productive business loans, encouraging thereby commercial banks, themselves, to make loans to solvent businesses in order to sustain economic and employment growth. Commercial banks would focus on production and commercial loans because solvent business loans, instead of U.S. Treasuries, could then be used by commercial banks as the *primary* eligible collateral by which to secure credit from the Fed as the lender of last resort. In a word, Treasury subsidies by the Fed should be replaced by productive business loans oriented toward economic and employment growth.

Mr. Chairman, this simple, proposed reform of Fed operations was the very monetary policy insisted upon by Carter Glass, a leading Democrat, who was the chief sponsor of the Federal Reserve Act of 1913. The congressional legislative leaders who created the Federal Reserve Act of 1913 designed the Fed to enable steady commercial investment and employment growth. The Federal Reserve Act was also designed explicitly to uphold and maintain a dollar convertible to gold in order to maintain a reasonably stable, general price level. Such a congressional reform of the Fed, *today*, consistent with the original Federal Reserve Act, would require no further legislative mandate to sustain employment growth and to rule out systemic inflation and deflation.

Today, the Fed reiterates at every meeting that the central bank must manage interest rates to fulfill a congressional mandate to maintain reasonable price stability and reasonably full employment. But the best way to do this is to remobilize the express intent *and* the techniques of the original Federal Reserve Act, namely the statutory requirement that the Fed uphold the classical gold standard; and, as was intended by the original Federal Reserve Act, to substitute commercial market credit for Treasury debt as the primary eligible collateral for bank loans from the lender of last resort, the Federal Reserve System.

Mr. Chairman, may I say, with respect, Congress has *defaulted* to the Federal Reserve System its sole and solemn constitutional authority to define and to regulate the value of the dollar, *and* to define the vital economic use of eligible collateral by which to obtain productive business credit from the Federal Reserve System.

It does not have to be this way. Thank you very much.

III. A Road to Prosperity: The Case for a Modernized Gold Standard

Gold, a fundamental, metallic element of the earth's constitution, exhibits unique properties that enabled it, during two millennia of market testing, to emerge as a universally accepted store of value and medium of exchange, not least because it could sustain purchasing power over the long run against a standard assortment of goods and services. Rarely considered in monetary debates, these natural properties of gold caused it to prevail as a stable monetary standard, the most marketable means by which trading peoples worldwide could make trustworthy direct and indirect exchanges for all other articles of wealth.

The preference of tribal cultures, as well as ancient and modern civilizations, to use gold as money was no mere accident of history. Nor has this natural, historical, and global preference for gold as a store of value and standard of measure been easily purged by academic theory and government fiat.

Gold, by its intrinsic nature, is durable, homogenous, fungible, imperishable, indestructible, and malleable. It has a relatively low melting point, facilitating coined money. It is portable and can be readily transported from place to place. Gold money can be safely stored at very low cost, and then exchanged for monetary certificates, bank deposits, and notes – convertible bills of exchange that efficiently extended the gold standard worldwide.

Like paper money, gold is almost infinitely divisible into smaller denominations. But paper money has a marginal production cost near-zero. Producing gold money, like other articles of wealth, requires real labor and capital.

This investment of real labor and capital gives gold an objectively grounded value on which to base proportional exchanges – a value that can be compared to that invested in producing a unit of any product or service. Prices for goods and services always vary with subjective preferences. But the real costs of production persist as an underlying market-price regulator. Despite subjective preferences, a mutual exchange of real money – a gold monetary unit – for a good or service is a transparent, proportional, equitable exchange, grounded by real costs of production, namely labor, capital, and natural resources.

In contrast, almost no marginal labor or capital is required to produce an additional unit of paper money. Thus, legal tender paper money is subject only to quantitative control and the discretion of political authorities. Historical evidence shows that inconvertible paper money is overproduced, tending always toward depreciation and inflation, interrupted by bouts of austerity and deflation. Over the long run, government-forced and spurious paper money has not maintained equitable exchanges between labor and capital. Market exchanges based on depreciating paper money and floating paper currencies issued through the banking system always lead to speculative privilege of insiders, generally the financial class.

Because of its imperishability and density of value per weight unit, gold can be held and stored (saved) permanently at incidental carrying costs. Precious metal monetary tokens (gold and silver) survived millennia of experiments with inferior alternatives such as shells, grains, cattle, tobacco, base metals, and many others. These alternatives are either consumable, perishable, bulky, or of insufficient value for large-scale commercial exchange over long distances. For example, perishables like wheat or cattle are not storable for long periods at very low cost; nor are they portable cheaply over long distances to exchange for other goods; nor are they useful and efficient to settle short- and long-term debts promptly.

Through a process of long-term economic evolution in tribal, inter-regional, and national trading markets, gold's natural properties were discovered and utilized in almost all cultures. Gold thus became universally marketable and acceptable as the optimum long-term store of value, uniform standard of commercial measure, and durable medium of exchange. Universal marketability and acceptability is a hallmark of global money. Silver, with its much lower value per unit of weight, was the suboptimal monetary metal of modern civilization, exhibiting many but not all of the properties required for large-scale international exchange.

Merchants, bankers, farmers, and laborers may not have consciously considered these facts, but over the long run, they behaved as if they did. Thus, gold became an unimpeachable, universally accepted currency, to be held as reserves and passed on as a reliable store of future purchasing power. People, even hostile nations, freely accepted gold, a non-national currency, from one another in exchange for other goods, even as they rejected the sovereign risk of holding national currencies as their exclusive reserves. All who cherished the value of their saved labor – pensioners, working people, those on fixed incomes – came to rely on the gold monetary standard as a stable, long-term proxy for goods and services to be purchased later, perhaps much later.

Today's global stock of aboveground gold in all its forms is approximately
5 to 6 billion ounces, perhaps more – close to one ounce per capita of the
world population. Because of gold's lasting value from time immemorial,
and the human incentive to conserve all scarce resources, these 5 to 6 billion
ounces represent most of the gold ever produced. Yet the aboveground gold
stock today may be enclosed in a cube of approximately 70 feet on each
side. Gold may be easily converted to substantial amounts of monetary coin
to underwrite convertible paper money and bank deposits or convenient
exchange in the market.

Moreover, the empirical data demonstrate that the stock of aboveground
gold has grown for centuries in direct proportion to the growth of
population and output per capita. The average, annual, long-run growth of
the stock of gold in the modern world is approximately 1.5 percent. This
remarkable fact accounts for the unique, long-run stability of its purchasing
power. New output of gold money, joined to its rate of turnover, is
sufficient for both economic growth and long-run stability of the general
price level, as modest but regular output of gold does not affect the relative
value of the large existing stock.

This hidden but crucial commercial equation of the social order was a
fundamental reason why the true gold standard, i.e., gold-based money,
became the foundation of the monetary institutions of modern civilization.
Gold-based money not only stabilized the long-term price level, but its
network effects also integrated and compounded the rapid growth of
the advanced, competitive trading nations of the Western world during
the Industrial Revolution. For the purpose of global trade, exchange
and investment currencies convertible to the universally acceptable gold
monetary standard had engirdled the earth by the beginning of the 20th
century.

As the technology and productivity of the payments mechanism evolved,
banknotes and checking account deposits (among other credit and transfer
systems), came into modern circulation as substitutes for physical, monetary
tokens. But these banknotes and checks derived and sustained their value
from the fact that everyone knew they were credit instruments convertible
to gold. Still, actual gold transfers were used to settle residual balance-of-
payments deficits among nations, a necessary and efficient international

adjustment mechanism by which to rebalance domestic and international trade and exchange.

Despite legal tender inconvertible paper money and the disabilities presently imposed on gold by the political authorities, gold retains the same inherent properties that make it the least imperfect monetary standard. Indeed, all inconvertible paper money systems, based on contemporary fractional reserve banking, use the vestigial forms but not the substance of their original convertible currency systems.

In sum, gold is natural currency, not least because it provides in a single, indestructible substance the primary functions of money – i.e., a standard unit of account, a stable medium of exchange, a stable store of value, and a stable deferred means of payment. By reason of these facts, the market guided the authorities over time to bestow on gold coin the status of an official monetary standard. Gold money was, moreover, endowed by nature with profound but simple national and international networking effects, the digital standard by which free prices could be communicated worldwide. Thus, the gold standard exhibited natural economies of global information scale, a necessary virtue in the present electronic age. The adoption of the gold standard by the major trading nations in the 19th century led to a radical reduction in the settlement costs of international trade and transactions, a crucial confidence and reliability factor stimulating an unparalleled boom in trade that was constantly and promptly rebalanced by residual deficit settlements in gold.

A Just Social Order and Economic Growth

To choose or to reject the true gold standard is to decide between two fundamental options: on the one hand, a free, just, stable, and objective monetary order; and on the other, manipulated, inconvertible paper money, the fundamental cause of a casino culture of speculation and crony capitalism, and the incipient financial anarchy and inequality it engenders.

Restoration of a dollar convertible to gold would rebuild a necessary financial incentive for real, long-term, economic growth by encouraging saving, investment, entrepreneurial innovation, and capital allocation in productive facilities. Thus would convertibility lead to rising employment and wages. Economic growth would be underwritten by a stable, long-term price level, reinforced domestically by a rule-based, commercial and central banking system subject to convertibility, and internationally by exchange rates mutually convertible to gold. Consider the past decade of hyper-managed paper currencies and manipulated floating-exchange rates wherein American annual economic growth fell to an anemic 1.7 percent. Under the classical gold standard (1879-1914), U.S. economic growth averaged 3 to 4 percent annually, the equal of any period in American history.

Different growth rates are not mere accidents of history. The gold dollar, or true gold standard, underwrites, among other things, just and lasting compensation, and purchasing power for workers, savers, investors, and entrepreneurs. It prevents massive, recurring distortions in relative prices created by manipulated paper currencies and floating-exchange rates, which misallocate scarce resources. It suppresses the incentives for pure financial speculation, everywhere encouraged under manipulated paper currencies and floating-exchange rates. It rules out the "exorbitant privilege" and insupportable burden of official reserve currencies, such as the dollar and the euro. It limits and regulates, along with bankruptcy rules, the abuse of fractional reserve banking that is commonplace under inconvertible paper-money systems. It minimizes the enormous premium exacted by the banker and broker establishment in the purchase and sale of volatile foreign exchange.

Moreover, the lawfully defined gold content of a stable currency encourages long-term lending and investment, stimulating more reliance on equity, less on leverage and debt. With currencies convertible to gold, long-term lenders receive in turn, say after 30 years, similar purchasing power compared to the capital or credit they surrendered to the borrowers. (Convertibility thus encourages stable, long-run domestic and international growth, not the austerity engendered by deficits.)

A dollar legally convertible to gold, reinforced by effective bankruptcy laws, sustains economic justice, regulating and disciplining speculative capital, and restraining political and banking authorities such that they cannot lawfully depreciate the present value or the long-term purchasing power of lagging dollar wages, savings, pensions, and fixed incomes. Nor under the sustained, legal restraint of convertibility can governments ignite major, long-run, credit and paper money inflations with their subsequent debt deflations. Under the gold standard, the penalty for excessive corporate and banking leverage is insolvency and bankruptcy. As the profits belong to the owners, so should the losses. Bankruptcy of insolvent firms shields the taxpayer from the burden of government bailouts. Under the rule-based gold standard in a free-market order, managers, stockholders, and bondholders must bear the responsibility for insolvency.

A stable dollar, convertible to gold, leads to increased saving not only from income, but also from dishoarding, a fact often neglected by economists. Dishoarding means releasing a vast reservoir of savings previously held in hedges such as commodities, antiques, art, jewelry, farmland, or other items purchased to protect against the ravages of inflation. These trillions of savings, imprisoned in hedging vehicles by uncertainty and inflation, are induced out of hedges, and the capital is then supplied in the market to entrepreneurs, business managers, and households who would create new income-generating investment in production facilities, thereby leading to increased employment and productivity. On the other hand, central bank subsidies to government and subsidized consumption, both enabled by inconvertible paper and credit money, lead – through deficit financing, transfer payments, paper money fiscal and monetary stimulation – to disinvestment, debt financing, speculative privilege, and growing inequality of wealth.

It is rarely considered by conventional academic opinion that the long-term stability of a rule-based currency convertible to gold brings about a major mutation in human behavior. In a free market, every able-bodied person and firm must first make a supply before making a demand. This principle effectively alters human conduct. It encourages production before consumption, balances supply and demand, rules out inflation, maintains balanced international trade, and upholds the framework for economic growth and stable money. In a free market and its banking system, grounded by the rule of convertibility to gold, new money and credit may be prudently issued only against new production or additional supply for the market, thus maintaining equilibrium between total demand and total supply. Inflation is thereby ruled out. Moreover, worldwide hoarding of real assets, caused by government overissue of paper money, would come to an end.

The irony of the gold standard and currency convertibility is that it ends speculation in gold. It restores the incentive to use and hold convenient, convertible paper currency and other gold-convertible cash balances. Thus can the road to economic growth, rising real wages, and growing employment be rebuilt on the durable foundation of a free monetary order – that is, money free from government manipulation.

Rebalancing the Global Economy

The overall balance-of-payments of a country, or a currency area, is in deficit when more money is paid abroad than received; a surplus occurs when more money is received than paid abroad. The United States, because of the dollar's role as the reserve currency of the world, has experienced an overall balance-of-payments deficit most of the past half-century and, over that full period, systemic inflation.

Under both the Bretton Woods agreement (1944-1971) and the subsequent floating, dollar-based, global reserve currency system, the U.S. budget and balance-of-payments deficits have been financed substantially by U.S. government trust funds, the Federal Reserve, and foreign purchases of dollars abroad. Since 2008, these deficits have been accompanied by unprecedented quantitative easing, a euphemism for large-scale central bank money and credit creation (or "money printing"). By this means the Fed finances not only the government budget and balance-of-payments deficits, but also overleveraged banks, insolvent debtors, and other wards of the state. The issue of new money by the central bank unaccompanied by the production of new goods and services leads ultimately to inflation because total demand in the market will exceed total supply.

With the dollar as the reserve currency, the U.S. balance-of-payments deficit causes Fed-created dollars to rush abroad, directed there by relative price differences. In foreign countries, many of these excess dollars are monetized by foreign authorities and held as official foreign-exchange reserves. But these reserves are not inert. They do not lie around in bank vaults. They are in fact reinvested in the U.S. dollar market – especially in U.S. government securities sold to finance the federal budget deficit. In effect, the United States exports its debt securities, thus receiving back the dollars it created and used to settle its balance-of-payments deficits abroad.

Everything goes on as if the deficits didn't exist. No adjustment is required of the United States to settle its debts, or to rebalance the deficits with surpluses. Thus again, total demand is enabled to exceed total supply. In a word, the world dollar standard enables America to buy without really paying, a fundamental cause of inflation. But when the Federal Reserve slows or ends quantitative easing, or money printing, total monetary demand declines and deflation threatens.

Rebalancing world trade is impossible under an official reserve currency system. (The International Monetary Fund and the central banks are pathetic shadows of "all the king's men" trying to put Humpty Dumpty – that is, global rebalancing – back together again.) This perverse international monetary system, whereby the reserve currency country issues its own money to finance and refinance its increasing deficits and debts, augments global purchasing power and potential worldwide inflation, because the newly issued central bank money is not associated with newly produced goods and services. Total demand has been divorced from supply. When total demand exceeds total supply, inflation usually occurs first in marketable, scarce commodities, equities, and inflation hedges (2009–2012); other more general price level effects may be deferred because of unemployed labor and other unutilized resources in excess supply. But ultimately, the general price level will rise as the economy approaches full employment. (The worldwide panic demand for the dollar over the past two years, during the European crisis, has mitigated the general price level effect of quantitative easing. The desire to hold the dollar in cash equivalents rather than to spend or invest it defers inflation.)

Under the rule-based gold standard, the regular settlement of balance-of-payments deficits eliminates a root cause of global imbalances, re-establishing equilibrium among trading nations. Under the true gold standard, residual payments deficits could no longer be settled in newly issued national paper and credit monies, such as the reserve currencies of the dollar or euro.

Instead, these deficits would be settled with an impartial, non-national monetary standard: gold. The requirement to settle in gold rules out the exponential debt increases of flawed reserve currency systems. A famous example of this is the flawed gold-exchange-reserve currency system of the

1920s, the collapse of which turned a recession into the Great Depression. Another case is the financial bubble and its collapse during the past decade (2002–2012).

Moreover, it is very much in the American national interest to terminate the reserve currency role of the dollar. This role is an insupportable burden borne by the United States since the end of World War II (even since the great powers' Genoa agreement of 1922). The U.S. taxpayer should no longer go further into debt in order to supply the world with dollar reserves denominated in U.S. debt. Terminating this burdensome "privilege," combined with the restoration of dollar convertibility to gold, will gradually end the long era of extreme global trade imbalances, secular debt accumulation and inflation, and currency depreciation. Furthermore, because the reserves of monetary authorities will be held only in gold and domestic currency claims, the exchange rate risk will be eliminated in all national banking systems.

The rule-based, true gold standard not only would end the official reserve currency role of the dollar, but also limit arbitrary Federal Reserve money issuance secured by spurious, defective, and illiquid collateral. Unstable mutations in the gold standard of the past – including the failed reserve currency-based "gold-exchange" system of Bretton Woods and the collapse of its predecessor, the reserve currency–based "gold-exchange system" of the 1920s and 1930s – must be ruled out. So, too, must floating-exchange rates. For almost a century, policymakers, politicians, historians, and economists have confused the flawed, interwar gold-exchange standard, based on official reserve currencies, with the true or classical gold standard. They have mistakenly blamed the Great Depression on the gold standard, instead of on the liquidation of the official reserve currencies underpinning the gold-exchange system established at Genoa in 1922, which, like Banquo's ghost, reappeared in 1944 in the form of the Bretton Woods system.

The Bretton Woods pegged-exchange rate system, based on the official reserve currency role of the dollar, collapsed in 1971 because the United States had accumulated more short-term debt to foreigners than it was willing to redeem in gold. Its collapse ushered in the worst American economic decade since the 1930s. The unemployment rate in 1982 was

higher even than the unemployment rate occasioned by the collapse of
the Fed-induced real estate bubble of 2007-2009. Similarly, the recession
of 1929-1930 became the Great Depression of the 1930s because of the
collapse and liquidation of the interwar official reserve currency system,
based as it was on the pound and the dollar. The liquidation of official
sterling and dollar currency reserves deflated the world banking system:
Without these foreign currency reserves the banks were forced to deleverage,
call in loans, or go bankrupt. They did all three.

Since 1971, the floating-exchange rate system, or the world dollar
standard, has been even more perverse and crisis-prone than Bretton Woods
and the Genoa interwar system. The dollar's role as the reserve currency has
caused not only extreme inflation and the subsequent threat of deflation,
but also industrial and manufacturing displacement in the United States. It
has resulted in declining American competitiveness, one witness of which
is the collapse of the international net investment position of the United
States (essentially, U.S. assets held abroad, less foreign assets held in the
United States). In 1980, the U.S. net international investment position
was 10 percent of GDP. In 2010, it was negative 20 percent of GDP. The
difference was equal to the increase of foreign-held official dollar reserves,
arising from continuous U.S. balance-of-payments deficits under the dollar-
based official reserve currency system.

Under the present system, the perennial U.S. balance-of-payments deficit
will, more often than not, continue to flood foreign financial systems
and central banks with undesired dollars, followed by brief periods of
dollar scarcity, the threat of deflation, and a cyclical rise of the dollar on
foreign exchanges. Foreign authorities may continue to purchase excess
dollars against the issue of new domestic money. This duplicates potential
purchasing power unassociated with the production of new goods, causing
total demand to exceed total supply – thus tending to sustain worldwide
inflation, generally followed by recession and the threat of deflation. So-
called sterilization techniques designed to neutralize central-bank money
printing are not fully effective. Without monetary reform, the excess dollars
purchased by foreign central banks, reinvested in U.S. government securities
and other dollar debt, will continue to finance excess consumption and
rising government spending in the United States.

Today, inflation of the general price level (or CPI) proceeds gradually in the United States because of unemployed resources, combined with the panic demand worldwide to hold the dollar rather than spend it, or to repay debt with the money rather than to consume. At full employment, inflation will pick up. Because the reserve currency system generally leads to a rapid increase in global purchasing power, without a commensurate increase in the supply of goods and services, the systemic tendency of the reserve currency system is monetary expansion or inflation. Yet the process can work dangerously in reverse, causing deflation, especially when the Fed tightens or there is panic out of foreign currencies into the dollar (the Asian Crisis, 1996-2002, and the Euro Crisis, 2012). Illiquidity abroad can cause foreign official dollar reserves to be resold or liquidated in very large quantities, reducing the global monetary base, as occurred in 1929-1933 and recently in 2007-2009.

In the absence of government rules that favor inconvertible paper and credit money, the historical evidence shows that gold, or paper and credit money convertible to gold, was preferred and accepted in trade and exchange from time immemorial. Until recent times the gold standard also underwrote, indeed required, global trade rebalancing, now the subject of empty exhortations by the International Monetary Fund and political authorities. But to desire a goal without the effective means to attain it – namely, the true gold standard – is to court political and financial disaster. In the absence of prompt balance-of-payments settlements in gold, the undisciplined official reserve currency systems have immobilized the international adjustment mechanism. The result has been increasing trade imbalances, ever-rising debt, and credit leverage at home and abroad. Under the world dollar standard, other nations have gained desired dollar reserves only as the United States becomes an increasingly leveraged debtor through balance-of-payments deficits. Whereas under the gold standard, the global economy may actually attain a balance-of-payments surplus as a whole vis-à-vis worldwide gold producers.

Among its monetary virtues as the least imperfect monetary system of civilization, the true gold standard, without official reserve currencies, is the sole rule-based monetary order that reliably and systematically rebalances worldwide trade and exchange among all participating nations.

Coda

How to Get From Here to There

Step 1. The President announces unilateral resumption of the gold monetary standard on a date certain, not more than four years in the future. Unilateral resumption means that the U.S. dollar will be defined by law as a certain weight unit of gold. The Treasury, the Federal Reserve, and the entire banking system will be obligated to maintain the gold value of the dollar. On the date of resumption, Federal Reserve banknotes and U.S. dollar bank demand deposits will be redeemable in gold on demand at the statutory gold parity. Further use by foreign governments of the dollar as an official reserve currency will entail no legal recognition by the United States.

Step 2. The President issues an executive order eliminating all taxes imposed on the buying, selling, and circulating of gold. Another executive order provides for the issuance of Treasury bonds backed by a proportional weight of gold. Since Federal Reserve notes and bank deposits (money) are not taxed by any jurisdiction, the executive order specifies that gold, being legal tender, is to be used as money and thus to go untaxed. Gold can be used to settle all debts, public and private. The Treasury and authorized private mints will provide for the creation and wide circulation of legal tender gold coin in appropriate denominations, free of any and all taxation.

Step 3. Shortly after announcing the intent to go forward to a modernized gold standard, the United States calls for an international monetary conference of interested nations to provide for the deliberate windup of the dollar-based, official reserve currency system and the consolidation and refunding of foreign official dollar reserves. The international agreement to be negotiated will inaugurate the reformed international monetary system of multilateral convertibility of major countries' currencies to the gold monetary standard. Stable exchange rates would be the result. The value of each participating currency would be a function of its stipulated gold parity.

Step 4. The conference, attended by representatives of the Bank for International Settlements, International Monetary Fund, World Trade Organization, and the World Bank, would establish gold as the means by which nations would settle residual balance-of-payments deficits. The agreement would designate gold, in place of reserve currencies, as the recognized international monetary reserve asset. Official foreign currency reserves, to a specified extent, would be consolidated and refunded.

Step 5. A multilateral, international gold standard – the result of the conference convertibility Agreement – would effectively terminate floating and pegged-undervalued exchange rates. The reformed monetary system without official reserve currencies, the true international gold standard, would establish and uphold stable exchange rates and free and fair trade, based upon the mutual convertibility to gold of major national currencies.

Now we are able to formulate an authentic, bipartisan program to restore 4 percent American economic growth over the long term: (1) tax rate reductions with an enlarged tax base; (2) government spending restraint aimed at a balanced budget; (3) simplification of business regulation designed to empower entrepreneurial innovation. But these reforms can only be made effective for America and the world by (4) a modernized gold standard and stable exchange rates. This is the very same platform which uplifted 13 impoverished colonies by the sea in 1789 to leadership of the world in little more than a century.

ACKNOWLEDGEMENTS

Not all of my friends, colleagues, and helpful critics have agreed with my views, but I have learned much from my conversations and debates with Benjamin Atkinson, Jeffrey Bell, Ralph Benko, Jonathan Bush, William H.T. Bush, Frank Cannon, Langdon P. Cook, Elizabeth Currier, Sean Fieler, Ed Feulner, Desmond FitzGerald, Paul Fabra, Mark Gerson, George Gilder, Richard Gilder, James D. Grant, William Kristol, John A. Levin, Seth Lipsky, James Lyle, John D. Mueller, Christopher Potter, Samuel T. Reeves, Anthony Roberts, Julian H. Robertson, Jr., Judy Shelton, David Stockman, Ann Thivierge, Frank P. Trotta, Jr., R. Emmett Tyrrell, and of course, my sons Leland, John, Thomas and Peter, and my daughter, Eliza. Above all, my wife, Louise, has cross-examined me on every argument of every essay, every speech, and every book.

I cannot say enough about the genius of Paul Fabra and his personal, intellectual, and cultural influence on me.

Cherished colleagues who have died include Robert L. Bartley, William F. Buckley, Jr., Theodore Forstmann, J. Peter Grace Jr., Jack Kemp, Jeremiah Milbank, Jr., C. Nicholas Potter, C. Howell Scott, Charles L. Stillman, Jr., and William E. Simon, Sr. Their advice and counsel has not been forgotten.

Special mention must be made of John P. Britton, my friend and collaborator from our years at Yale University – a brilliant mathematician, astronomer, outdoorsman, and businessman. He wrote his Yale Ph.D. on how the Greek astronomer Claudius Ptolemy derived the parameters for his solar and lunar theories in the 2nd century AD. In the 1980s, John returned to Yale to study Akkadian and Sumerian languages and research Babylonian astronomy. In my own early work in developing the statistical foundation for my ideas, John was an invaluable counselor, colleague, statistician, and chart-maker. John will long be remembered for his sublime intellect; his deep capacity for true friendship; his devotion to reasoned argument; his mastery of the English language; his unstinting loyalty to family and friends; his tutored and refined esthetic sensibility. His was a restless and indomitable spirit of incomparable modesty.

More recently, I lost another cherished friend who had a strong impact
on the development and distribution of my writings about monetary policy,
the Federal Reserve, and the gold standard. Barton M. Biggs was a world-
respected senior partner at Morgan Stanley for more than three decades. In
that role, he took an interest in the publication of my views. He recruited
me for Morgan Stanley as a managing director in the late 1980s. I had the
opportunity for several years to work alongside him. He was an original.
When he was made, the Maker broke the mold.

Barton's prescience about financial markets is well known – whether
about the promise of emerging markets or the excesses of the dot-com
bubble in technology stocks. Barton always kept his own counsel even
when he respected the experience and advice of those he trusted. Barton
was a serious man – spartan in his personal habits. His values were inner-
directed, born of an era gone by. Grit, determination, and unstinting hard
work pervaded his every calling and commitment – including his role as
"Commissioner" of the over-40 football league in which I played.

Much of my writing, after I left university, concentrated on the analysis
of monetary and economic issues, all viewed from an historical perspective.
I summed up my arguments in a book with three university professors in
1976, *Money and the Coming World Order*, which was republished in 2012.
The decade of the 1970s witnessed the collapse of the post-World War
II Bretton Woods international monetary system. The major economic
debates of the 1960s and 1970s reminded me of the national banking,
currency, and economic debates of the Lincoln era. I did not fail to make
that connection, writing on the contemporary controversies for the *Wall
Street Journal*, *Harper's* magazine, *New Times*, and other publications. Those
were avocational efforts, as my commitment to a demanding business
schedule kept me constantly on the road, at home and abroad.

I owe so much of my intellectual development in the 1970s to a man
forty-two years my senior – the French scholar and statesman, an *eminence
grise* of President Charles de Gaulle's Fifth Republic, Jacques Rueff. Rueff
played a major part in the 1959 de Gaulle economic reforms of the Fifth
Republic, which raised France from the depths of the Algerian crisis and
near civil war to one of the fastest growing developed economies in the
decade of the 1960s. As an economist, Rueff was a younger contemporary,

a friend, and a peer of John Maynard Keynes, with whom Rueff debated. Rueff was older, but a friend and peer of Milton Friedman. At the epicenter of monetary theory and diplomacy in France throughout the period between World War I and World War II, Rueff remained a key figure in the intellectual, economic, and diplomatic debates of the post-World War II era until his death in 1978.

I write of him because, without his interest in my intellectual development, my economic and historical understanding would have been less integrated. He also encouraged my writing style. President de Gaulle had publicly described Rueff as the "Poète de finance" and I took notice. He was recognized by his intellectual peers as the first economist ever elected to the "Academie Francaise." With him I studied the monetary history of the Western world so intimately that I decided, with the French publisher, Plon, to assemble and publish Rueff's collected works in seven French volumes (including his scientific essays, plays and autobiography), subsequently overseeing their translation into English by Roger Glemét, the chief economic translator of the United Nations in Geneva. A polymath who was fluent in English, Professor Rueff caused me to rethink causes and consequences in American history, to try to link international diplomacy, economic and monetary institutions with the national politics, ideas, and institutions of our unique American history. In the Anglo-Saxon-dominated world, Jacques Rueff is now a neglected French scholar. No acknowledgment here could repay him sufficient tribute, nor give his gentle genius adequate praise. The coherent and comprehensive analysis of his magnum opus, *L'Ordre Social* (1945), helped me to plumb the intellectual coherence and integrity of Mr. Lincoln's integrated worldview.

All these treasured colleagues and friends helped shape me and *Money, Gold, and History*. Of course, the views are mine. Responsibility for the errors are mine alone.

BIOGRAPHY

LEWIS E. LEHRMAN has written widely about economic and monetary policy in publications such as *Harper's, The Washington Post, The Wall Street Journal, The Weekly Standard, Policy Review, Crisis, New York Post, Greenwich Time, The American Spectator, The Washington Times, The Washington Examiner, National Review* and *The New York Times*. His writings about monetary economics earned him an appointment by President Ronald Reagan to the Presidential Gold Commission in 1981. Along with Congressman Ron Paul, Lewis Lehrman collaborated on a minority report of the commission, which was published as *The Case for Gold* (1982). He is also the author of *The True Gold Standard: A Monetary Reform Plan without Official Reserve Currencies* (2012) and *Lincoln at Peoria: The Turning Point* (2008). He edited the 2012 edition of *Money and the Coming World Order*.

In April of 1987, Lehrman joined Morgan Stanley & Company, investment bankers, as a Senior Advisor and a Director of Morgan Stanley Asset Management. In 1988, he became a Managing Director of the firm. He is presently Senior Partner of L. E. Lehrman & Co., an investment firm he established.

Lehrman has been named to the advisory board of the American Principles Project's Gold Standard initiative. He heads The Gold Standard Now – *www.TheGoldStandardNow.org* – a project of The Lehrman Institute. Established in 1972, The Lehrman Institute is a public policy foundation focused on history, economic and foreign policy, education, and local communities. He has been a trustee of the American Enterprise Institute, the Morgan Library, the Manhattan Institute, the Heritage Foundation and New-York Historical Society. He is a former Chairman of the Committee on Humanities of the Yale University Council.

Lehrman received the National Humanities Medal at the White House in 2005 for his teaching and studies of American history. In 2010, he was awarded the William E. Simon Prize for Lifetime Achievement in Social Entrepreneurship.

Lehrman earned his B.A. from Yale where he became a Carnegie Teaching Fellow on the Yale faculty and an M.A. from Harvard where he was a Woodrow Wilson Fellow. Lehrman has been awarded honorary degrees from Babson College (Babson Park, MA) where he was made a member of its Entrepreneurial Hall of Fame; Gettysburg College (Gettysburg, PA); Lincoln College (Lincoln, IL), Marymount University (Arlington, VA); and Thomas Aquinas College (Santa Paula, CA).

CPSIA information can be obtained at www.ICGtesting.com
Printed in the USA
BVOW081527150513

320815BV00001B/1/P